Essential Bicycle Maintenance & Repair

Essential Bicycle Maintenance & Repair

Daimeon Shanks

Human Kinetics

Library of Congress Cataloging-in-Publication Data

Shanks, Daimeon, 1980-
  Essential bicycle maintenance & repair / Daimeon Shanks.
    p. cm.
  ISBN 978-1-4504-0707-6 (soft cover) -- ISBN 1-4504-0707-2 (soft cover)
  1. Bicycles--Maintenance and repair--Handbooks, manuals, etc. I.
Title.
  TL430.S48 2012
  629.28'772--dc23

                          2012004823

ISBN-10: 1-4504-0707-2 (print)
ISBN-13: 978-1-4504-0707-6 (print)

The web addresses cited in this text were current as of March 2012, unless otherwise noted.

Acquisitions Editor: Tom Heine
Developmental Editor: Laura Floch
Assistant Editor: Elizabeth Evans
Copyeditor: Erin Cler
Permissions Manager: Martha Gullo
Graphic Designer: Bob Reuther
Cover Designer: Keith Blomberg
Photographer (cover): Neil Bernstein
Photographer (interior): © Human Kinetics
Photo Asset Manager: Laura Fitch
Visual Production Assistant: Joyce Brumfield
Photo Production Manager: Jason Allen
Printer: United Graphics

Human Kinetics books are available at special discounts for bulk purchase. Special editions or book excerpts can also be created to specification. For details, contact the Special Sales Manager at Human Kinetics.

Printed in the United States of America   10 9 8 7 6 5 4 3 2 1

The paper in this book is certified under a sustainable forestry program.

Human Kinetics
Website: www.HumanKinetics.com

United States: Human Kinetics
P.O. Box 5076
Champaign, IL 61825-5076
800-747-4457
e-mail: humank@hkusa.com

Canada: Human Kinetics
475 Devonshire Road Unit 100
Windsor, ON N8Y 2L5
800-465-7301 (in Canada only)
e-mail: info@hkcanada.com

Europe: Human Kinetics
107 Bradford Road
Stanningley
Leeds LS28 6AT, United Kingdom
+44 (0) 113 255 5665
e-mail: hk@hkeurope.com

Australia: Human Kinetics
57A Price Avenue
Lower Mitcham, South Australia 5062
08 8372 0999
e-mail: info@hkaustralia.com

New Zealand: Human Kinetics
P.O. Box 80
Torrens Park, South Australia 5062
0800 222 062
e-mail: info@hknewzealand.com

E5443

Contents

Foreword

The world of professional cycling is a tense one. Inside the peloton a mistake of 1 inch can mean many trips to the hospital. A fractional error in tactics can mean the loss of the most important of races. A minute mistake in management can mean the loss of a multimillion-dollar sponsor. Most of this high-stakes tension plays out in the press and on TV screens across the world for all viewers to pontificate on. However, the one element that causes more tension inside a team, behind the curtains, and outside public view is the mechanical side of cycling.

Cycling, by nature, is a unique combination of human and machine. If the human breaks, no race can be won. However, the same is true for the machine. Much is spent on perfecting training, nutrition, and physical therapy techniques to keep the human engine from breaking. But unbeknownst to most, just as much effort is spent on ensuring the machines don't break. Mechanics for professional cycling teams must be absolutely precise in their work, because any flaw could mean a loss of millions of dollars for the sponsor and team. Even the small mistake could cause a failure leading to a crash, injuries, and even death. To say their work inside a team is important is an enormous understatement.

The riders at the professional level put the bike through stresses most do not, all the while demanding the lightest equipment—which sometimes makes it fragile and prone to breakage. The riders must trust the work that's been done on their bikes, beyond a doubt, so they can get on with their high-speed work. It's a tightrope, and few mechanics can take the pressure of walking it—all this while being asked to live in hotels year round and improvise when proper replacement equipment can't be found on the never-ending road. The pressure the mechanic crews live under is every bit as intense as that of the riders, and they take their work every bit as seriously. You may not get to see them on TV, but no team is ever a winning team without a top wrench.

Daimeon Shanks came to my professional team while it was still a growing and blossoming dream. We were far from the best, the largest, or the best funded back then. As with any small start-up, the hurdles were numerous and the hours were very long. Despite still being a scrappy start-up, mainly based on hope rather than results or real organization, we were given an invitation to the inaugural Tour of California in 2006. However, unlike the largest pro teams, we were low on the sponsorship totem pole when it came to delivery times for our equipment. We had received our shipment of new bikes and parts just a few days before the biggest event of this small team's brief history. Our sponsors demanded that we use the new equipment, and not any from the year before, so we were faced with the task of building all the bikes up for an entire team in such a short time. And my other mechanic had just quit in frustration. I had one person to rely on: Daimeon Shanks.

"Daimo," as we all knew him, was an angst-filled young wrench with a lot of ambition and drive. That much was obvious to me, right from the start. Whether or not his unique energy could be precise enough for the high-stakes game of professional cycling remained to be seen, but he was all I had in that moment. Over the next few days, he worked 24 hours a day, literally, building and tuning every one of our bikes. His bloodshot eyes still smiled because he was doing what he loved, and the challenge of doing something no other mechanics could do in the pro peloton appealed to him in some sort of sadistic way. By the start of the race, all the bikes were built.

Now, it's one thing to have put all these bikes together in such short time; it's quite another to have them actually work. No mechanic I'd ever met (or met since) could accomplish this as a solo act. My assumption was that the first day of the race would be riddled with shifting problems, bolts coming loose, and maybe even a rolled tire. So, with crossed fingers of both hands on the steering wheel, I drove behind stage 1 of the Tour of California, waiting for disaster. Twenty miles passed with no problem, then thirty, then halfway. . . . We made it to the end of stage one without even a complaint from a single rider. I was amazed and forever indebted to Daimo.

*—**Jonathan Vaughters***
Former racer and current manager of the Garmin-Barracuda professional team

Acknowledgments

I would like to thank my parents for their support and understanding of my passion for cycling; Dave Campbell, my first teacher of all things cycling; Jonathan Vaughters for taking a chance on me; Tom Danielson and my business partner and best friend, Nick Legan, for their praise; Mike Friedberg for inspiring me to become an author; and Flora Duffy for putting up with my hectic schedule.

Last, but certainly not least, I'd like to thank the guys at Cycletopia and Hutch's Bike Shop, especially Len and Luke, who taught me at least half of what I know. Sorry for the mess—I'll clean it up after lunch.

Preface

When I began the writing process for this book, my goal for the finished product was divided between two ideals: to provide a straightforward, easily comprehendible guide to the utilitarian task of maintaining a modern road bike and to convey the passion for cycling that led to my becoming a mechanic in the first place.

This book is a compendium of the practical knowledge and tricks that I've learned during my long career as a professional mechanic. You do not need any previous mechanical knowledge in order to begin maintaining and repairing your bicycle. Although the focus of this book is on road bikes, you'll be given a basis of skills that can be applied to all types of bikes.

Each chapter is dedicated to a specific part of the bicycle. With a brief explanation of how these bike parts function, specific repairs and maintenance tips are laid out in step-by-step instructions combined with illustrations. A glossary of bike terminology is included, but each repair is explained in the simplest of language that even the greenest of mechanics can easily follow and understand.

Few things in life are more rewarding than diagnosing and repairing a problem on your own. A road bike needs regular and proper maintenance not only to function well but to function at all. With just a little self-reliance and practical know-how, you can avoid costly trips to your local bike shop and gain the satisfaction of doing a job right.

In an attempt to inspire your passion for cycling with my own passion, I've included Pro's Point of View sidebars—some of my favorite stories from my years as a pro wrench. I hope you enjoy.

—Daimeon Shanks

CHAPTER 1

The Modern Road Bike

In some ways, today's modern road bikes differ from the bikes that were available 15 to 20 years ago, but, overall, today's bikes function the same way that bicycles from even earlier generations functioned. Despite the many innovations and advancements of today's racing machines, the basic skills and principles needed to tune and repair a bicycle have changed little in the past 50 years. The upshot is, once you've mastered the basic skills of bike repair, you can easily work on any bike out there!

Understanding Your Bike and How It Works

Most modern bicycles will have two spoke-tensioned wheels, a cable-actuated caliper brake system, a linked chain and cassette drivetrain, and a derailleur shifting system. Let's take a look at how the different parts of your bike function.

Frame

The most basic element of a bicycle is its frame: it's the heart of the bike and is the most important element in deciding the fit and function of your bike. New bicycle frames come in a dizzying variety of materials and designs and are finely tuned to provide an improved ride quality. Most of the ride quality of your bike is determined by the angles of your frame. Today's bike frames are typically a double-triangle configuration, just like in older bikes, which has proven to be the simplest way of creating a light, stiff platform that can easily be adjusted to accommodate different-sized riders.

Ride quality also depends on the construction materials used. Steel is the traditional choice for a road bike, but most manufacturers of modern bikes opt for more advanced materials, such as lightweight aluminum, titanium, or carbon fiber or any combination of these materials. Each material has its own advantages and disadvantages.

Steel

Steel has been the traditional choice of frame manufacturers for most of the past century. In fact, not until the early 1980s did an alternative to the steel frame become available, when Vitus, a French bike manufacturer, began mass-producing aluminum frames. Many cyclists today choose steel frames for their supple ride quality and their ease of repair. Unlike aluminum or titanium, if bent, steel frames can be straightened without significant loss of strength. Steel frames, even boutique pieces, are usually much less expensive than frames made from more exotic materials. The low cost comes with some penalties, however: steel frames tend to be much heavier than other types and are susceptible to damage from corrosion.

Aluminum

Aluminum frames tend to be budget racers' choice because of their high stiffness-to-weight ratio and imperviousness to corrosion. Aluminum, although not quite as strong as steel, is considerably lighter, so frames can be made with large, beefy tube profiles that can transmit maximum pedaling power to the wheels. Aluminum frames are often mated with other materials, usually carbon fiber, at the seatstays to counteract the harsh ride quality that is the result of such a stiff frame. It's not recommended to try to repair a bent or dented aluminum frame because any deformation in the aluminum inherently weakens the frame, so these frames tend to have the shortest life span.

Titanium

Titanium was first used to make road frames in the 1970s and was brought to a larger market in the 1980s by Litespeed. Ti frames are not made from pure titanium but are actually a titanium and aluminum alloy, usually in a 3:2.5 or 6:4 ratio of aluminum to titanium. Titanium is an exotic material that produces a supple ride quality similar to that of steel but with the light weight of aluminum. These frames are extremely durable and do not corrode; therefore, they last much longer than steel frames and retain their ride quality throughout their use. Although costing considerably less than when they were introduced, titanium frames are still much more expensive than other noncomposite frame styles.

Carbon Fiber

Carbon is quickly becoming the most popular choice for modern road frames, and for good reason. Most modern racing bikes are made from carbon fiber to produce an extremely light, efficient bike that is comfortable as well. Carbon graphite thread is either woven together (carbon-fiber weave) or layered in one direction (unidirectional fiber) within a mold and impregnated with resin. When the resin is cured, the result is an extremely strong and lightweight composite material that is excellent for use in bicycle frames. Carbon frames are usually made with unidirectional fiber, which can be laid in any direction the frame manufacturer chooses. Because the fiber will be very strong in one direction (across the grain of the fiber) and still be compliant in another (with the grain), the frame can be infinitely tweaked to produce various ride characteristics while maximizing the transfer of pedaling power to the wheels. Weave carbon fiber, the traditional "carbon fiber look," is usually only applied on the top layer of a carbon frame for aesthetic purposes. Unlike metal frames, carbon will not bend; therefore, any failure tends to be catastrophic. While small cracks are repairable (at a considerable cost), any large crack or break necessitates the replacement of the entire frame.

Today's frames sport new and innovative ways of housing the bottom bracket and headset bearings. The bicycle frame, as shown in figure 1.1, does much more than just provide a mounting point for the two wheels: each part of the frame is designed for a specific task. The headset houses the bearings on which the fork rotates, and the bottom bracket shell holds the crank bearings (or bottom bracket). The seatpost sits inside the seat tube and is held in place with the seatpost clamp. The seatstays and chainstays meet at the rear dropouts, which are slotted to allow easy installation and removal of the rear wheel axle.

Figure 1.1   Parts of a road frame.

Fork

Forks, as shown in figure 1.2, are designed in conjunction with the frame to produce the desired angles of the head tube and seat tube. Forks can have various crown lengths (distance between the fork dropouts and fork crown) and various rakes (the perpendicular distance from the fork dropouts to the steering axis angle). Both the crown length and the rake can greatly affect the handling and feel of a bicycle. A longer or shorter crown length will either slacken or steepen, respectively, the head tube angle of a frame, while a change in fork rake will affect both the steering axis angle and the overall wheelbase length. I'll discuss forks in greater detail in chapter 3 and explain how the fork design can affect how your bike handles and feels.

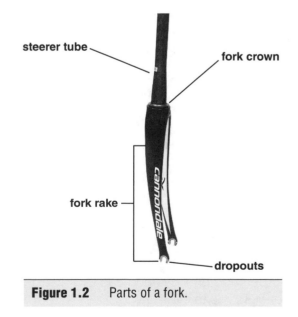

Figure 1.2   Parts of a fork.

Stem and Handlebars

The stem and handlebars represent the cockpit of your bike and allow you to steer. The handlebars are one of the three contact points between you and the bike (the other two being the saddle and pedals). Bicycle stems were traditionally built in a "quill" style, a one-piece stem and neck combo that used an expander plug to affix the stem to the steerer tube of the fork (see figure 1.3). Most bikes today use what is called a "threadless" headset (see figure 1.4), which allows the stem to clamp directly to the fork, thus eliminating the need for a heavy and redundant stem neck. Handlebars, despite advantages in shape and materials, have changed little since their inception. Road bars are built in a traditional drop shape, which allows riders to place their hands in three distinct positions to allow for changes in comfort and performance.

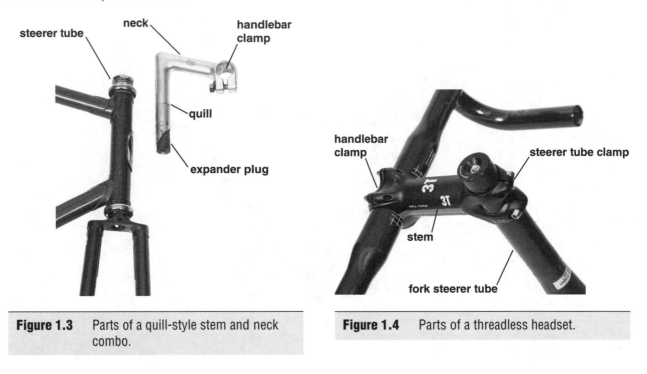

Figure 1.3   Parts of a quill-style stem and neck combo.

Figure 1.4   Parts of a threadless headset.

Saddle and Seatpost

The saddle and seatpost, as shown in figure 1.5, may be the most uncomplicated parts on your bicycle. The saddle can be adjusted fore and aft on a rail system, which is affixed to the head of the seatpost using one of a dizzying array of clamping systems. The seatpost slides into the seat tube of the frame and is held in place by either a binder bolt or quick-release seatpost clamp. Perhaps the most interesting thing about the saddle and seatpost system is its enduring mystery as to why the term *seat* isn't used when it's attached to a seatpost or why the term *saddlepost* is not preferred when a saddle is perched on it. No one has ever been able to explain this to me!

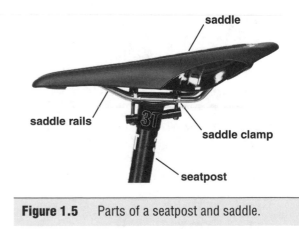

Figure 1.5   Parts of a seatpost and saddle.

Wheels and Tires

A road wheel, as shown in figure 1.6, is measured by its radius, the most popular being 29 inches (700C), while 26-inch (650C) wheels are available for shorter riders who require a very small frame size. The wheel is centered on its hub, which houses the axle and the wheel bearings on which it rotates. The axle is attached to the frame and fork dropouts with a clamping skewer mechanism called a quick-release skewer. The rim of the wheel is attached to the hub by a system of tensioned spokes, which keep the pressures exerted on the wheel evenly distributed and the overall shape of the wheel round and true. Rims can be either clincher compatible or tubular compatible, but never both! A clincher tire uses a hook-and-bead system to attach to the rim and a replaceable inner tube to provide inflation. A tubeless tire setup is mechanically similar to a clincher, except the tire and rim combination is airtight and does not require an inner tube, similar to modern car tires. A tubular tire completely encases the inner tube within the tire casing and is glued to the rim using special tubular cement. Tires are measured by their width and can vary from a very narrow 19 millimeters up to 40 millimeters or more, depending on their intended application.

Most bicycle wheels still use tensioned spokes to create a strong, durable wheel, just as they did when the bicycle was invented, but you'll be hard pressed to find anyone using wood rims anymore. Today, rims are made with lightweight aluminum or carbon fiber and use as few as 16 spokes to achieve what used to take 32 or more. Also, in the past 20 years, clincher-style tires, those with a hook-and-bead rim interface (see figure 1.7), have far surpassed the traditional glued-on tubular sewn-up tire (see figure 1.8) for almost all styles of cycling, much to the applause of the home mechanic, who no longer needs to deal with messy glue jobs. However, tubular tires are still the most popular choice for racing cyclists, so tubular gluing has not become a dead art yet!

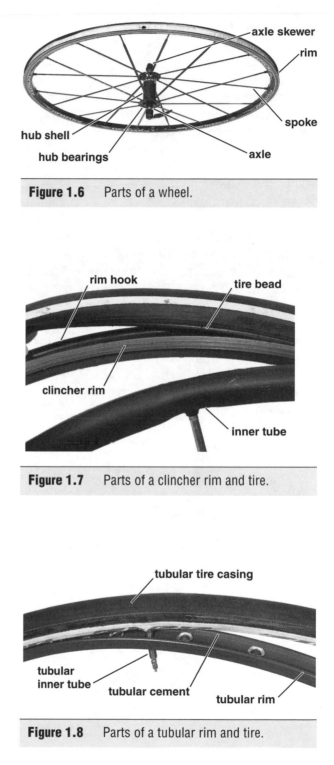

Figure 1.6   Parts of a wheel.

Figure 1.7   Parts of a clincher rim and tire.

Figure 1.8   Parts of a tubular rim and tire.

Brakes

The standard braking system used on road bikes is the so-called caliper brake (see figure 1.9). The caliper brake is a cable-actuated system affixed at one central pivot point and consists of two arms that wrap around the wheel and press the attached brake pads into the rim. The brake cable is attached to one arm of the brake, and the brake cable housing is stopped on the opposing arm. When the brake lever is squeezed, the pull of the brake cable against the immovable brake housing causes both arms to pivot into the rim. Most modern brakes are actually of a dual-pivot design, which allows each arm of the brake to pivot independently of the other, thus producing greater mechanical advantage for greater braking power. The caliper design loses much of its power as the brake arms become longer; therefore, you would be hard pressed to see them on anything other than a road bike. Tandem, cyclocross, and mountain bikes use either cantilever or disc brakes, which are much more powerful but are also much heavier and are considered overkill for road bikes.

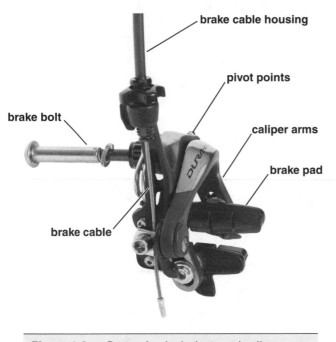

Figure 1.9   Parts of a dual-pivot road caliper.

Drivetrain

If the frame were considered to be the heart of a bicycle, then the drivetrain would be analogous to its legs. The drivetrain, as shown in figure 1.10, is what allows riders to convert their muscle energy into the mechanical energy that powers the wheels and propels the rider and bike. The first point of contact between the rider and the drivetrain is the pedals. Road cyclists wear special stiff-soled shoes that attach to the pedals using a cleat and retention system in much the same way a ski boot attaches to a ski. The pedals are attached to the crankset, which consists of two cranks that are affixed to an axle that rotates around bearings housed in the frame's bottom bracket shell. The front chainrings are attached to the right, or drive, side of the crankset. The drivetrain transfers the rotation of the crankset to the rear wheel via a chain that rests on the front chainrings and on cogs attached to the rear wheel.

A group of cogs is called a cassette. The cassette is attached to the rear wheel using a freehub, which allows the wheel to spin independently of the cassette when the rider is not pedaling (called coasting) and to engage and power the wheel forward when the rider resumes pedaling. Chainrings and cogs are measured by the number of teeth they have, and each size combination of chainring and cog produces a different mechanical advantage, or the amount of revolutions the crank must turn to move the wheel one revolution.

The chain can be moved between chainrings and cogs by the front and rear derailleurs. The derailleurs are a cable-actuated shifting system that allows the rider to decide on the fly which gears to use. The shifter (usually incorporated into the brake lever on modern bicycles) has a ratcheting system that pulls the shifter cable in one direction and holds it in place. Each derailleur has a spring that pulls the chain in the direction opposite to the one that the shifter is pulling it. The cable pulling the derailleur in one direction and the derailleur spring pulling the chain in the opposite direction achieves shifting.

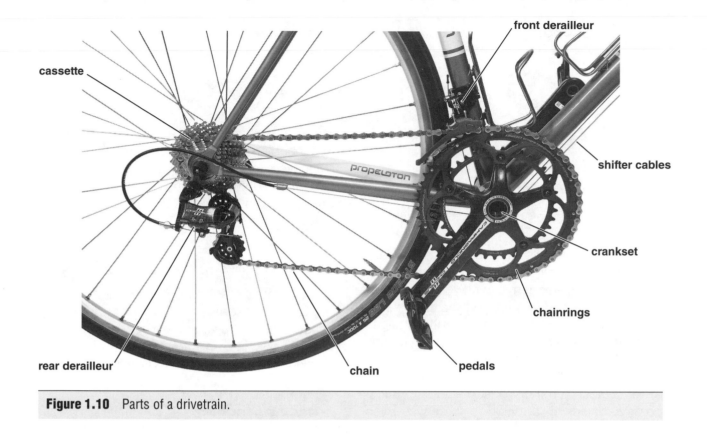

Figure 1.10 Parts of a drivetrain.

Building Your Home Tool Kit

Gathering the necessary tools to properly repair and maintain your bike can seem like a costly and intimidating enterprise. But not to fear! Many of the tools needed aren't even bicycle specific, and those that are can often be borrowed from your mechanic friends, provided you ask with a six-pack of their favorite beer or other bonus item. This list, although comprehensive, is not necessarily everything you might need to work on your bike. Many of today's bicycle products are so advanced that they require their own proprietary tools to work on them (as was the case with BB30 bottom brackets before they became widespread), so, if you have special equipment, double-check that you have all the tools you need. *Note:* All of the bolts and parts of a modern bicycle are metrically calibrated, so, unless specifically stated, SAE or imperial unit tools (inches) are not required or recommended.

Basic Tools

The basic tools that you need are the tools that you most likely have around your home already, lurking in the garage or tucked away in a junk drawer. While some of them are bicycle specific, the majority are multipurpose tools that can easily and inexpensively be purchased at your local hardware store.

Allen Wrenches

Allen wrenches are also referred to as "hex head" wrenches, for their unique hexagonal shape. Most bolts on the modern bicycle are of this style, so these wrenches are probably the most important of your basic tools. Buy a set that ranges from 2 to 10 millimeters to be prepared for any circumstance. I recommend buying an extra 4- and an extra 5-millimeter wrench because these are the most commonly used—and the most commonly lost! In addition, a three-way Allen wrench (4,5,6 mm) and a 5 mm T-handle Allen wrench can come in handy in certain situations.

Torx Wrenches

Although much more common on mountain bikes, some road bicycle parts are now incorporating Torx bolts into their designs, so Torx wrenches may be needed. Torx bolts are star shaped instead of hexagonal and allow for greater torque accuracy and a tighter tool interface. A small, foldable set of Torx wrenches is recommended.

Torque Wrench

Many would consider a torque wrench an advanced or supplemental tool, but I consider it a necessity for today's bicycles. Modern parts are extremely lightweight, and improperly torqued bolts can lead to catastrophic (though preventable!) failures.

Screwdrivers

A couple of different sizes of both flat-blade and Phillips-head screwdrivers are handy for the variety of size screws you may find on a bike and bike accessories. An extra-small, eyeglass-style screwdriver is great to have as well.

Other Wrenches

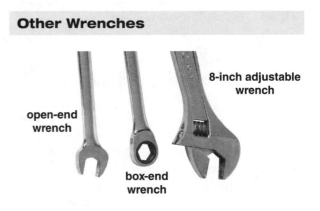

Although used less and less often on modern bikes, the common open-end wrenches and box-end wrenches come in handy from time to time, especially when adjusting hubs. A basic set of 10- to 15-millimeter wrenches should suffice in most cases. An 8-inch adjustable wrench is also recommended for when you need the leverage that the longer handle can provide.

Pliers

A pair of channel-lock pliers and a pair of needle-nose pliers are great for when finger strength is just not enough, such as when pulling a derailleur cable taut or tightening a valve stem.

Hacksaw

A hacksaw with extra 24-tooth blades, which is a general-purpose tooth count, works well with most bicycle applications, such as cutting steerer tubes or seatposts.

Files

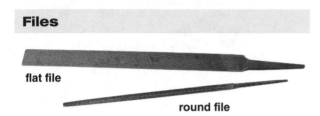

flat file

round file

One round file and one flat file can be used to finish cut parts or clean brake pads. Having both flat and round files allows you to easily get to any part of the bike that may need finishing.

Hammers

A regular claw hammer or a ball-peen hammer and a rubber mallet are necessary for when brute force is required. The rubber mallet protects expensive paint jobs from damage.

Dental Tool or Pick

A dental tool or pick is an invaluable tool used for a dizzying amount of small jobs. A spoke sharpened on one end and bent into a handle on the other works just as well. This is used for any application where a sharp point is required, such as opening the end of a cable housing or extracting an o-ring.

Scissors

Scissors are mainly used in cutting handlebar tape or electrical tape. A high-quality pair of scissors will last a long time and make your work easier.

Side Cutter

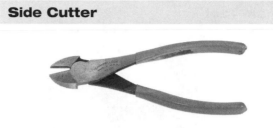

A side cutter is a side-angle cutting device similar to cable cutters. It is used for cutting zip ties and crimping cable ends.

Cable Cutter

A cable cutter is a cutting device used to cut cables. Use bicycle-specific cable cutters, and use them only on bicycle cables and cable housings so they stay sharp!

Pedal Wrench

A pedal wrench is a 15-millimeter open-end wrench with a long handle, specifically designed for removing stubborn pedals.

Bottom Bracket Tool

A bottom bracket tool is the tool that engages the bottom bracket and facilitates installation and removal. Use a splined-cartridge bottom bracket tool or an external-bearing bottom bracket tool, depending on which one is used on your bike.

Chain Tool

Chain tools break and connect the chain links and are specifically designed to work with 9-, 10-, or 11-speed chains, so make sure your chain tool is compatible with your drivetrain.

Chain Wear Tool

A chain wear tool is used to measure the amount of stretch (or wear) on a chain and allows you to accurately decide when to replace it.

Chainring Nut Tool

A chainring nut tool is used to hold the chainring nut while tightening a chainring bolt. This tool is specific to Shimano-style chainring bolts, which are found on most bicycles.

Cone Wrenches

Cone wrenches are very thin open-end wrenches used for hub maintenance. Buy the sizes used on your hub or a whole set if you plan on working on several different-sized wheels.

Lockring Tool

A cog lockring tool that is designed for installing and removing your cogset is recommended.

Chain Whip

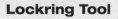

A chain whip is a tool used to hold the cogset in place as you remove the lockring.

Spoke Wrench

A spoke wrench is a very small wrench that turns a spoke nipple to adjust spoke tension. There are several standard spoke-nipple sizes; get either several spoke tools or a multitool that can handle the various sizes. If your bike tires have internal nipples or the nipples are an odd-duck style (e.g., Mavic Ksyiriums), get the specific spoke wrench for your wheels because a standard spoke wrench will not work on them.

Tire Lever

A tire lever is used to remove clincher tires. Have several on hand because they can break!

Spare Tubes

Spare tubes in your tires' size and a good patch kit are recommended. Tubes can be replaced when they go flat or repaired with a patch kit in an emergency.

Bike Stand

A bike stand is used to hold your bicycle while you're working on it. You can get one that's either designed to clamp onto the seatpost or one that has a fork mount, whichever you prefer.

Floor Pump

A floor pump is used to inflate your bike's tires. Get one with a tire pressure gauge and a head that is compatible with both Schrader and Presta valves. Pumps have only one head for maximum versatility.

In addition to these basic tools, there are other items that are great to have as part of your tool kit. A tube of bicycle grease; your favorite chain lube; and a multipurpose lube, such as Tri-Flow, all have their place on your bike's threads, pulleys, links, and other various moving parts. Also, it's great to have several colors of electrical tape available for finishing and other projects, zip ties in various lengths and widths for securing stray parts or housing, and both red grease rags and white lint-free rags (old T-shirts work superbly).

Advanced Tools

The tools previously listed are enough to get you through most of the basic repairs you'll be doing as a home mechanic. However, they are not enough to allow you to live without a bike shop. Advanced tools are those that are used infrequently and that are the most costly to acquire. Buy them as you need them, or better yet, borrow them if you can on the rare occasions that you'll need them.

Headset Press

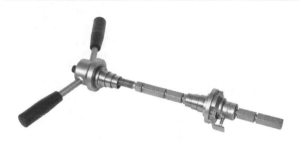

A headset press is used for pressing nonintegrated headset cups into frames. They are also used in BB30 bottom bracket installations.

Headset Cup Remover

A headset cup remover is necessary if you have press-fit headset cups, which need to be pounded out with a hammer.

Crown Race Setter and Remover

crown race setter

crown race remover

The crown race is a headset part that is installed on the fork crown. A crown race setter and removal tool are needed for both press-fit and integrated headsets.

Truing Stand

A truing stand holds the wheel and is used for gauging the straightness of the wheel's rim. A truing stand is essential for complicated wheel repair and building. It is advised that you get a newer model that is designed to work with 29er mountain bike tires.

Dishing Tool

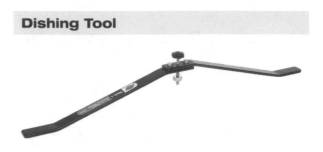

When building a wheel, a dishing tool is used to ensure the rim is centered over the hub.

Spoke Tensiometer

A spoke tensiometer is used to measure the tightness of a single spoke. It is used primarily in wheel building but is also good for difficult wheel-truing jobs.

Derailleur Hanger Alignment Tool

Most frames today have replaceable derailleur hangers, but, even so, a derailleur hanger alignment tool is great for diagnosing shifting ailments.

Metric Thread Taps

Metric thread taps are used for repairing damaged threads by recutting and cleaning the thread grooves. The most common taps needed are 4, 5, and 6 millimeters.

BB30 and BB90 Bearing Remover

BB90 bearing remover

BB30 bearing remover

A BB30 and BB90 bearing remover pushes bottom bracket bearings out of the bottom bracket shell without damaging the frame.

Bottom Bracket Tap

A bottom bracket tap can be used to repair bottom bracket threads by recutting and cleaning the thread's grooves and, with extra accessories, face the bottom bracket and ream and face the head tube.

Seatbag Tools

It's always a good idea to bring along several important tools whenever you head out for a ride. Should an emergency bike repair be necessary, you'll always be prepared. Many companies make lightweight and compact multitools that allow you to carry all the necessary bits in one small package. As with your home tool kit, double-check that you have the necessary tools to work on any special or unique equipment you might be running on your bike. Here are the recommended tools to carry with you on the road:

- **Tubes.** Carry at least one spare inner tube (or two if it's a long or rough ride) in the correct size and valve style.
- **Tire Levers.** One tire lever is usually all that is required to remove a stubborn clincher, but, if you find it easier, feel free to bring two.
- **Patch Kit.** A patch kit is needed because sometimes your flats are more numerous than your tubes and you should always have one for just such emergencies.
- **Inflation Device.** Bring either a portable pump or a CO_2 inflator.
- **Allen Wrenches.** Carry 3-, 4-, 5-, 6-, and 8-millimeter wrenches to cover your bases. If you have any Torx bolts on your bike, carry the appropriate Torx wrench as well.
- **Chain Tool.** After the Allen wrenches, a chain tool is probably the most important tool you can bring.
- **Spoke Tool.** Ensure that you have the proper size and design for your wheel. Without one, you might be walking home!
- **Screwdrivers.** Carry both a Phillips and a flat blade.
- **Cash.** Cash is probably the most versatile of all of your portable tools! You can use it to buy food if you're bonking or arrange for a pickup if your bike is beyond repair, and the structure of a dollar bill is excellent for booting sidewall cuts.

Setting Up Your Home Workshop

Though often overlooked, a good workspace is vital to your success as a mechanic. While you may not need a dedicated bike shop in your home, it's a good idea to use the same place each time you do repairs. Working is much easier when you can easily find your tools, lubes, and other parts in a familiar place.

Find a space, such as in your garage or on your patio, that has good ventilation because you'll be using some products that contain harmful vapors. Have good overhead lighting that illuminates your entire work area well so you'll never have to scramble after a dropped bolt in the dark. A dedicated workbench is not a necessity but is great to have if you have the space for it. Set up a pegboard above the workbench so you can hang all of your tools. Keep your tools in the same place so you'll always be able to quickly find what you're looking for. The most important rule for your home shop is simple: keep it clean! Not only is a clean workspace the calling card of a competent mechanic, it makes all of your repairs easier. An organized, clean space is essential for finding tools quickly and operating them safely, especially when dealing with power tools.

CHAPTER 2

Basic Maintenance

The most successful mechanics are those who prevent major problems from occurring by properly maintaining their bikes before and after each ride. Small, easily addressed issues can develop into dangerous (and expensive!) failures if left unattended. In about the time it takes to down a postride espresso at your local coffee shop, you can give your bike the same attention that the pro's bikes receive following each race.

In this chapter, I'm going to teach you how to check your bike before and after your ride to ensure that small problems don't become big ones. You'll learn how to wash your bike properly and how to lube and adjust your freshly cleaned ride. Finally, I'll show you how to determine whether your bike needs more than the day-to-day maintenance and it's time for a complete tune-up. *Note:* If some of the skills covered in this chapter seem too advanced for you, don't worry; they'll be covered in subsequent chapters. Any advanced skill will include a note on where to find instructions in this book.

Preride Checks

After strapping on your shoes and helmet, it's important to do a quick check of your bicycle before heading out for a ride. Small issues can result in big problems if they go unnoticed. A quick run-through of your bike's most important working parts (i.e., wheels, tires, brakes, and shifting) is all that's necessary. Practice your preride check until it becomes second nature before you begin your ride.

1 Check the Wheels

- Make sure the quick-release skewers are tightened correctly. Spin the wheels to check that they are true and that they don't rub on the brake pads or anywhere on your frame or fork. If there is a wobble in the rim, go ahead and true it before you head out for your ride (see chapter 6).

- Check that the wheels turn freely and that there are no grinding noises coming from the hub. If the wheel stops turning after only a few revolutions or if there is a grinding sound from the wheel, then you'll need to adjust the hubs. Note that, on the rear wheel, most freehub bodies will make a rapid-fire clacking sound as the wheel is rotated. It does this only while coasting and will be silent while pedaling (see chapter 6).

2 Inspect the Tires

- Check that there is adequate air pressure in the tires. Most tires will have the proper tire-pressure range printed on the sidewall. For the majority of road tires, a pressure of 110 to 120 pounds per square inch is best, depending on your size and riding style (in wet conditions, use 5 psi less than you normally would).

- Check that there aren't any cuts or nicks in the sidewall or tread of the tires, where the inner tube can bulge through and cause a flat. Visually inspect the tires for pieces of glass or thorns stuck in the tread, which can work through the casing of the tire and puncture the inner tube.

- Check that there is adequate tread on both tires. A tire needs to be replaced when the tire's cross section is no longer round; it will take on a square shape. Replace the tire if it is severely worn or has cuts.

3 Test the Brakes

- Spin the wheels and apply the front and rear brakes independently of each other. Check that the brakes engage before the brake lever reaches the handlebars and that there is enough stopping power to be safe.

- Make sure the brake pads are not worn. Inspect where the brake pads hit the rim; they should contact the rim evenly on both sides and not rub the tire in any way because this will cause a flat.

- Adjust the brakes or brake pads if needed (see chapter 8).

4 Lube the Chain

- If you haven't done so previously (after washing your bike since your last ride, for example), then lube the chain. There are many, many styles of lube available, and each works differently in different conditions. If you're unsure what to use or if you like to keep only one type around for all conditions, then use a light oil, such as Tri-Flow.

- Apply a small amount to the inside of the chain as you pedal backward so the entire chain gets an even coat. It's a good idea to run through the gear range to get a little lube on the cassette and chainrings as well. Note that you should always apply lube to the inside of the chain so that, as you pedal, centrifugal force will push the lube into the chain parts. If you apply the lube to the top of the chain, the centrifugal force will simply fling the lube off the chain before it does any good.

- Use a rag and wipe off the excess lube. Too much lube is worse than not enough. A chain coated in oil or grease will collect dirt and sand and will quickly wear out the drivetrain.

5 Check the Shifting

- Check that the rear derailleur shifts evenly and smoothly between all the gears on the cassette.
- Check that the chain doesn't fall off the front chainrings when performing front derailleur

shifts and that it shifts smoothly between the small and large chainrings. Adjust as necessary (see chapter 10).

Now you can head out on your bike ride knowing that your bike is safe and ready to perform optimally!

Postride Checks

After your ride, you'll need to determine whether you should do a full bike wash or whether you can get away with a simple wipe down. If you're like me and you live in a moderate climate, such as Colorado's, then most days your bike won't be exposed to much of the elements and you can simply wipe down your bike and put it away. Use a rag to wipe off the drivetrain, and then grab a lint-free rag and some cleaner to wipe down the frame. Glass cleaner is a quick and cheap frame cleaner, or, if you want to baby your paint job, then use a specialty frame cleaner, such as Pedro's Bike Lust.

However, if you've been caught out in a rainstorm or exposed to blowing sand, or you simply live in the Pacific Northwest, then you should probably give your bike a full wash. Regardless of the riding conditions, you should wash your bike at least every 10 rides to keep it in tip-top shape. A proper bike wash should take less than 10 minutes (and will go much faster as you do it more often) and will allow you to inspect all the parts of your bike as they're being cleaned.

1 Prepare the Supplies

A wash kit can be easily and cheaply assembled from products found at any hardware store. Keep all of your washing kit stored in your wash bucket someplace out of the elements to make sure it's always ready for your next wash. Following is a list of the supplies you will need:

- Bucket for soapy water
- Large natural-bristle brush
- Small, thin, flexible brush
- Water bottle, cut in half
- 2-inch paintbrush

- Chain keeper
- Dish soap
- Biodegradable degreaser
- Lint-free rags
- Garden hose with spray nozzle

2 Put the Bike in the Stand

- Clamp the bike in the stand and shift the chain onto the largest chainring and the smallest cog.
- Remove the wheels and set aside.
- Insert the chain keeper into the rear dropouts so that the chain is able to move freely through the drivetrain with the rear wheel removed. Pedro's makes an excellent and inexpensive chain keeper, or you can use an old hub or wheel axle, or even the rear skewer from your wheel will work in a pinch. ▶

3 Prep the Washing Supplies

- Add a liberal amount of dish soap to the bucket (Dawn seems to be the preferred choice of pro mechanics), and fill with water until almost full.

- Add a small amount of biodegradable degreaser to the cut-in-half water bottle, and place in the water bottle cage on the seat tube. Many companies produce bike-specific biodegradable degreasers that work excellently, but, if you can't find any, then Simple Green will work well enough, though you may have to run through the degreasing process twice.

4 Degrease the Drivetrain

- Dip the 2-inch paintbrush into the degreaser and apply liberally to all the parts of the drivetrain. Always apply degreaser to a dry drivetrain; the degreaser works best when undiluted with water. Degrease the front and back of the chain, the chainrings, the derailleur pulleys, and the derailleurs themselves. Let the degreaser sit on these parts while you apply the degreaser to the rear wheel's cassette.

- Remove the cut-in-half water bottle and set aside. Then use the large natural-bristle brush and the soapy water to scrub the drivetrain and cassette. Always use a natural-bristle brush because plastic bristles tend to collect grease and then smear it on other parts of your bike. If you only have plastic bristle brushes available, then have two brushes: one for only the drivetrain and the other for the rest of the bike.

5 Rinse the Entire Bike

- First, spray off the drivetrain and cassette. With a good degreaser and soap, all the dirt and grease on the drivetrain should come right off. If there is persistent grease, then repeat the degreasing process.

- Then spray down the rest of the bike and wheels with water to rinse off the loosest grime.

6 Wash the Wheels

- Use the large brush and scrub the rims of the wheels, the tires, the spokes, and the hubs.

- Use the small, thin brush to get the hub shell and any other crevices hidden behind the spokes.

- Rinse well and set aside.

7 Wash the Bike

- Grab the large brush, and, beginning with the saddle, scrub the bike from top to bottom. Always start with the top of the bicycle and work your way down so that dirt falls off the bike and not onto freshly washed areas.

- Use the small brush to get the hard-to-reach spaces around the brakes and the drivetrain and in the water bottle cages.

- Rinse well.

8 Dry the Bike

- Use a lint-free rag or towel and wipe down the bike and wheels.

- While drying the bike, inspect it for damage. Look for cracks in the frame, worn brake pads, damaged or frayed cables and housing, cuts in the tires, broken spokes, or anything that looks out of the ordinary.

9 Lube and Adjust the Bike

- Remove the chain holder and reinsert the wheels.

- Lube the chain and derailleurs.

- Use a couple of drops of light oil on the pivots and moving parts of both the front and rear derailleurs and on the derailleur pulley seals.

- Check the shifting and adjust as necessary. Check the wheels, tires, and brakes as you would when doing your preride check.

10 Prepare for the Next Wash

Rinse the brushes and bucket, and let them dry before putting them away. Put all of the wash kit in the wash bucket, and store it someplace where it won't stay wet or freeze, such as in a heated garage or a basement, to prevent rusting and rotting. Remember, good mechanics take care of their tools, as well as their bikes.

Tune-Ups

Unlike most aspects of bike care, when to schedule your bike for a tune-up is not an exact science. The following scheduled maintenance chart will give you a good idea of when to perform certain tasks but should only be used as a rough guide. Several factors can influence the wear and tear on your bike, including, but not limited to, living in particularly rainy areas, the quality of your bicycle's components, and how often you perform regular bike maintenance.

It's a good idea to buy a chain wear indicator tool and check your chain for stretch regularly. These are simple tools that will let you know when your chain needs to be replaced—when the chain has stretched between .75 and 1 percent of its original length. A modern road chain should last you around 2,000 miles (3,219 km), but again, this depends on several factors. Replacing your chain before it's completely worn out is the easiest way of keeping expensive repairs at a minimum (for more on drivetrain maintenance, see chapter 11).

Just like chains, the cables stretch as well. Worn-out brake and shift cables can result in poor performance or even failure of the braking and shifting systems. Cables may also lose performance from dirt and grime inside the cable housing. A stretched or dirty cable will feel sticky when you pull the brakes, and you'll feel a loss of braking power. When shifting, the derailleurs will move slowly and will not give you crisp, accurate shifts. It can be impossible to accurately adjust a derailleur with dirty or worn-out cables, and they have caused many mcchanics to wring their hands in exasperation (for more on brake cables, see chapter 8; for more on shifter cables, see chapter 10).

With proper maintenance, your bike should last as long as you care to take care of it! See the figure on page 20 for a sample maintenance schedule to help you keep track of what should be done when.

BIKE MAINTENANCE SCHEDULE

Before Every Ride

___ Check wheels for proper adjustment

___ Inspect tires for wear and damage

___ Test brakes

___ Check chain for adequate lubrication

___ Check shifting performance

Every Month or 500 Miles (805 Kilometers)

___ Measure wear on the chain and visually inspect for tight links and other damage Replace as necessary

___ Inspect cassette for damage

___ Inspect and lubricate brakes, brake levers, derailleurs, and cables

___ Lubricate pedals

___ Use torque wrench to check proper tightening of all bolts (stem bolts, handlebar bolt, seatpost binder bolt, seat fixing bolt, crank bolts, chainring bolts, and brake mounting bolts)

___ Inspect shoe cleats

Every Three Months or 1,500 Miles (2,414 Kilometers)

___ Inspect frame and fork for cracks or bulges, which are indicative of failure, and pay particular attention to frame joints

___ Check brake pads for wear and alignment

___ Visually check entire bike for bent or damaged components including saddle, saddle rails, seat-post, stem, handlebars, chainrings, and cranks

Every Six Months or 3,000 Miles (4,828 Kilometers)

___ Inspect and adjust headset bearings, hub bearings and cones, pedal bearings, and bottom bracket

Every Year or 6,000 Miles (9,656 Kilometers)

___ Disassemble and overhaul all bearings

___ Remove and replace all brake and shifter cables

___ Remove seatpost and stem and reinstall with proper lube

The Importance of the Bike Wash

I've always had a soft spot in my heart for the sport of cyclocross. I grew up in the Pacific Northwest, where cyclocross was more than just a niche sport to us; it was a way of life. I owned and raced a 'cross bike long before I ever threw a leg over a road bike.

These days, cyclocross is just as important to me, but for a very different reason. Races are typically run in the fall and early winter months and go on no matter what Mother Nature throws at you. In Oregon, this meant rain, rain, and more rain. It is truly the one sport in which a good mechanic is essential to success. A cyclocross course is a 1.5- to 2-mile (2.4 to 3.2 km) loop that includes barriers, which riders have to leap over, and running sections that force riders to dismount and carry their bikes. Every course also includes a mechanic's pit, where riders can, twice a lap, swap out their muddy bikes for freshly cleaned ones. That means in a race that lasts for one hour, a rider could conceivably change his or her bike 20 times! So, what does the mechanic do between bike swaps? The fastest bike wash and lube you'll ever see!

In the fall of 2008, I was working for the Clif Bar Development Cyclocross Team, a mix of junior- and elite-level riders. The second leg of the U.S. Grand Prix cyclocross series that year was held in New Jersey, and the weather was miserable. The course featured a long sand section, a wooden stair step, and mud. Lots and lots of mud. Our riders were forced to swap bikes every time they came through the pit to keep the mud from completely clogging their wheels and making the bikes unridable. The only problem was there was only one power washer for the entire race, and, with 40-plus mechanics vying for use of the hose, it was impossible to get the bikes done before our riders came back through.

Luckily enough, the race venue was situated beside a beautiful—but cold—lake. Each lap, I and our other mechanics would grab our muddy machines, dash across the racecourse, and leap knee deep into the lake, bikes first. After a quick, cold scrub down, we'd remount the bank and sprint back to the pit with just enough time to lube the chains and derailleurs before handing the bikes back to our riders. This was repeated for a solid hour in the pouring rain. It was easily one of the coldest experiences of my life.

The rider I was pitting for, Troy Wells, earned an excellent second place in the elite race, behind his older brother, Todd. It's a great feeling to know that, at least in a small way, that podium appearance wouldn't have been possible without my hard work.

CHAPTER 3

Frame and Fork

The frame and fork are the most elemental parts of your bicycle and the most important in determining its fit and function. More important, not having a properly maintained frame and fork can be a huge safety concern. A damaged or improperly maintained frame or fork can cause a catastrophic failure while riding.

Bicycle frames are designed to create very specific ride characteristics. By changing the angles, frame materials, and construction details, two bicycle frames that may superficially resemble one another can have drastically different ride qualities. Most modern frames resemble the traditional bicycle design, that of a double-triangle main frame, a fork with two legs, and two equal-size wheels. This design has been around for more than a century and has been relatively unchanged for one good reason—it works extremely well. In general, these frames have pretty standard angles that may vary by a couple of degrees either way. When designing a road frame, each angle has to be given special consideration because a change of just one degree somewhere can affect how the entire bike will feel. Designing a road frame is as much an art as it is a science.

Even with the same model of road frame, each size may have different angles. Shorter bikes have shallower head tube angles and forks with more rake to prevent toe overlap while turning. They'll also have a steeper seat tube angle to compensate for a shorter rider's lack of reach. Larger bikes will have the opposite: steeper head tube angles to keep the wheelbase from becoming ridiculously long and a shallower seat tube angle to make room for long, monkeylike arms. As we learned in chapter 1, material selection also goes a long way in determining how a bike rides. Using different materials (or a mix of materials) will create very different riding frames, even if the angles are exactly the same. See figures 1.1 and 1.2 on page 3 for an example of these parts.

In this chapter, we'll cover how to install a headset and fork in the frame, diagnose and resolve issues that can occur while building your bicycle, and maintain the frame and fork to ensure years of safe, enjoyable riding. There will also be a step-by-step guide on packing your bike safely when you need to take it with you on an airplane or when you need to ship it.

Installing a Headset

A headset is the system of cups and bearings that are installed in the head tube of the frame and on which the fork turns. A properly installed and adjusted headset allows the handlebars to move smoothly and easily while steering. Headsets come in one of two varieties: threaded or threadless. This designation refers to the way that the fork is held in place in the frame.

Threadless headsets, although invented fairly recently, have completely replaced the older, threaded style on modern bicycles. They are much easier to install and adjust and, unlike threaded headsets, allow for use of carbon steerer tubes, which could not be threaded like a traditional steel steerer tube. Steerer tubes have traditionally been a 1-inch (2.5 cm) size, but in recent years, 1 1/8-inch (2.9 cm) has become the norm. But, like many parts of the modern bike, standards are changing, and larger steerer tube designs have been invented and implemented. Make sure that you have the correct headset to fit your frame and fork combo.

Threaded Headset

In a threaded-style headset, the steerer tube of the fork is threaded, and the uppermost part of the headset threads onto the fork and is used to hold the fork in place. A quill-style stem (one that slides into the steerer tube and is held in place with an expanding wedge) is needed when using a threaded fork. For more on quill-style stems, see chapter 4.

Threaded Headset Installation

Installing a threaded headset involves pressing the headset cups into the frame's head tube. Installing the cups requires the use of a special headset press tool. If you don't have the correct tool, do not attempt to install cups using any other method. *Note:* With some threaded headsets, the upper cup is not actually a cup at all but is instead a cone on which the bearings turn. In this style, the threaded adjusting cap acts as the bearing cup instead. Installation, however, remains the same.

1 Install Cups

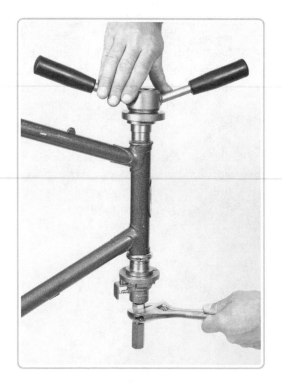

- Lightly grease the head tube of the frame where the headset cups will contact. If you have a titanium frame, use an antiseize compound.

- Slide the top cup onto the upper race of the headset press, and insert the headset press through the top of the head tube.

- Slide the bottom cup onto the lower portion of the headset press, and install the lower race of the headset press. Hold the bottom of the headset press with a wrench so that the tool does not spin as you press in the headset cups. As you install the cups, make sure that the cups are straight and are not binding in the head tube. ▶

- Stop when the cups make flush contact with the head tube. Do not overtighten because the cups can be damaged if they are pressed after they are firmly seated in the head tube.

2 Install Fork Crown Race

The fork crown race sits on the crown of the fork and is the contact point for the lower bearing assembly. Use a crown race setter and the correct attachment for your specific size and type of crown race.

- Slide the crown race down the steerer tube until it reaches the flange at the bottom.
- Slide the crown race setter over the crown race. ▶
- Strike the crown race setter with a hammer until the race is flush with the crown of the fork. Check that there are no gaps between the crown and crown race.

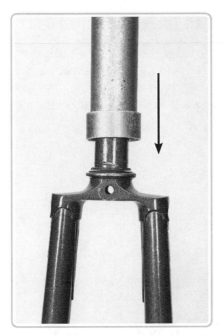

3 Install Lower Bearing

- Liberally apply grease to the crown race, and slide the lower bearings over the steerer tube and onto the crown race. Liberally apply a layer of grease to the lower bearing cup. If the steerer tube is steel (and most likely it is if you're using a threaded-style headset), apply a thin layer of grease on the entire length of the steerer tube to prevent corrosion.
- Slide the fork into the head tube from the bottom.

4 Install Upper Bearing

- Liberally apply a layer of grease to the upper bearing cup.
- Slide the upper bearings over the steerer tube until they are seated in the upper bearing cup. Apply a thin layer of grease on top of the bearings after installation. ▶

5 Install Threaded Bearing Cap

This is the adjustable cap that is used to center the fork in the frame and that properly loads the headset bearings. Thread onto the steerer tube until finger tight on the upper bearings. ▶

6 Install Lock Washer and Threaded Lockring

- The lock washer is notched and simply slides over the steerer tube.
- The lockring threads over the top of the entire system and is used to lock in the headset adjustment. ▶

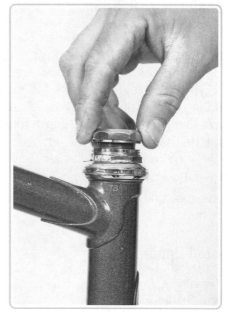

Adjusting a Threaded Headset

A properly adjusted headset, whether threaded or threadless, will allow the handlebars to turn smoothly and easily without any play in the system. To check adjustment, hold down the front brake, and, while standing over the bike, push the handlebars forward and backward. If you feel any movement of the handlebars, then the headset is too loose. Pick the bike up and turn the handlebars to the side. Let them go and see how they return to center. If the movement is not quick and smooth or if there is binding anywhere, then the headset is too tight.

To adjust a threaded headset, you will need a headset wrench and a large adjustable wrench. The headset wrench will fit the threaded bearing cap of the headset and will be flat enough to allow the lockring to be turned freely while holding the bearing cap in place.

1 Loosen the Lockring

Hold the bearing cap in place with the headset wrench, and use the large adjustable wrench to loosen the lockring. Using this technique, determine whether the headset is too tight or too loose. ▶

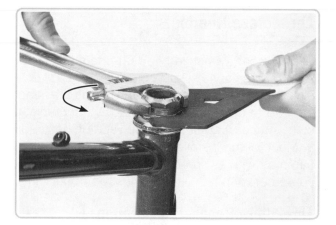

2 Adjust the Bearing Cap

Hold the front wheel with your knees, and adjust the threaded bearing cap until there is no play in the headset but the handlebars still turn freely. ▶

3 Tighten the Lockring

- Once correct adjustment is made (and while still holding the front wheel with your knees), hold the bearing cap in place with the headset wrench, and tighten down the lockring with the large adjustable wrench. Check that the headset is still adjusted correctly; often, when the lockring is tightened, the headset becomes too tight. ▶

- If the headset is too tight, loosen the lockring, and back off the bearing cap before retightening the lockring.

Threadless Headset

In the threadless-style headset, the steerer tube is smooth and passes through the entire headset. A threadless-style stem is clamped directly to the steerer tube, and adjustments are made using an expanding bolt and top cap that loads the headset bearings. Also, instead of using a threaded bearing cap to achieve bearing load, the threadless headset uses a top cap that pushes the stem (and stem spacers) against the top race of the headset to load the bearings.

Much of the installation and adjustment procedures used on a threadless headset are exactly the same as with a threaded system. That's because the basic principle of top-loaded bearings is the same between the two; they just go about it in different ways.

Threadless Headset Installation

Threadless headsets are much more common on road bicycles these days and may or may not have bearing cups. Installing headset bearing cups requires the use of a special headset press tool. If you don't have the correct tool, do not attempt to install cups using any other method.

1 Install Bearing Cups

Before you begin, note that many modern bicycles do away with external bearing cups altogether and use an integrated cup system. If your bicycle has this style, simply apply grease to the integrated cups and set the bearings into the frame by hand. Integrated threadless headset bearings come in two popular sizes (the International Standard and the Campagnolo Standard) and are differentiated by having different bearing contact angles. Refer to your bicycle's instructions to make sure that you have the correct bearings.

If you do not have integrated bearing cups, follow these steps:

- Lightly grease the head tube of the frame where the headset cups will contact. If you have a titanium frame, use an antiseize compound.

- Slide the top cup onto the upper race of the headset press, and insert the headset press through the top of the head tube.

- Slide the bottom cup onto the lower portion of the headset press, and install the lower race of the headset press. Hold the bottom of the headset press with a wrench so that the tool does not spin as you press in the headset cups. As you install the cups, make sure that the cups are straight and are not binding in the head tube. ▶

- Stop when the cups make flush contact with the head tube. Do not overtighten because the cups can be damaged if they are pressed after they are firmly seated in the head tube.

2 Install Fork Crown Race

The fork crown race sits on the crown of the fork and is the contact point for the lower bearing assembly. Use a crown race setter and the correct attachment for your specific size and type of crown race.

- Slide the crown race down the steerer tube until it reaches the flange at the bottom.
- Slide the crown race setter over the crown race and strike the crown race in an up-and-down motion until the race is flush with the crown of the fork. Check that there are no gaps between the crown and crown race. ▶

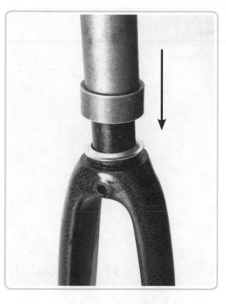

3 Install Lower Bearing

Apply a thin layer of grease on the fork crown race and slide the lower bearing onto the race. Liberally apply grease onto the lower bearing cup and slide the fork into the head tube from the bottom until the lower bearing is seated into the lower cup.

4 Install Upper Bearing

Liberally apply grease to the upper cup and install the upper bearing into the upper cup. Apply a thin layer of grease on top of the upper bearing. ▶

5 Install Centering Cone and Top Cover

Threadless headsets use a centering cone (sometimes called a compression ring) that is pressed into the bearing by the top cover to achieve bearing load. ▶

6 Install Stem and Spacers

Using headset spacers, determine the correct stem height. If the steerer tube needs to be shortened, see the instructions on cutting on page 32. ▶

7 Insert Expansion Plug or Star Nut

The top cap presses the stem and spacers down on the top cover to achieve bearing load. To do this, the top cap is anchored to the fork using either a star nut (for use with steel, aluminum, or titanium steerer tubes) or an expansion plug (for use with carbon steerer tubes) and a long bolt that is set in the top cap.

To install a star nut, you must use a special star nut setter. This tool consists of two sleeves: the inner sleeve has a threaded post on which the star nut is threaded, and the outer sleeve slides over the steerer tube. The inner sleeve is hit with a hammer to drive in the star nut, and the outer sleeve keeps the inner sleeve straight and has a lip to stop the star nut from being inserted too far. ▶

If you are using an expansion plug, install the plug so that the top cap has room to be adjusted both in and out. The expansion plug will have an Allen bolt that can be tightened to expand the plug in the steerer tube and hold it in place. ▶

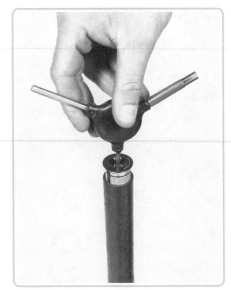

Adjusting a Threadless Headset

Check the headset adjustment in the same manner that you would a threaded headset—remember, if there is movement in the headset, it's too loose, and, if the handlebars do not swing freely, then the headset is too tight. Note that if it seems like your headset is constantly coming out of adjustment, check that the star nut or expansion plug is not loose. If either is not properly installed, it can migrate up the steerer tube and cause the headset to come out of adjustment.

1 Loosen the Stem Bolts

Loosen both of the stem bolts. The stem, when clamped in place, essentially becomes the headset's lockring and must not be tightened when doing the adjustment.

2 Check Headset Cap

Check that the headset top cap is not bottoming out on the top of the steerer tube. If the bottom of the top cap reaches the top of the steerer tube before the bearings are properly loaded, then it will seem like the cap is fully bolted down but the headset will still have play. If this is happening, you will either need to add another spacer on top of the stem or cut the steerer tube down a small amount. ▶

spacer width

greater than headset spacer

3 Adjust Top Cap

Tighten the top cap bolt until all the play is taken out of the headset. Check that the handlebars still swing freely with no binding and there is no play in the headset.

4 Tighten Stem Bolts

Tighten the stem clamp bolts to lock the system in place. ▶

Installing a Fork

Many of the steps necessary to install a fork have already been covered in the section "Installing a Headset," on page 24. The only thing left to determine is how to cut the steerer tube to fit your bicycle.

When replacing a fork, it's not recommended to simply measure the existing steerer tube and cut the new fork without installing it first. If the new fork has any different measurements or angles from the existing fork's, then it may necessitate a change in the stem's position. For this reason, it's best to install a replacement fork following the same steps used when installing a brand new fork.

Cutting a Threaded Steerer Tube

If you're installing a new headset onto an existing frame and fork combo, chances are that the steerer tube is already cut to the right length. If, however, you are installing a new fork, then it may be possible that you will have to cut the steerer tube to fit the frame. The top of the steerer tube should be flush with the top of the lockring when the headset is adjusted correctly. If the fork does not reach the top of the lockring, then the fork is cut too short for the frame and should not be used.

First, install the threaded headset as described above. Follow all of the steps to install the fork, threading the lockring onto the top of the fork as far as it will go. The distance between the top of the notched lockring washer and the bottom of the lockring is the measurement of how much needs to be cut off the fork. Make sure you take the correct measurement because you can always cut more if you need to but you can never add to a steerer tube! Use a fork cutting guide and a hacksaw to remove the correct amount of steerer tube. ▶

Cutting Threadless Steerer Tube

To determine how much of the steerer tube needs to be removed, first install the headset and fork onto the bike (see "Threadless Headset Installation," on page 28). Use headset spacers to move the position of the stem until the desired height is reached. If you're unsure as to exactly where you want the stem to be, leave extra room on the top of the stem with some spacers—it can always be cut down later! I always recommend leaving at least one 5-millimeter spacer on top of your stem—even with noncarbon steerer tubes. This ensures that the entire clamping force of the stem is evenly distributed on the steerer tube and does not crush the topmost section. This could potentially lead to a dangerous failure.

1 Mark the Steerer Tube

With the correct amount of stem and spacers on the fork, mark the fork 5 millimeters below the highest point. This means that if you're using only one 5-millimeter spacer on top of the stem, then mark the fork flush with the top of the stem. If you're using spacers above the stem, leave one 5-millimeter spacer before marking the top. The mark can be made either with a pen or something sharp to etch a line, such as a flat-blade screwdriver or a dental tool. ▶

2 Cut the Steerer Tube

Remove the stem and spacers from the steerer tube and install the fork cutting guide. Line up the fork cutting guide with the mark that you've made and tighten. I usually leave the fork in the bike while cutting and drape a rag underneath the guide to catch the shavings. You can also remove the fork entirely and use a vise to clamp the cutting guide if you'd like to keep your frame pristine. Use a hacksaw with a fine-tooth blade (I usually use a 24-tooth blade for most applications) to cut the steerer tube. Some companies produce a special hacksaw blade for carbon, but they are quite costly. I've found that a new 24-tooth blade works quite well. Use a flat file to lightly finish the cut edges. ▶

Removing a Crown Race

Crown races are specific to each headset; therefore, to replace an existing fork, you must reuse the crown race that had been installed on the fork that is being replaced.

Crown races can be removed with a special crown race removal tool. This tool has a clamp that is bolted around the crown race and a sliding hammer that is used to pull the race up using swift, solid strokes. ▶

Some older forks (especially steel ones) are narrow enough at the crown that the crown race actually sits over the edge of the crown itself. With this type of fork, the race can be removed by placing the lip of the crown race on the inner edges of a vice and gently tapping the fork with a mallet to loosen. ▶

Repairing a Frame

Traditional steel frames and forks have long been revered for their ability to be repaired in the event of damage. Unlike aluminum or titanium, steel retains much of its strength after being bent. Carbon frames are essentially irreparable after being damaged. That is why most newer frames come with replaceable derailleur hangers—in the event of damage, unlike the frame itself, they can easily be replaced.

Once a very common occurrence in bike shops, frame repair is becoming something of a lost art. Large-scale production techniques and new advances in materials have done away with the once-necessary frame prep needed to build a new bike. Still, it's good to know the basics of frame repair if you do come across a traditionally built bike or need to make a diagnosis.

Chasing and Facing the Bottom Bracket Shell

The bottom bracket shell is probably the most commonly damaged frame part. If the bottom bracket shell is not perfectly flat on its face, then the bottom bracket installed can creak mightily. Damaged threads may make it impossible to install a bottom bracket at all.

Bottom bracket shells come in a variety of sizes, shapes, and standards. Traditionally, the shell has been threaded to accept a thread-in bottom bracket style, but more and more bicycle manufacturers are adopting press-in bottom bracket styles, such as BB30 and BB90. The many different standards and their installation and adjustment will be covered in chapter 9.

FRAME AND DROPOUT ALIGNMENT

Although straightening dropouts and frames remains solely in the realm of steel rigs, learning how to check the alignment of each one still serves as a great diagnostics tool. A frame's alignment is actually a measurement of where the rear wheel sits in relation to the front triangle of the frame. A frame alignment gauge rests against the head tube and seatstay, and the measurement is taken from the rear-wheel dropout to the alignment gauge. Measurements are taken on both sides of the frame. If the measurements

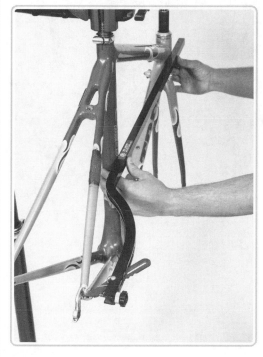

aren't equal, then the frame is bent! If you are running a steel bike, each side of the rear end can be bent using a frame bending tool. ◄

Dropout alignment gauges are tools that have a handle on one side and a cylindrical cone on the other. They are affixed to the frame or fork dropouts, with the cylindrical cones facing in. The cones should match up perfectly if the dropouts are aligned correctly. If you have a steel fork or frame, you can use the gauge's handles to bend the dropouts until the cones are aligned. ▼

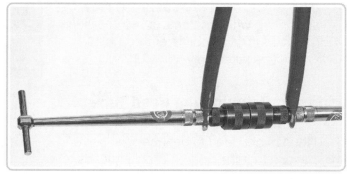

Chasing the Bottom Bracket Threads

A bottom bracket thread tapping tool is an expensive purchase that probably won't be used very often by the home mechanic. Ensure that you are using the correct thread taps for your bottom bracket shell.

1. Apply a light covering of cutting oil on the thread taps.

2. Insert both taps into the bottom bracket shell. Chasing both sides simultaneously ensures that the tap will remain straight and limits the chances of cross-threading. If the threads are damaged or cross-threaded, there will be resistance while turning the tap handles. When no more resistance is felt and the taps turn smoothly and easily, the frame is ready to have the bottom bracket installed. ▶

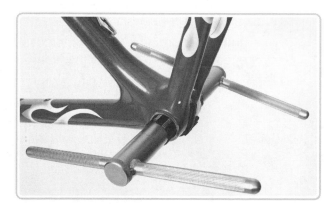

Facing the Bottom Bracket Shell

Often the face of the bottom bracket shell is not perfectly flat, which can cause creaking while riding. Uneven paint or imperfect manufacturing can result in an uneven surface. The same tool that is used to chase bottom bracket threads is used to face the bottom bracket.

1. Remove the thread tap from one side of the tool and replace it with the facing bit.

2. Insert the side of the tool with the thread tap into the bottom bracket on the side opposite to the side being repaired (this keeps the tool centered and the facing bit perpendicular to the line of the bottom bracket). ▶

3. Apply a light layer of cutting oil on the facing bit, and turn the handle in a clockwise motion while applying pressure. Stop when material is being evenly removed from all points of the shell. Often, this takes only a few turns.

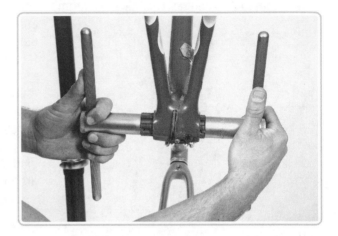

Facing and Reaming the Head Tube

A head tube might need to be faced for the very same reasons that the bottom bracket needs to be faced. In fact, in most cases, the same facing bit is used for the head tube and the bottom bracket. A head tube facing and reaming tool consists of a spinning handle on one side and a spring-loaded compression plug on the other. If the inner part of the head tube is not perfectly round, a reaming bit can be used in place of the facing bit to even out the inner walls.

1. Insert the tool on the side being faced. The compression plug on the opposing end keeps the tool centered and applies pressure to the facing bit. ▶

2. As with the bottom bracket shell, remove only enough material to make the face flat.

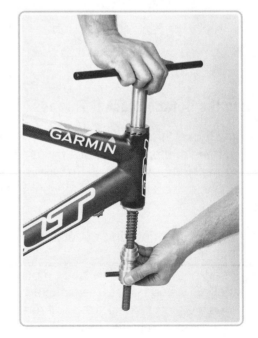

Reaming the Seat Tube

If your bike's seatpost does not easily fit into the frame, then you may need to ream the seat tube. But, before beginning to ream, double-check that you have the correct size seatpost!

Often, only a small amount of corrosion, paint, or other imperfection needs to be removed, and reaming would be overkill in this situation. A specially designed hone that can be attached to a power drill is often enough to prep the seat tube.

If the hone does not remove the imperfection or if the seat tube is simply not even on the inner walls, then a ream will be needed. Most seatpost reaming tools can be adjusted to the correct size. Use a liberal amount of cutting oil while reaming the seat tube. *Note:* Never attempt to ream a carbon seat tube; only a hone should be used. ▶

PACKING A BICYCLE

When you must take your bike with you on an airplane or ship your bike anywhere, there are a couple of easy things you can do to prevent your ride from arriving damaged. Keep a small supply of packing supplies so you'll always be prepared. These supplies include a bicycle box, cardboard or otherwise; bubble wrap or other protective wrap; zip ties of various sizes; dropout savers; and packing tape (if using a cardboard box). Following are the instructions on how to pack your bike:

1. Remove the wheels from your bike. Set them aside.

2. Remove the pedals. Secure them to the top tube with zip ties.

3. Secure the chain to the large chainring with zip ties. This is to protect the chainring teeth from being bent or broken in the box.

4. Remove the rear derailleur. Place a zip tie through the rear derailleur cage, and attach it to the inside of the chainstay. This is to protect the rear derailleur hanger if the bike takes a whack from the side.

5. Place the dropout savers in the frame. Plastic dropout savers can easily be acquired from any bike shop. Always, always use dropout savers to protect your frame!

6. Wrap the frame and fork in bubble wrap. Use the packing material (bubble wrap, other protective wrap, etc.), and wrap it around the down tube and the nondrive side of the fork. Secure with zip ties. Tape can be used, but use masking tape so it won't stick to the bike and ruin the paint job.

7. Remove the handlebars. Make sure to reattach and tighten the headset cap.

8. Place the stem next to the down tube, and attach with a zip tie. Notice how the shifter threads through the fork legs; that's the reason for wrapping the nondrive side in packing material.

9. Remove the saddle and seatpost, and wrap both in packing material. Retighten the seatpost clamp.

10. Slide the bike into the box. Wedge the saddle and seatpost in so that they won't flop around and damage your bike. Slide the wheels in on each side of the bike. Use packing material or a couple of pieces of cardboard to keep the wheels from scratching anything.

Choosing the Right Frame for Your Riding Style

Walking into a bike shop can be a bewildering experience. There are so many different styles and makes of bikes, not to mention the plethora of accessories and clothing options available today. While most bike shops have friendly, experienced staff to help guide you in your selection process, it's still a good idea to have a general idea of what you're looking for before you start shopping. So, if you're reading this book, let's assume that you're shopping for a road bike. That narrows down the selection significantly and cuts out all the cruiser, hybrid, track, and mountain bikes. But that still leaves a large, varied, and confusing selection process.

When you're looking for a new road bike, the most important factor in determining which is best for you will be the frame: what materials the frame is made out of, its geometry and fit, and its overall construction design. Two $1,600 bikes may have the same price tag but have nothing else in common. One bike may have nicer parts and wheels hanging on it but features a heavier frame with a lower ride quality. Between the two, I would always choose the bike with the nicer frame because it's much easier to upgrade the parts and wheels down the road than it is to swap out the frame.

So, which frame is right for you? It all depends on what you're wanting the frame to do. Do you want a touring bike that's comfortable over many long miles and has various rack options? Are you a hill climber obsessed with light weight? Or are you a budget-conscious rider looking for a do-everything bike? Knowing what you're looking for before you head into the shop will also keep the salesperson on track so she or her can give you the best options possible. That way you're not talked into an $8,000 carbon boutique bike when all you really wanted was a steel beast to get you through the winter months.

Steel frames, although technologically primitive, have not yet become obsolete for many good reasons. They offer an exceptionally smooth ride quality and comfort that are hard to match. They're heavier than other types of frames but also have a style factor for those with a retro or traditionalist bend. Steel frames are best for riders who are budget concerned and want a smooth ride for long distances and those with a flair for style.

Aluminum frames are similar to steel frames inasmuch as they are typically designed for a very specific reason. Aluminum frames tend to be extremely stiff, fairly light, and responsive and are therefore usually sought after by racers and larger folks looking for the most power transfer they can find. Many companies offer lower-priced aluminum bikes that are designed for comfort, but generally these will still be stiffer and have a rougher ride than similarly priced steel bikes.

While working my way through college in various bike shops, I learned that titanium frames were sometimes referred to as "doctor's bikes." The majority of high-end titanium bikes that we sold went to affluent, older customers who wanted something light, very comfortable, and with a reputation for being expensive—the cycling equivalent of driving a Porsche to the country club. But crass stereotypes aside, ti bikes are very nice—great for riders who are looking for a steel-like ride with lighter weight and who don't mind paying the higher price tag.

Finally, carbon bikes are on the cutting edge of technology and the hottest material in the industry now. Because of the myriad of ways that carbon fibers can be laid up in a frame's mold, they can be manipulated to create any kind of ride quality that the designers want. For this reason, it's hard to classify the average carbon-frame customer. The most advanced, high-end racing bikes are made of carbon fiber, but so are many of the mid- and lower-range bikes. Carbon can be super light, very stiff, comfortable, responsive, stable, and pretty much any other adjective that could be used to describe a bike.

What separates carbon frames from one another is often the carbon fiber itself. More-expensive fiber has a better strength-to-weight ratio so less can be used, resulting in a lighter frame. Budget carbon bikes will often be as heavy, if not heavier, than similar aluminum frames and employ so much carbon fiber (to make it strong enough) that the result is a "dead feeling" bike. Carbon has a natural ability to dampen road vibration; too much carbon, and the bike will feel unresponsive and boorish.

So, when looking for a new bike, do your research, read reviews, and ask the experts, but remember that you're the one who's going to be riding it. Take any bike you might be interested in out for a test ride and feel the differences for yourself

CHAPTER 4

Handlebars and Stem

Referred to as the cockpit of the bike, the handlebar and stem combo is one of the three contact points between the rider and the bicycle. While handlebars can slightly vary the way a bicycle fits, different length stems can radically alter a bike's handling characteristics. A longer stem will create a larger turning radius and slow down the bike's steering compared to a shorter stem.

The traditional drop handlebars that are invariably found on today's road bikes became popular around the turn of the 20th century, and little has changed since. The drop handlebars allow a rider to choose among three distinct hand positions: on the drop part of the bend for sprinting and descending, on the brake hoods for general riding, and on the top of the bars for comfort and climbing. Brake levers have always been situated on the handlebars. On modern bicycles, the shifters have been moved from the down tube and are now incorporated into the brake levers so that all of the bike's controls are operated without removing your hands from the bars. Handlebars, despite being generally the same shape, come in a variety of widths and configurations. The width, brake lever reach, and depth and shape of the drop are all variable. For a good rule of thumb, the bar should be about as wide as your shoulder, and you should be able to comfortably reach the brake levers in both the tops and drops.

Until recently, stems have enjoyed a similarly long, unchanged existence. Stems came in only the quill type until the advent of the threadless headset, but these are practically an extinct species on new bicycles. Quill-style stems are so named because of their resemblance to a quill pen and ink pot. Stems and bars can be made out of pretty much the exact same materials as bike frames—steel, titanium, aluminum, and carbon fiber. They're often built to complement a certain frame's ride characteristics or aesthetic style. Just like frames, each material has its own advantages and drawbacks. Steel and titanium are both durable and comfortable, titanium being more costly but lighter. Aluminum is popular for its light weight and low cost. Carbon fiber has recently become the standard for racers and light-bike enthusiasts but is expensive and easily damaged in crashes. Stems come in a variety of lengths and angles and can easily be swapped to adjust the fit of your bicycle. For more information on deciding which stem is best for your fit, see chapter 13.

Installing and Adjusting Stems and Handlebars

Both the stem and the handlebars serve a utilitarian purpose, but a failure in either of these would result in instant and serious consequences. It may seem that a bicycle's handlebars and stem are a permanent, unmoving, and completely forgettable item, but nothing could be further from the truth. Stems and bars take quite a bit of abuse during the life of a bike; they absorb a lot of road vibration and are extremely susceptible to damage due to a crash or the bike's being knocked over. It's important to check your stem and bars frequently for damage and signs of wear.

Installing Quill-Style Stem and Handlebars

If your bike has a quill-style system, follow these instructions to install both a stem and handlebars:

1 Grease the Stem

Cover the stem quill, expander plug, and stem bolt with a liberal amount of grease.

2 Check the Bolt

Tighten the stem bolt enough so that the expander plug is close to the quill but not so far that it will not slide into the steerer tube.

3 Install Stem Quill

Slide the stem quill into the steerer tube to the desired height. Check that the stem is inserted far enough to pass the minimum insertion line found on the stem. ▶

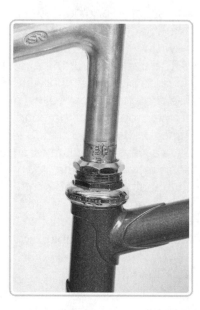

4 Install Handlebars

Quill stems will have a single pinch-style handlebar clamp. Before installing brake levers or shifters on your bars, you must slide the handlebars through the stem's pinch clamp and center them. Pinch clamps can be more finicky than newer faceplate-style clamps, so make sure you have the proper bar diameter. If you cannot get your bars tight enough, a shim cut from a soda can works great for taking up extra space. ▶

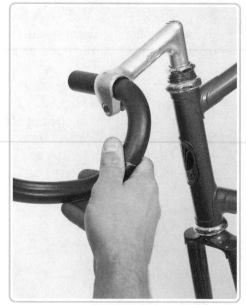

5 Straighten Stem

Tighten the bolt enough that it will hold the stem's height but not so tight that it won't move at all. Straighten the stem so that it lines up with the front wheel. *Note:* An easy way to get the stem straight every time is to turn the stem and wheel to one side so that you can line up both the front and the rear of the wheel with the stem. ▶

6 Tighten Stem Bolt

Tighten the stem bolt so that the stem will not move. It's hard to overtighten a quill-style stem, but too much force can damage the steerer tube. To check the stem's tightness, stand in front of the bike and clench the front wheel between your knees. Try to rotate the bars from side to side; if the stem moves, it's not tight enough.

Installing Threadless-Style Stem and Handlebars

If your bike has a threadless system, follow these instructions to install both the stem and the handlebars:

1 Loosen the Stem Bolts

There's no need to grease the stem or steerer tube unless you're using carbon fiber components. For carbon, use a specifically designed carbon paste (such as Finish Line's Fiber Grip™) because it will add friction so that your stem and bars will not slip when properly torqued.

2 Install Stem

Slide the stem onto the steerer tube. With the stem bolts loose, it should slide on easily. If it does not, check that you have the correct size stem. ▶

3 Insert Expander Plug or Head Cap

- If you're using an aluminum or steel steerer tube, a star-fangled nut will be installed in the steerer tube, and an expander plug will not be required. Place the headset cap over the stem, and thread the cap bolt into the nut. Tighten just enough so that any play is taken out of the headset. ▶

- If you have a carbon steerer tube, insert the expander plug and tighten before installing the headset cap and bolt. If the headset cap bottoms out on the steerer tube before tightening the headset, add a headset spacer between the stem and headset cap. For more on installing headsets and headset caps, see chapter 3. ▶

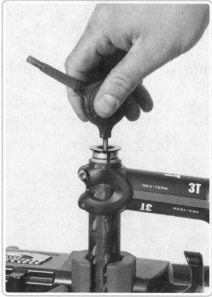

4 Install Handlebars

Most threadless stems have removable face-plates so you can install handlebars that already have the brake levers attached.

- Thread the faceplates in evenly, but don't tighten them yet.
- When all of the bolts are threaded into the stem, tighten evenly so that the gap between stem and faceplate is even on the top and the bottom of the bars. If the faceplate has four bolts, tighten them in a star pattern to keep the load even. Use a torque wrench to ensure proper tightness. ▶

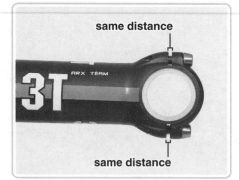

5 Tighten Stem Bolts

In the same way that you tightened the stem faceplate, tighten the stem bolts evenly with a torque wrench. Check that nothing slips before you go out to ride. To check the stem's tightness, stand in front of the bike and clench the front wheel between your knees. Try to rotate the bars from side to side; if the stem moves, it's not tight enough. ▶

Wrapping the Handlebars

Wrapping the handlebars on a road or cyclocross bike is a fine art, indeed. Nothing can make a tired bike look revived like a new bar tape job, and nothing can ruin the look of a great bike more easily than a poorly done job.

Bar tape has evolved from the simple cloth affair that was used only to add grip to slippery bars. Modern bar tape comes in a dizzying array of designs, styles, and features. The tape can be extra grippy for wet conditions, padded for comfort, or even custom designed to match your bike or your kit. Choosing which style of bar tape to use is a completely personal choice. There are soft cork and gel tapes, thin cotton tapes, slick vinyl tapes, and many more. Pick whichever feels nice to you and give it a try; tape is not very expensive, so it can easily be replaced. Even though there are many tape styles and types, there remains just one way to apply it correctly.

1 Unroll the Tape

Take the tape out of the package and completely unroll one side. If there's a backing adhesive, remove the paper that covers it. Be careful not to get the tape dirty or let it snag on something that might tear it.

2 Cut One End at an Angle

Cut the tape so that the pointed end is on the inside of the bars when the tape is pulled toward the back of the bike. ▶

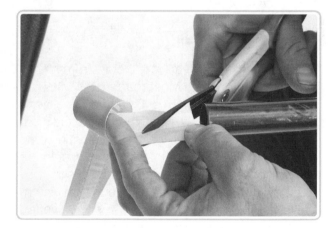

3 Insert Tape and Begin Wrapping

Insert the angled end of the tape into the bottom of the open end of the handlebar and begin wrapping to the outside, leaving about a .25 inch (.64 cm) of tape hanging over the end of the bars. Always wrap from the inside to the outside so that as you grip the bars, the way your hands rotate will tighten the wrap job instead of loosening it. Pull gently on the tape as you wrap so that the tension is tight and even. Overlap about a quarter of the tape with each pass. ▶

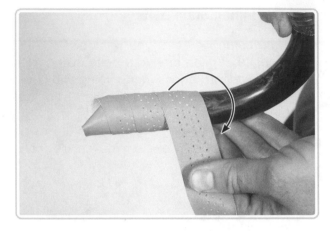

4 Wrap Tape in a Figure Eight Around the Brake Levers

Most tape comes with two small strips that are meant to be placed behind the bar levers. I don't know why; please throw them away. When you've reached the brake lever, continue wrapping up and over the top of the bar lever, then around the inside, back to where you started. Wrap around in front of the bar and up the back to the top again in a figure-eight motion. It sounds complicated, but it will make intuitive sense as you do it. You'll know that you did it right if the tape is still wrapping in the same direction—from the back to the front. ▶

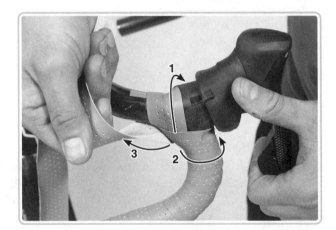

5 Finish the Wrap

You can stop wherever you like; it's a matter of personal preference. Most road riders will wrap up to 1.5 or 2.0 inches (4 or 5 cm) from the stem, and track riders will wrap all the way to the stem to give more grip while using the tops in some races. Wrap past the point where you'll stop the wrapping job, and use a pair of scissors to cut a straight line to the bar. Finish the end with electrical tape. Pull on the tape slightly as you overlap the edge, and you'll get a nice clean finish. ▶

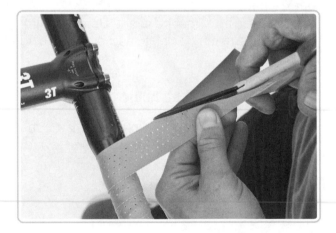

6 Insert the Bar Plugs

Use your finger to push the overlapping end of the bar tape into the end of the handlebar, followed by the bar plug. The extra tape will give the bar plug a tight fit and prevent it from coming out. *Note:* Always ride with the bar plugs installed; in the event of a crash the open end of the handlebar can be a danger.

Installing Grips

In certain situations, some road bikes will have mountain bike–style grips instead of bar tape. Many track sprinters prefer a rubber grip for maximum security, and some commuters prefer the weather resistance. Unlike bar tape, there are many different ways to install grips, all of them valid and useful in certain applications.

Compressed Air

Installing grips using compressed air is the most common method used in bike shops, and this method works really well on clean, new parts. Here are the instructions:

1. Attach a blow gun nozzle to a compressed air system and slip under the grip.
2. Shoot the compressed air into the grip as you wiggle it onto the bar.

Rubbing Alcohol

So you don't have a compressed air system? Rubbing alcohol works well for installing most types of grips. Just know that you need to work fast because rubbing alcohol will evaporate quickly! Once the rubbing alcohol has evaporated, the grips should be stuck fast. Here are the instructions:

1. Liberally apply the rubbing alcohol to the inside of the grip (and a little on the bar if you want).
2. Slide grip onto the bar.

Hairspray

So the grips aren't stuck fast? Using a common hairspray, such as AquaNet, will coat the inside of the grips with a sticky adhesive after it dries. This method is great for installing grips on older bars that may not have a clean, new surface. Here are the instructions:

1. Spray hairspray inside the grip.
2. Slide grip onto the bar.

Working With Special Styles of Bars

While most road handlebars are in the traditional drop configuration, there are alternatives. Riders looking for an aerodynamic advantage may opt for special aero bars used for time trialing and triathlon racing. Older riders or those just looking for comfort may install a mountain bike flat bar to create a hybrid machine.

Aero Bars

The recent explosion in the popularity of triathlons and road races has created a boom in aerodynamic cycling parts, created specifically to cut through the wind with the least amount of drag. Triathlon and time-trial bikes no longer have regular-style drop bars and clip-on extensions; now almost all of them come equipped with specialized aero handlebars.

The typical aero bar consists of a U-shaped base bar (what used to be referred to as bullhorns), aero extensions, and elbow pads. New technology and design concepts have resulted in a vast array of setups. Here are some of the common problems that result from working with these bars.

Internal Routing

Moving the brake and shift housing inside the base and aero extensions reduces drag by making the lines of the bars and extensions unbroken. Most of the bars will have an internal guide or be open.

Internal Guide   Installation of housing through a bar with an internal guide is about as easy as it gets for these bikes.

1. Simply slide the housing from the base. ▶

2. The housing will pop out of the other side of the bar, ready to be attached to the brake lever. ▶

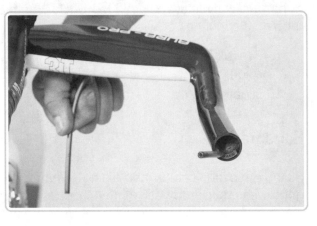

Open Design   If the aero bars are open, basically a hollow shell, it's best to start at the end of the bar and then fish the housing out at the base. There will be a larger opening at the base (often with a plastic or rubber plug to fill the gap after the housing is routed) that will allow you to extract the housing.

1. Slide the housing into the front of the bar until you can see it in the opening.
2. Use a tool such as a dental pick (with a 90-degree bend) or a hook (I use a spoke folded over on itself) to grab the housing and pull it out. ▶

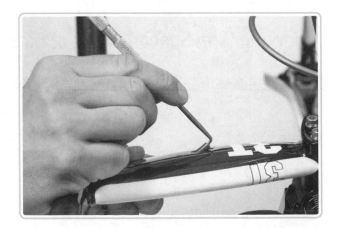

Aero Extensions

Aero extensions attach to the base bar and allow riders to get their hands out in front of them while riding—a very aerodynamic position. The bike's shifters are affixed to the end of the aero extensions, allowing riders to shift without moving from their aero position.

Installing Aero Extensions Aero bars are typically made very thin to shave down weight. They don't carry much load, so they can be made thin, but you need to be very careful when clamping them. Use carbon fiber paste (if they're carbon), and carefully follow the torque specs provided by the manufacturer. They only need to be tight enough so they don't move in your hand!

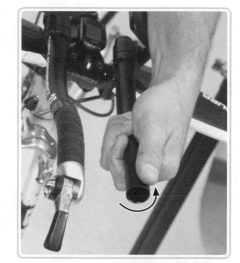

1. Liberally apply carbon paste to the end of the extension to be inserted into the aero bars.

2. Position the bars for the correct length and angle.

3. Using a torque wrench, tighten the clamp bolts to the manufacturer's specs.

4. Check for tightness by attempting to rotate the aero extensions by hand. ▶

Shortening Aero Extensions If you'd like to shorten the extensions, a fork cutting guide can be used to trim excess. It's best to cut from the back of the extensions rather than the front; often this area is specially designed to allow for the shifter installation. If you cut this section off, you might not be able to install a shifter at all!

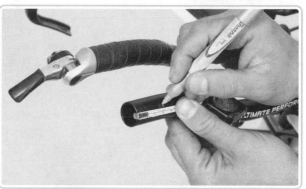

1. Determine how much material needs to be removed from the aero extension. ▶

2. Measure how much of the aero extension needs to be inserted into the aero bar; there is usually a labeled minimum insertion line. ▶

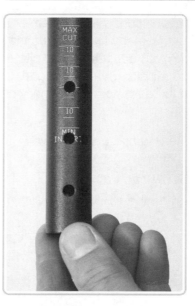

3. Check to make sure that, if you remove the desired amount of material from the aero extensions, you will still be able to insert the extensions into the bar to the minimum insertion line. ▶

4. Remove the aero extension and use a fork cutting guide and a hacksaw to cut off the desired amount. ▶

5. Reinstall the aero extension following the previous instructions in the "Installing Aero Extensions" section.

Elbow Pads

Elbow pads may seem straightforward, but they can be anything but! As one of the main contact points for a rider in an aero position, making them comfortable is of the utmost importance. Because they are often adjusted many, many times during the life of an aero bar, it's important to be ginger with the pad bolts. Small bolts with delicate thread pitches can easily be stripped, requiring a large amount of unnecessary work to repair. While working for pro teams, I would often replace the lightweight alloy bolts that came with the aero bars with slightly heavier stainless steel bolts that would provide greater durability.

1. Determine where to place the elbow pads.

2. Grease the elbow pad bolts.

3. Install and tighten the elbow pad bolts. ▶

Wrapping Aero Bars

Many riders prefer to have bar tape on their aero bars for extra grip and comfort. Wrap them the same way you would a road bar, beginning at the brake lever or shifter and finishing where you see fit.

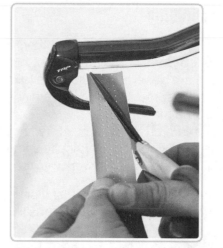

1. Instead of inserting the bar tape into the bar, cut the beginning tape at an angle. ▶

2. Lay the tape flat against the bar as you begin taping. This will keep the look and feel of the tape consistent from one end to the other, using the same process described for wrapping bars on page 43. ▶

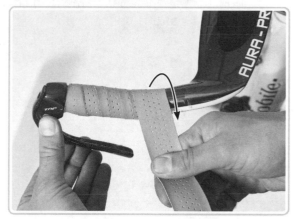

Flat Bars

Flat mountain bike–style handlebars have become much more popular in recent years as the baby boomer generation began taking up cycling as a way to stay fit. The upright position and stable handling associated with these bars make cycling more comfortable for aging athletes and riders with special anatomic needs. While they might look like a mountain bike with skinny tires, typically these bikes are true road bikes and require road bike–specific equipment. Flat bars are installed in the same manner as road bars, whether threadless or quill style, using the instructions beginning on page 40.

Brake Compatibility

Most mountain bikes that are not equipped with disc brakes will have V-brakes. V-brake–specific brake levers pull more cable than road brake levers, therefore you need to have road-specific brake levers to work road caliper brakes properly.

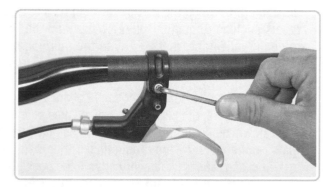

1. Slide the brake clamp onto the handlebar and position as you'd like.

2. Tighten the clamp bolt to the manufacturer's torque specs. ▶

Shifter Compatibility

It may seem intuitive that all 9-speed shifters will work with all 9-speed derailleurs, all 10-speed shifters with all 10-speed derailleurs, and so on, but that's not the case. Shimano and Campagnolo shifters and derailleurs are generally compatible (although not perfectly!), and SRAM shifters are hit and miss whether they're interchangeable. Generally, it's a good idea to keep your shifters and derailleurs supplied by the same manufacturer.

Another problem arises when you try to use mountain bike shifters with road derailleurs. The rear derailleur and shifter combo is typically compatible, but often the fronts are not. It's best to use flat bar shifters specifically designed to work with road derailleurs; all of the major manufacturers produce them.

1. To install the shifter, slide the shifter clamp onto the handlebar and position as you'd like.

2. Tighten the handlebar clamp to the manufacturer's torque specs. ▶

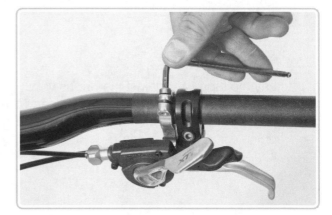

PRO'S POINT OF VIEW

Aero Bars and the Athlete's Hour Record

The hour record is one of the most prestigious feats in all of cycling. Cycling luminaries such as the great Eddy Merckx, Chris Boardman, Francesco Moser, and the late Jacques Anquetil have all held the hour record during their careers. Boardman called it "the blue-ribbon record in cycling."

The first officially recognized hour record (cycling's international governing body came into existence in the same year) was set at 35.325 kilometers in 1893 by a Parisian legal clerk, Henri Desgrange, who would go on to create cycling's greatest race, the Tour de France. The record moved forward in fits and starts, sometimes stagnating for a decade or more until another legend of cycling would again set the mark during the height of World War II.

Fausto Coppi, known as "Il Campionissimo," or Champion of Champions, bested the previous mark by a miniscule 31 meters under what could conservatively be called difficult circumstances, scheduling his attempt between the RAF's bombing runs over Milan. Over the next 20 years, the record would fall to greats such as Anquetil, Roger Rivière, and Ole Ritter until Eddy Merckx put down what many thought to be an unbeatable mark. Early in the morning of October 25, 1972, in the rarified air of Mexico City, the "Cannibal" Merckx rode 49.431 kilometers in one hour, beating the previous record by almost a full kilometer.

Merckx's record would stand for 12 years, a period that would see great advances in cycling technology. Aerodynamic handlebars, carbon disc wheels, tear drop–shaped helmets, and innovative new positions were slowly being adopted by the professional peloton to gain maximum advantage in time trials—races that are often won by the most efficient riders, not the strongest.

Francesco Moser used every advantage possible—front and rear disc wheels, aero helmet, skinsuits, and bullhorn bars—to push the record past 50 kilometers. The aerodynamic edge was so great that

Moser was able to beat his own record a scant four days later. Merckx's disgust with the new technology was palpable; he was quoted as saying of Moser, "For the first time in the history of the hour record, a weaker man has beaten a stronger man."

The next chapter in the hour-record saga was dominated by technological innovation, as well as by sporting achievements. Graeme Obree, a Scottish amateur, held the record with a homemade bicycle (pieced together with parts from a washing machine, among other things) and an extreme riding position dubbed the "praying mantis." With the handlebars high and hands and arms tucked into his chest, Obree took the title in 1993 and again in 1994, after it was held for a brief time by British track star Chris Boardman (employing the same praying mantis position).

During subsequent years, the record would be held by five-time Tour de France champion Miguel Indurain and Giro d'Italia champion Toni Rominger. In 1996, using a monocoque carbon-fiber bike designed by supercar design firm Lotus and a stretched position dubbed "the Superman," Chris Boardman blasted to an incredible 56.375 kilometers, the absolute hour record, which still stands today.

Meanwhile, the UCI, the sport's governing body, had decided that enough was enough. Technology was taking too much precedent in cycling, they argued, making smaller teams and poorer countries in the Olympics compete at a significant disadvantage to those with money for advanced bicycle technology. The UCI passed regulations that limited a bicycle's design and the rider's position and instituted a mandatory weight limit.

The upshot was that Eddy Merckx was once again the hour record holder. The official UCI hour record, often called the "athlete's hour record," was only recognized if undertaken on a traditional track bike, similar to the one that Merckx himself rode. The UCI mandated that the frame was to have round tubes, the rims could be no deeper than 2 centimeters, each wheel must have 16 spokes minimum, and no aero helmets or triathlon bars would be allowed.

Undaunted, Chris Boardman, in the gloaming of his career, in the fall of 2000, used a traditional track bike to break Merckx's 28-year-old record by just 10 meters, proving that he deserved his hour title. It would be broken again in 2005 by the Czech Ondřej Sosenka, who would later be disgraced in a doping scandal.

The irony of the athlete's hour record is that Merckx's bike was anything but traditional. Holes were drilled in the handlebars and cranks to shave weight, a unique titanium stem was crafted in the United States, and even lighter-than-air helium was used to pressurize the tires. If Merckx's bike were employed today, it would not be close to legal by the UCI standards.

Today, richer teams and richer countries still use vast resources to produce the most advanced bicycles. Technology is used to develop the fastest bikes allowable by the somewhat arbitrary rules; modern time-trial bikes are as dissimilar to 1970s' time-trial bikes as Boardman's absolute hour record bike was to Merckx's.

Imagine if you could see Mike Tyson and Muhammad Ali fight for the heavyweight title. Or Tiger Woods tee off at Augusta against Jack Nicklaus in his prime. For me, at least, the athlete's hour record is the ultimate test of a cyclist's ability, the only true metric in cycling: Chris Boardman *was* faster than Eddy Merckx, with or without aerodynamic equipment.

CHAPTER 5

Saddles and Seatposts

A rider makes three contact points with the bicycle—the handlebars, the pedals, and the saddle. While all three are extremely important for determining the best riding position and contribute to overall comfort, the saddle is by far the point of contact that makes the greatest impact on your general happiness on the bike. Even short rides can become excruciatingly painful if you have an uncomfortable saddle or an incorrect saddle position.

The saddle's position is the most important measurement on your bike and the reference point for all of the other fit measurements. The saddle height refers to the measurement from the center of the bottom bracket to the very top of the saddle and is one of the main determining factors when choosing a bicycle size. The setback of a saddle refers to the distance the tip of the saddle is behind (or in front) of the bottom bracket. For more information on determining your saddle height and setback, see chapter 13.

Until Cinelli developed the first plastic composite renditions in the 1980s, saddle construction consisted of one extremely tough piece of leather riveted to a steel frame. These saddles took an inordinate amount of time to break in before they would become comfortable to ride on, and often the use of special leather conditioners were needed to assist in the process. Modern saddles are made with a hard shell covered in padding (or not!) with two rails suspended between the front and back of the shell. The seatpost clamps onto these rails, and the setback is determined by where on the seatpost clamp the rails sit. Some saddle and seatpost combos do away with rails altogether and have innovative and unique attachment systems, but these are few and far between.

While a saddle may seem like a very simple piece of equipment, there's absolutely no shortage of differing designs. Saddles can have a lot or a little padding, cutouts to relieve pressure points, built-in suspension, various construction materials, and many other design features.

So how do you determine which saddle is the best for you? Ultimately, what it all comes down to is comfort. Saddles are about as personal a preference as you can get on a bike. No two riders will have exactly the same experience on the same saddle so it's difficult to solely read reviews or take opinions and come to a good decision as to which saddle is best for you. Often you'll have to try many different saddles before you hit upon one that is just right for you.

Saddles can be so personal that once you find one you love, you may never switch. Lance Armstrong famously rode his beloved Concor saddle long after Selle San Marco stopped producing it. His adherence to that particular piece of equipment eventually convinced the company to resurrect the design.

Seatposts, unlike saddles, are a fairly simple product. Whether they are built with a top clamp or a side clamp, as long as they keep the saddle from slipping from front to back or up and down, they're doing their job well. They can be made out of any of the major bicycle materials (steel, aluminum, carbon fiber, etc.). The only major difference between them are weight and efficacy of their clamp design.

Installing a Seatpost

Seatposts require very little maintenance and are very simple to install. Before you attempt to install any seatpost, double-check that you have the correct seatpost size for your frame. Seatposts are measured to the millimeter, so what may seem like the correct size when you slide it into the frame may result in a constantly slipping saddle and even a catastrophic failure.

1   Measure the Seatpost

If your seatpost's size isn't clearly labeled, use a caliper and measure the circumference. Then double-check the inner diameter of your frame's seat tube. If you don't have a caliper, you can usually find the specifications of your frame's seat tube on the Internet or in the instruction manual. ▶

2   Grease the Seatpost

Spread a thin layer of grease on the seatpost to prevent corrosion and the dreaded stuck seatpost that can result. Spread a little inside the seat tube, as well, to ensure a proper coating. If you're using a carbon seatpost or a carbon frame, use carbon paste instead of grease. This will keep the carbon parts (inherently more slick than other materials) from slipping when clamped at a proper torque specification.

3   Clamp the Seatpost Binder

Always use a torque wrench to clamp a seatpost. If the torque specification is not clearly labeled on the clamp (and they almost always are these days), start with 4 N-m and continue to tighten until the post can no longer be moved when you twist on the saddle with your hands. If you overtighten the seatpost binder, it can pinch the seatpost and damage it, especially carbon posts. This is why it's so important to use carbon paste if you have carbon parts.

Note: When using a carbon seatpost, it's a good idea to turn the seatpost binder clamp 180 degrees so that the binder bolt isn't directly over the slot in the seat tube. This helps evenly distribute the clamping force and prevents pinching and damaging the post. ▶

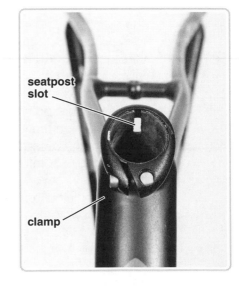

seatpost slot

clamp

Installing a Saddle

Most seatposts function by having two pieces of a clamp that affix either to the top and bottom of the saddle rails or on each side of the rails. There will be one or two bolts used to tension the two halves of the clamp to prevent the saddle from moving. Seatpost clamps come in four major designs. Each design, if done properly, can work perfectly well, but each design has its own strengths and weaknesses.

Single-Bolt Clamp

Single-bolt clamps are easy to work with and easy to adjust, but they can lack adjustments for fine-tuning. Because of their simple design, they often are overbuilt to provide strength and reliability and are therefore typically heavy and inexpensive.

1 Loosen the Main Bolt

Loosen the bolt enough so that the top half of the clamp can be turned and the saddle rails slid in between the two halves of the clamp. It may be necessary to completely remove the top half of the clamp to insert the saddle rails. ▶

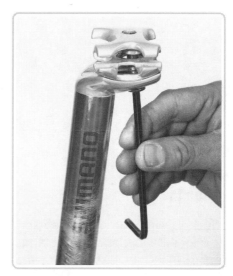

2 Insert Saddle

Slide the rail in between the two clamp halves. Position close to where you think might be an appropriate fore/aft position. To adjust the fore/aft position of the saddle after it has been installed, you must loosen the clamp bolt and slide the saddle forward or backward.

3 Tighten the Clamp Bolt

Hold the saddle in the position you think you might want it to be in and tighten the clamp bolt using the correct size Allen wrench. Usually the clamp bolts are larger (6 mm or more) than typical seatpost clamp bolts and are difficult to damage by overtightening. Tighten until you can no longer move the saddle by pulling up and down on it with your hands. ▶

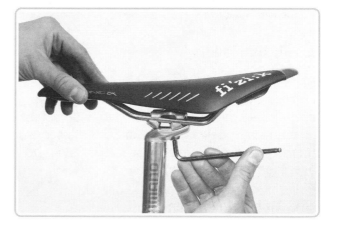

4 Adjust the Tilt

To adjust the tilt of the saddle, you must loosen the clamp bolt and physically rock the saddle up or down. Typically a single-bolt style seatpost will have a ratcheted surface so that tilt adjustments are done incrementally. After you have reached the desired tilt, retighten the clamp bolt.

Single-Bolt Clamp With Adjustment Grub Screw

Single-bolt clamps with adjusting grub screws are easier to fine-tune but are not quite as simple to work with. They use a similar clamping structure as a single-clamp bolt seatpost, but the bottom half of the clamp can be fine-tuned with a separate grub screw that tilts the base up and down.

1 Loosen the Grub Screw

Loosen the grub screw with the correct size Allen wrench so that the base of the clamp is close to level. ▶

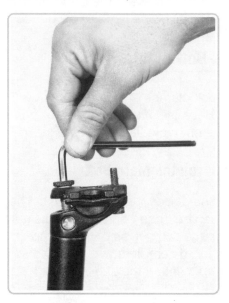

2 Loosen the Clamp Bolt

Loosen the bolt with the correct size Allen wrench enough so that the top half of the clamp can be turned and the saddle rails slid in between the two halves of the clamp. It may be necessary to completely remove the top half of the clamp to insert the saddle rails. ▶

3 Insert Saddle

Slide the rail in between the two clamp halves. Position close to where you think might be an appropriate fore and aft position. To adjust the fore and aft position of the saddle after it has been installed, you must loosen the clamp bolt and slide the saddle forward or backward.

4 Tighten the Clamp Bolt

Hold the saddle in the position you think you might want it to be in, and tighten the clamp bolt using the correct size Allen wrench. Usually the clamp bolts are larger (6 mm or more) than typical seatpost clamp bolts and are difficult to damage by overtightening. Tighten until you can no longer move the saddle by pulling up and down on it with your hands. ▶

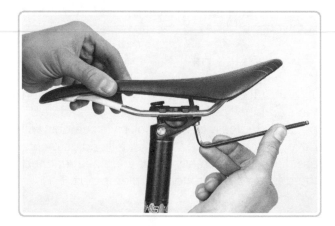

5 Adjust the Tilt

To adjust the tilt, loosen the clamp bolt with the correct size Allen wrench and adjust the grub screw. Retighten and check the tilt. It may take several tries to get the tilt perfect. ▶

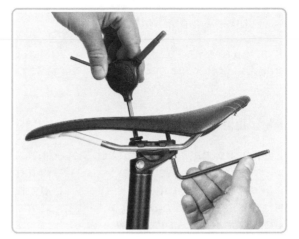

Side Clamp

Side-clamping seatposts make for quick and easy adjustments but tend not to be as secure as other designs. The two clamp halves pinch the rails from the sides instead of on the top and bottom. Often, but not always, a separate bolt adjusts the saddle's tilt so the setback and tilt can be adjusted independently.

1 Remove One Side of the Clamp

To install the saddle rails, you will need to remove at least one side of the clamp. Loosen the clamp bolt until one side opens completely and there is room to insert the saddle rail on the opposite side. ▶

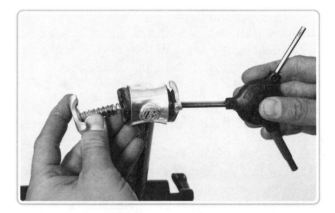

2 Insert Saddle

Insert the saddle rail between the two halves of the clamp. Reattach the removed side of the clamp by holding with one hand while you thread the clamp bolt with the other hand. ▶

3 Tighten Clamp Bolt

Adjust the fore and aft position, then tighten the clamp bolt to torque specification with a torque wrench. ▶

4 Adjust Tilt

If the seatpost has a separate bolt that adjusts tilt, loosen the bolt with the correct size Allen wrench to adjust the tilt. This style of seatpost, especially titanium versions, tends to slip easily, so make sure to use the correct torque specification. If your saddle still slips, use a carbon paste on the clamping surface (even if it's not a carbon post). If the seatpost does not have a separate tilt adjustment, you must loosen the clamp bolt with the correct size Allen wrench to adjust the tilt.

Two-Bolt Clamp

Clamps that use two bolts fore and aft of the seatpost make adjustments easy and secure, but they are more difficult to use when installing a saddle. The bottom half of the clamp sits on a concave surface that allows it to tilt. Two bolts are threaded through eyelets on the front and back of the seatpost and attached to the top half of the clamp. Adjusting these two bolts changes the tilt of the saddle.

1 Loosen Both Clamp Bolts

Loosen both clamp bolts with the correct size Allen wrench until it is possible to slide the saddle rails in between the two halves of the clamp. If you cannot slid the saddle rails in between the clamp halves, then completely undo one of the bolts so the top half will open freely. ▶

2 Insert Saddle

Slide the saddle rails into the clamp and begin tightening the clamp bolts. If you had to open the clamp completely, use one hand to hold the clamp together as you thread the loose clamp bolt with the other hand. Tighten both bolts evenly.

3 Tighten Clamp Bolts

Tighten both bolts evenly to torque specification using a torque wrench.

4 Adjust Tilt

The tilt is adjusted by tightening one side of the clamp while simultaneously loosening the other. Loosen the rear bolt, and, depending on which way you want to tilt the saddle, either tighten or loosen the front bolt. If you tighten the front bolt, the nose will tilt downward; if you loosen the bolt it will tilt upward. Retighten the rear bolt to torque specification, leaving the front bolt untouched. Check the tilt adjustment. You'll often have to do this process several times to get the desired result. ▶

Adjusting an Integrated Seat Mast

Some new carbon road frames do away with the traditional seatpost setup altogether and instead have an integrated seat mast. Basically, the seatpost becomes an integrated part of the frame, and the saddle mounts directly to the masthead. The benefits of an integrated seat mast are lower weight, increased stiffness, the possibility of aerodynamically shaped seat masts, and a striking aesthetic appeal. The downsides are difficult to travel with (fitting the frame and seat mast in a bike bag or box), loss of resale value if seat mast is cut, and increased cost.

When working with a bike with an integrated seat mast, it's important not to clamp the seat mast in a work stand unless an adaptor is provided by the frame's manufacturer. You must use a euro style repair stand that holds the bike by the fork dropouts and the bottom bracket shell. ▶

There are several types of integrated seat masts, but they generally fall into two categories—either the seatpost clamp is inserted into the top of the mast or a cap fits over the mast top. An inserted seatpost clamp can be installed on a bike by a wedge system, by an external bolt that holds it in place, or it might even be a very short seatpost that is held by a traditional clamp. ▶

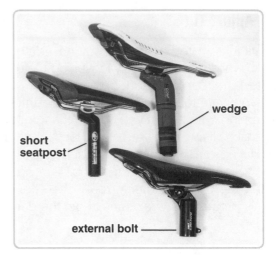

short seatpost

wedge

external bolt

Of the two styles, the mast cap is more common. Ridley, Trek, Scott, and most of the other major brands that offer frames with integrated seat masts all use a mast cap. The cap will have one or two pinch bolts and may or may not have elastomers (rubber bumpers) or shims that are inserted between the top of the mast and the clamp. As is true whenever you are clamping something to a frame, pay extra attention to the torque specifications provided with the frame. ▶

Frames that have an integrated seat mast must be cut down to achieve proper saddle height. It's extremely important to be sure of your measurements before you cut the seat mast because, once it is cut, more mast cannot be added. Most mast caps have a centimeter or two in adjustment built in, but this is not much of a safety net. Some frames are designed in such a way that if you did mess up your measurements or wanted to resell your frame, you can cut the seat mast off near the junction of the seat tube and top tube and install a standard seatpost clamp. Then you can simply install and use a standard seatpost. Before you take a hacksaw to your new frame, pull out your old bike and double-check that your saddle is in the correct position and that you're happy with those measurements.

1 Measure Saddle Height

On your existing bike, measure your saddle height from the center of the bottom bracket to the top of your saddle. Measure along the line of the seat tube. ▶

If you're using different size cranks than what is currently on your bike, measure from the pedal axle, with the crank arm in the down position and aligned with the seat tube. ▶

2 Install Saddle and Clamp

Install the saddle and clamp on your new frame, leaving the seat mast uncut. Fully bottom out the clamp on the mast.

3 Measure New Saddle Height

Using the same method described in step 1, measure the saddle height of your new frame with the seat mast uncut. Subtract the measurement from your old bike from your new. This is the amount of seat mast that is to be cut off. ▶

4 Mark Seat Mast

Carefully measure from the top of the seat mast the amount to be cut, and mark with a pen or notch with a flat-blade screwdriver or other utensil. ▶

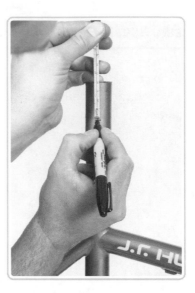

5 Install Cutting Guide

If your frame came with a cutting guide, install on the seat mast where it is marked. Park makes an excellent seat mast cutting guide that will work for almost all frames if one isn't provided. If the seat mast is round, you can use a standard steerer tube cutting guide. ▶

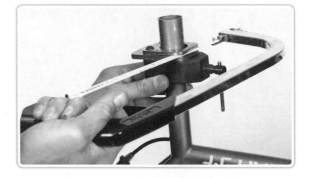

6 Cut the Seat Mast

Use a hacksaw equipped with either a fine-toothed blade (24 teeth or more) or a carbon-specific blade. Lightly smooth the cut with a fine file or sandpaper.

7 Install Seat Clamp and Saddle

Install the seat clamp, bottoming out on the seat mast. Some frames require the use of elastomers between the seat mast and seat clamp. Measure the saddle height and adjust if necessary. If the saddle height is a little too low, you may be able to raise the clamp a small amount either with shims or by simply raising the clamp (within the minimum insertion mark). If the saddle is too high, you must cut the seat mast again. ▶

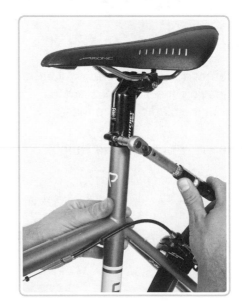

Eddy Merckx and the Never Right Saddle

Saddle position is important for any cyclist, whether it be a weekday commuter, avid mountain biker, or weekend racer. For a professional cyclist, it can become an obsession. Think of all the miles that you've ridden in the past year . . . now think of doing a lot more. The average pro will ride as much as 25,000 miles (40,234 km) per year, so you can imagine how a small error in saddle position can result in a lot of problems for someone who makes his or her living pedaling a bike.

Eddy Merckx, for me, is the greatest cyclist to have ever lived. His palmarès read more like an encyclopedia of cycling races rather than a list of achievements. In a career that spanned 13 years, he amassed more victories than any other pro cyclist (525), the most victories in one season (54), and the most grand tour wins (11), as well as having a professional win rate of nearly 30%. That means for every three professional races he entered, he won one of them—an astounding feat.

But many experts agree that his achievements could have been even more impressive if not for a back injury that plagued him for the second half of his career. In 1969, near the end of the season, Merckx was competing in a derny race at the Blois velodrome when tragedy struck. Derny racing is a mass start event where each rider is paced behind a motorbike on the track; both rider and pacer must work together to be competitive. A crash occurred, and Merckx and his pacer both went down heavily. Fernand Wambst, Eddy's pacer and good friend, was killed instantly. Merckx suffered a cracked vertebra and a severely twisted pelvis. While his wounds eventually healed, he was left with an imbalance that made cycling difficult and painful.

"After that crash it was never the same," Merckx said in an interview with *Cycle Sport* magazine. "After that day I could never sit comfortably on my bike again. I tinkered with my position and changed my frame angles. I would keep many bikes, all subtly different, all ready to race on, but I never found comfort. Before Blois I cannot say that I suffered in a bike race."

Eddy Merckx became notorious for constantly changing his saddle position, often in the middle of a race. In most race situations, it's not practical to stop on the side of the road and adjust your saddle height, so it must be done on the fly, out of the car window. His mechanic would lean out of the team car and adjust Merckx's saddle height while moving at a pretty good clip. I've had to do these types of adjustments during races, and I can attest that they never became comfortable for me. After a crash, riders who aren't hurt enough that they must abandon the race, immediately remount their bikes and continue with the race. Often, it isn't until they're riding again that they'll realize their bikes are in need of repair.

You may have to adjust derailleurs, brakes, saddles, and bottle cages, pretty much anything that can be adjusted on a bike. I've even had a rider once adjust his bars out of the window, and, even though he pulled it off, I still believe it was a horrible idea!

CHAPTER 6

Wheels

Wheels are the quintessential element of the bicycle. From their early invention to the most advanced racing bikes available today, the bicycle's wheels are what gives a bike its distinctive design and amazing mechanical efficiency. The invention of the wheel is one of the greatest breakthroughs in human history, and its origin can be dated back more than 5,000 years ago. The first bicycle wheels were very similar to those used on horse-drawn wagons. They consisted of a central hub with wooden spokes attached to a wooden rim that was wrapped with a metal band to increase durability. Those wheels were incredibly harsh and led to early bicycles being dubbed "boneshakers."

With the invention of the high-wheeler, or penny-farthing, type of bicycle in the 1870s, a new type of wheel was born. Because of the extremely large front wheel on these bikes (they could be up to 5 feet [1.52 m] across) the traditional wooden wheel was simply too heavy and cumbersome to be effective. Advances in metalworking led to the creation of metal rims laced with tensioned metal spokes and wrapped in a solid rubber tire.

These new types of wheels were a great advancement, but it wasn't until the invention of the safety bicycle in 1880 that the modern wheel design was finalized. These were the precursors to today's modern bikes and featured front and rear wheels of equal size and a pneumatic tire and tube, which greatly increased comfort and efficiency. Despite many advances in construction and materials, this is essentially the same design used today.

Around the turn of the 20th century, the first modern freewheel was developed by Ernst Sachs. (Sound familiar? Sachs, Inc. produced bicycle hubs and components until 1997 until it was bought by SRAM.) The freewheel threaded onto the rear hub and allowed the rear wheel to spin independently of the drivetrain, which was referred to as "coasting." Originally the freewheel had only one cog, but, with the invention of derailleurs, they would grow up to eight cogs until advancements in hub design made the freewheel obsolete.

Modern road wheels no longer use freewheels but instead use what's called a freehub. Essentially, the freehub is a freewheel stripped of the cogs and incorporated into the hub itself. There are many advantages to a freehub design, such as the simplicity of changing cogs (or a "cassette" as a set of cogs is referred to), simpler and lighter hub design, and better axle support by having wider bearing placement in the hub.

The standard wheel size for most road bikes today is called 700C, which is a reference to a French standard that measured the outer diameter of the wheel with a 35-millimeter tire attached. In reality, the diameter of a 700C rim is actually 622 millimeters, hence the International Organization for Standardization's label of ISO 622. The ISO label allows all rims of equal dimension to be labeled identically, therefore making compatibility decisions simple. Some shorter riders may require a smaller than standard wheel size (usually to avoid toe overlap while turning the front wheel), so a smaller, second standard was introduced. Referred to as 650C (ISO 571 [26 inches]), these are pretty much the only alternative to the 700C wheel size available for road bikes. Interestingly, the new 29-inch standard for mountain bikes actually has an ISO of 622 and is completely interchangeable with road 700C rims—at least as far as the wheel diameter is concerned. There may be some compatibility issues that come up when dealing with a wider mountain bike rim.

Adjusting Skewers

Modern road bikes use quick-release skewers to attach the wheels to the frame. Invented by Tullio Campagnolo (founder of the eponymous component manufacturer) in 1927 as a replacement for the wingnut mounting system, the quick-release skewer revolutionized bicycle design. It is essentially a lever that gives enough mechanical advantage so that a wheel can be clamped in the frame without tools.

Correct skewer installation and adjustment are extremely critical—incorrect adjustment can cause your wheel to fall out of your frame while riding. A lot of bikes come with "lawyer tabs," as shown in figure 6.1, named for their lawsuit-prevention function, which are nubs on the front fork that prevent the wheel from falling out when the skewer is opened, but these are at best an emergency-only safety feature.

Figure 6.1   Lawyer tabs.

1 Lubricate the Skewer

Make sure there's a thin film of grease on the skewer and the skewer's threads. This prevents corrosion and the potential seizure that could result. Any bicycle lube would work as well, but I prefer grease for durability.

2 Insert Skewer in Hub

There are two springs on the skewer, one for each side of the hub. They should be situated so that the smaller end of the spring points toward the hub. The springs gap the skewer ends away from the hub to make wheel installation quick and easy. On road bikes, the skewer arms are always installed on the nondrive side of the bike. ▶

3 Insert Wheel in Frame Dropouts

Insert the wheel in the frame between the fork or frame dropouts, depending on which wheel you're installing. On the rear, it may be necessary to pull the rear derailleur away from the frame to allow the wheel to slide in easily.

4 Adjust Skewer Tension

Try closing the quick-release skewer. When clos- ing a skewer, you should begin feeling resistance halfway through the lever throw, and, when there is only a quarter of the throw left, resistance should become stiff. If the skewer arm closes with no resistance, then you'll need to screw in the skewer nut on the opposite side of the skewer. If there is too much resistance, then unthread the skewer nut and try again. ▶

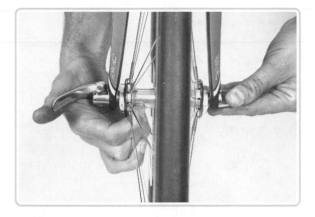

5 Check Adjustment

Position the skewer arm so that nothing interferes with its fully closing. I usually close the front skewer arm so that it is horizontal and facing backward and to the rear so that the skewer is facing slightly forward and down and away from the frame. This keeps any part of the frame or fork from interfering with the skewer arm's closing. ▶

6 Opening the Skewer

To open the quick-release skewer and remove the wheel, simply flip open the skewer arm. If it's the rear skewer, you can immediately remove the wheel. If it's the front wheel, you may need to back the skewer nut off a couple of turns to get the lever past the lawyer tabs. ▶

Truing a Wheel

When truing a bicycle wheel, there are three adjustments that can be made. The *trueness* of a wheel refers to the straightness of the rim on a horizontal plane. The *roundness* of the wheel is a measurement of the rim's levelness on a vertical plane. The *dish* is a measurement of where the rim sits in relation to the center of the hub.

When truing a wheel, you must take all three measurements into account, although the dish is usually adjusted only when the wheel is built. When truing a wheel, the trueness is adjusted first, then the roundness, and finally the dish if necessary. You may need to readjust the trueness after adjusting the roundness or dish because each adjustment can affect the others. ▶

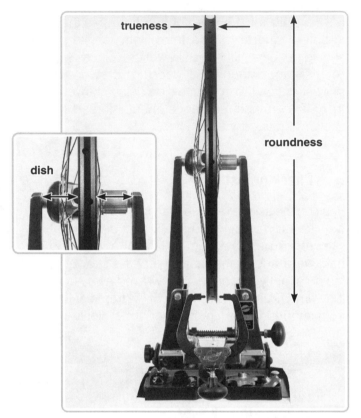

Adjust the Trueness

If your wheel is out of true, it will move side to side between the brake track while the wheel is spinning. Follow these steps to straighten the rim:

1 Place the Wheel in a Truing Stand

A truing stand has two arms that move in or out toward the rim so that you can determine where the wheel is out of true. Adjust the arms up or down until they are aligned with the rim. Dial the arms in until any part of the rim hits the arm—if the wheel is true, then all points of the rim will hit the arms at the same adjustment. ▶

2 Select the Correct Spoke Tool

Spoke nipples come in various sizes (called gauges), so you need to have the correct spoke tool for the nipple size. The fit should be tight so that there's no slippage, which can damage the nipple. Most high-end road bikes use 15- or 16-gauge nipples, and cheaper bikes use larger nipples. The gauge number grows larger as the diameter gets smaller; therefore; a 15-gauge nipple is smaller than a 13 gauge. ▶

3 Determine Where the Rim Is Out of True

A properly built wheel will have the rim centered between the two outer flanges of the hub. If the rim has any spot that is to the left or the right of that center line, it is considered to be out of true. Most truing stands have two arms that can be dialed in so that proper left and right boundaries can be established for trueness. If your truing stand has only one arm, you can true one side and then remove the wheel and turn it around to true the other.

4 Adjust Trueness

The rim is centered between the outer flanges of the hub by the spokes on either side pulling on the rim. When the spokes on both sides of the rim are tensioned evenly, then the rim is centered. To pull the rim to the right, tighten the right-side nipples and loosen the left-side nipples equally. It's best to do adjustments a bit at a time; a couple of turns can make a large difference. *Note:* Spokes are right-hand threaded (righty, tighty—lefty, loosey), but, because the spokes are upside down as you're adjusting them, you'll actually turn the spoke tool to the *left* to tighten the nipple. ▶

5 De-Bind the Nipples

Often when you tighten a nipple, the spoke will bind a bit, and the nipple will turn in the rim a small amount. This will add tension to the entire spoke and nipple system, but, when the nipple resettles in the rim bed (usually the first time you ride it), it will lower the tension and cause the wheel to go out of true. When truing the wheel, it's a good idea to periodically grab parallel spokes and squeeze them together with your hands. This helps settle any binding nipples so that you can properly true the wheel. Be careful—you don't need to squeeze too hard! Use about as much force as you would to open a car door handle. ▼

When truing a wheel that has bladelike aero spokes, you must use something to hold the spoke as you tighten the nipple to prevent the spoke from turning. Most wheels that have aero spokes will come with a spoke holder, but in a pinch, a pair of pliers can be used. ▼

Adjust the Roundness

If the wheel is out of round, the rim will move up and down while the wheel is spinning, creating a lumpy ride. Follow these steps to adjust the roundness:

1 Place the Wheel in a Truing Stand

If you have just trued the wheel laterally, then there's no need to move it! Adjust the truing stand's arms so that they sit below the rim instead of being aligned next to it; it's best to remove the tire and tube while doing this. You can adjust the roundness of the wheel with the tire installed, but there may be imperfections in the tire that aren't actually in the wheel itself. ▶

2 Select the Correct Spoke Tool

Spoke nipples come in various sizes (called gauges), so you need to have the correct spoke tool for the nipple size. The fit should be tight so that there's no slippage, which can damage the nipple. Most high-end road bikes use 15- or 16-gauge nipples, and cheaper bikes use larger nipples. The gauge number grows larger as the diameter gets smaller; therefore, a 15-gauge nipple is smaller than a 13 gauge.

3 Determine Where the Rim Is Out of Round

Just as the left and right tension of the spokes pulls the rim out of center, the tension of the spokes above and below the hub can pull the wheel out of round. Adjust the arms of the truing stand so that the rim scrapes the arms where it's out of round. If all parts of the rim scrape the arms equally, then the wheel is round. ▼

4 Adjust Spoke Tension

Where the rim is scraping the arm is called the high point of the wheel (if you inverted the truing stand so the arms were on the top, then that part of the rim would be taller than all other parts). To pull the high point in toward the hub, tighten the spokes that are immediately under the high point (once again, think of inverting the wheel). Tighten the left- and right-side spokes evenly to maintain trueness. Low points of the wheel can be brought toward the arms by doing the opposite—loosening the spokes under the low points. Adjust the high and low points until the wheel is evenly round. *Note:* Often when the rim has a high point, the opposite side of the wheel will have a low point. Do small adjustments at both sides of the wheel to help maintain proper overall tension. ▶

5 De-Bind the Nipples

Just as when you're truing the wheel, periodically grab parallel spokes between your fingers and squeeze to help de-bind any nipples that have turned in the rim. Use as much pressure as you would to open a car door handle.

6 Check Trueness

Often, when you've gotten your wheel perfectly round, it may have come a bit out of true. Re-true your wheel (see page 68) and check the roundness. You may have to go back and forth between adjusting the trueness and adjusting the roundness before you get both perfect.

Adjust the Dish

If your wheel is dished incorrectly, it will not sit evenly in your frame and may cause the tire to rub the frame on one side. Follow these steps to adjust the dish:

1 Determine the Proper Dish

Use a dishing tool to determine if the wheel is dished properly, meaning the rim is centered between the outer ends of the hub's axle. The dishing tool sits on the rim, and a gauge can be threaded in or out to touch the end of the axle. Place the tool on one side of the wheel and adjust the gauge so that it touches the axle. Without touching the gauge, place the dishing tool on the opposite side of the wheel and check where the gauge is. ▶

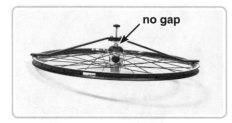

- If the gauge is touching the axle and the dishing tool is touching the rim, then the rim is centered and dished properly. ▶

- If the gauge is not touching the axle but the dishing tool is touching the rim, then you must adjust the dish. The amount of space between the gauge and the axle is the distance that the rim is off center. Move on to step 2. ▶

- If the gauge is touching the axle but the dishing tool is not touching the rim, readjust the gauge to fit this side of the wheel. Then put the dishing tool on the other side of the wheel to determine how much the wheel should be dished. ▼

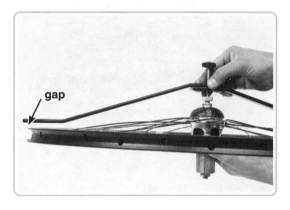

2 Place Wheel in Truing Stand

Make note of which side of the wheel needs to be adjusted. A truing stand has two arms that move in or out toward the rim so that you can determine where the wheel is out of true. Adjust the arms up or down until they are aligned with the rim.

3 Adjust the Dish

The spokes opposite to the side of the wheel that has a gap to the dishing tool gauge need to be tightened, and the spokes on the side with the gap need to be loosened. If the drive side of the wheel has the gap, think of pulling the nondrive side of the rim *away* from the gap so that it pulls the hub *toward* the gap and thus evens the dish. ▶

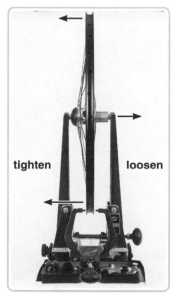

tighten   loosen

Start at the valve hole and tighten every nipple on the correct side a quarter turn, then loosen every nipple on the other side a quarter turn. Recheck the dish. Repeat until there is no gap on either side of the axle when the dishing tool is applied. Sound confusing? There's an easy way to make sure you're doing it right. If, after adjusting the dish, the gap between the axle and the dishing tool has gotten larger, then you're adjusting the spokes the wrong way! ▼

4 De-Bind the Nipples

After you've adjusted the nipples on both sides of the wheel, grab each set of parallel spokes between your fingers and squeeze to help de-bind any nipples that have turned in the rim. Use as much pressure as you would to open a car door handle.

5 Check Trueness and Roundness

Re-true your wheel (see page 68) and check the roundness (see page 70). Either adjustment may have been altered while adjusting the dish.

Replacing Spokes and Nipples

If a spoke or a nipple breaks altogether, obviously you cannot simply true the wheel to get it right again. You'll have to replace the broken spoke or nipple. This usually involves removing the tire and rim strip (or tubular tire if you're not using clinchers) and the cassette if the spoke is on the rear wheel. This may seem like a daunting task at first, but the process of installing a spoke is essentially the same as truing the wheel (see page 68).

If the nipple is broken, you may be able to reuse the spoke that's on the wheel. If the spoke is broken (and the part threaded in the nipple can be removed), then you can reuse the nipple inserted in the rim. Figure out what needs to be replaced, and then follow the appropriate steps.

Broken Spoke

If a spoke is broken and the broken part of the spoke can be removed from the nipple, you can reuse the nipple, saving you some time and a tiny bit of money.

1 Remove Broken Spoke

First, remove the lower portion of the broken spoke (the part that is not threaded into the nipple). If it's on the rear wheel, you may need to remove the cassette to facilitate this (see page 171). ▶

2 Unthread Spoke From Nipple

No need to take off the tire and rim strip; simply hold the spoke with the spoke tool (or pliers) and unthread the upper portion of the broken spoke from the nipple. Be extra careful to hold on to that nipple with your hand or spoke tool because, if it falls into the rim cavity, you may never see it again. If this does happen, remove the tire and rim strip (or tubular tire), and try to shake the nipple out of the rim through the spoke holes (or, if you can simply live with the rattling critter in the wheel, it won't hurt anything). ▶

3 Install New Spoke

Install the new spoke (make sure you have the same size and gauge as the previous spoke) by installing it the same way the old one came out. If you don't remember which way it came out, take a note of how its adjacent neighbor is laced, especially how it laces over or under other spokes, and do the same. Remember, if it doesn't look right, it probably isn't right. ▶

4 Tension the Spoke

Thread the existing nipple onto the new spoke until you feel a little resistance on the spoke tool. Keep turning a half turn at a time until you reach the proper tension. If you have a tensiometer (a device that measures spoke tension), you can use that to get the spoke to the same tension as the rest of the wheel. However, most at-home mechanics don't have a tensiometer; in fact, I never use mine except when building a new wheel. The best way to check tension is also the traditional way—by using pitch. Pluck the spokes around the new spoke as you would a guitar string. Then pluck the new spoke. If the pitch is lower, you need to add tension and vice versa. Seems low tech, but it works every time. ▶

5 True the Whole Wheel

True the whole wheel as you would normally (see page 68). Other spokes' tension and the overall trueness may have been affected by the broken spoke.

Broken Nipple

If the nipple itself is broken (or the spoke is broken in the nipple and cannot be removed), then you'll have to replace the nipple or both the nipple and the spoke.

1 Remove the Tire

To get the nipple out of the rim, you must first remove the tire and tube (or tubular tire if applicable) and then remove the rim strip. The rim strip may be a single plastic or rubber lining, or it may be a strip of cotton cloth with adhesive backing. Either way, save the rim strip because it can be reused. ▼

2 Remove the Broken Nipple and/or Spoke

Hold on to the broken nipple, and rotate the wheel so that the broken nipple is facing straight down. Simply let go of the nipple and let it fall out of the rim. Be careful not to let the nipple fall into the rim because it's difficult to remove once in there. If this does happen, try to shake the nipple out of the rim through the spoke holes. If the spoke is broken as well, remove that from the hub. If it's the rear, you may need to remove the cassette to facilitate its removal. ▼

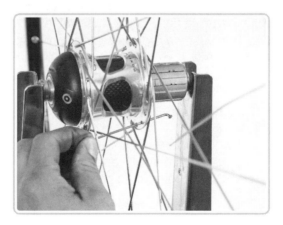

3 Install New Spoke

Install the new spoke (make sure you have the same size and gauge as the previous spoke) by installing it the same way the old one came out. If you don't remember which way it came out, take note of how its adjacent neighbor is laced, especially how it laces over or under other spokes, and do the same. Remember, if it doesn't look right, it probably isn't right. ▶

4 Install New Nipple

Insert a new nipple into the rim. If it's a deep-section rim or has spoke eyelets that are not closed off from the inside of the rim, then use something to hold the nipple while inserting it into the rim. I use another spoke of the same gauge, threading it into the back of the nipple and using it as a handle. ▶

5 Tension the Spoke

Thread the nipple onto the new spoke until you feel a little resistance on the spoke tool. Keep turning a half turn at a time until you reach the proper tension. If you have a tensiometer (a device that measures spoke tension), you can use that to get the spoke to the same tension as the rest of the wheel. However, most at-home mechanics don't have a tensiometer; in fact, I never use mine except when building a new wheel. The best way to check tension is also the traditional way—by using pitch. Pluck the spokes around the new spoke as you would a guitar string. Then pluck the new spoke. If the pitch is lower, you need to add tension and vice versa. Seems low tech, but it works every time.

6 True the Whole Wheel

True the whole wheel as you would normally (see page 68). Other spokes' tension and the overall trueness may have been affected by the broken spoke.

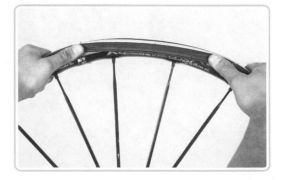

7 Install Tire

Reuse the rim strip, tube, and tire that you've removed to replace the spoke or reglue the tubular tire. Installation of clincher and tubular tires will be covered in chapter 7. ▶

Adjusting Hubs

Bicycle hubs have traditionally been built using loose ball bearings seated in cups built into the hub shell. Attached to the axle are angled hub cones that, when properly adjusted, roll smoothly on the bearings with no binding and no play. These so-called cup-and-cone hubs are smooth, infinitely adjustable, and easily serviced. This section will cover the adjustment of these types of hubs.

Most modern wheels, however, no longer use cup-and-cone hubs. They incorporate what are called cartridge bearings—the cup, cone, and ball bearings are built into a single unit that is installed into the hub shell. These types of bearings may have a very small amount of adjustability to them, but in large part, they are either in perfect working order or need to be entirely replaced.

cup and cone bearing

cartridge bearing

1 Determine Hub Adjustment

With the wheel installed in the bike, grab the rim and rock it side to side. If there is play in the wheel, the hub is too loose and needs to be tightened. Spin the wheel and check that it rolls smoothly. If the wheel stops spinning after only a couple of rotations or if it feels rough and you hear a crunching sound, the hub is too tight and you may need to replace the cone(s) (see page 86). ▶

2 Remove the Skewer and Cassette If Needed

For both front and rear wheels, remove the skewer, and, if you're adjusting the rear, remove the cassette as well (see chapter 11).

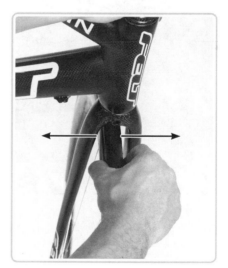

3 Tighten One Side of Axle

Pick one side of the axle to tighten; it doesn't really matter which one you choose. One side needs to be fully tight so that the other side can be adjusted. If both sides are loose, then it becomes impossible to adjust the hub correctly. Select the correct size cone wrench and place on the cone. Use an adjustable wrench and place on the locknut. Hold the locknut in place, and tighten the cone against the locknut by turning it counterclockwise. ▶

4 Place Locknut in Vise

Place the locknut on the side of the axle that you have just tightened into a vise. Clamp just the flat part of the locknut so that the wheel is securely held in the vise. *Note:* Some hubs may have a locknut that doesn't have a large flat surface that will fit in a vise. In this case, you'll have to use an axle clamp. An axle clamp fits into the vise and holds the axle rather than the locknut. ▼

5 Loosen Locknut on Opposite Side

Loosen the locknut on the side of the axle that is not clamped in the vise. Hold the cone with a cone wrench, and use a large adjustable wrench to loosen the locknut by turning it counterclockwise. ▶

6 Inspect the Cones

If the hub was making a crunching noise or was running particularly rough, inspect the cones for signs of pitting or wear. If the cones need to be replaced, see page 86. ▶

7 Grease the Bearings

While the hub is opened, it's a good idea to put new grease in the hubs. A grease gun is handy for injecting new grease into the hub without removing the axle. It's impossible to overgrease a hub, so don't be stingy. ▶

8 Adjust the Cone

- Use the cone wrench to adjust the cone in or out, depending on which adjustment needs to be made. Adjusting the hub is a process of trial and error. ▼

- Once the cone is adjusted, then hold the cone with the cone wrench and tighten the locknut. ▼

- Remove the wheel and check the axle's adjustment. The wheel should turn freely and smoothly with no play in the bearings. If the hub isn't perfectly adjusted the first time, put it back in the vise and start again. It usually takes several adjustments to get it perfect!

9 Check Adjustment in Wheel

When you think that you have the axle adjustment just right, replace the skewer and put the wheel in the bike. Spin the wheel and check the adjustment. The hub becomes a bit tighter when the skewer is tightened, so you may need to have a tiny bit of play in the wheel when it's off the bike to get it perfect when it's in the bike and the skewer is tightened.

10 Install Cassette

If you are adjusting the rear wheel, reinstall the cassette (see chapter 11).

Making Special Wheel Repairs

Sometimes you may need to go above and beyond a simple adjustment to the wheel. If the wheel is getting a bit old, you may need to overhaul it to keep it running smoothly. Or you may have had a crash and need to do an extensive wheel repair. Here are some of the more common special wheel repairs.

Lubricating the Freehub

The freehub is basically a shell with a ratcheting system that sits on the hub body. The shell will turn freely in one direction but will engage in the other direction. This is accomplished by use of tiny spring-loaded clips called *pawls*. The pawls are attached to the hub body and will lay flat as the ratcheted freehub body moves in one direction (coasting) but will catch the ratchets in the other direction (pedaling), thus turning the hub body and wheel.

To keep the freehub body turning smoothly on the hub shell and the pawls working properly, you should periodically lube the freehub and check for damage. This should be done at least every six months of riding, more often if you live in a rainy or snowy climate. An easy way to check whether your freehub needs lubing is to spin the rear wheel forward and see if it "pushes" the chain and cranks—this happens with a dirty freehub that doesn't move smoothly over the pawls and hub shell.

Before working on the freehub, find a clean, well-lit work space. The pawls are spring loaded and can easily pop out as you remove the freehub from the wheel. They're tiny and can readily be lost.

1 Remove Axle End Cap

- If you have a cup-and-cone–type hub, put the nondrive side of the rear wheel into an axle vise. Hold the drive-side cone with a cone wrench, and use a large adjustable wrench to loosen the locknut. Unthread both from the axle and set aside. ▶

- If you have a cartridge-style hub, there are several ways the axle end cap might come off. It's common for the axle end caps to have flats for Allen wrenches (usually two 5 mm flats on each side), and they are unthreaded. They might simply slide off or be held on with a small grub screw. ▼

With others, particularly the DT Swiss hubs, you may need to pull the entire cassette or freehub body off, taking the axle end cap off with it. ▶

- Some hubs use a combination of these styles, such as the Mavic rear hubs. They use a 5-millimeter hex key on the drive side and a 10-millimeter hex key on the nondrive side. To get to the 10-millimeter hex, however, you have to pull the nondrive-side cap off with your fingers. ▶

2 Remove the Freehub

With the axle end caps off, the freehub body will easily slide off the hub shell (or already has if you have a DT Swiss hub). Go slowly; the pawls will pop up as they're released and may have a tendency to go flying. Set the freehub aside. ▶

3 Remove the Pawls

You can leave the pawls on while wiping down the hub body, but, in my experience, they always fall off anyway. Make a mental note of how they fit into the hub body—they'll usually have a slot that the pawl ends slide into and an indent where the spring is positioned. Lift them up from the body, and they should release easily. ▶

4 Clean Hub Body and Freehub

Use a clean, lint-free rag and wipe down the inside of the freehub body and all of the surfaces of the hub shell. You can use a light degreaser such as Simple Green, but in my experience, simply wiping these surfaces down cleans them spotlessly.

5 Lube Hub Body and Freehub Body

Use a lightweight grease (Shimano makes an excellent freehub-specific grease) and apply liberally to the inside of the freehub and on the hub body. To get the best performance, but with less longevity, use mineral oil to lube the freehub instead of grease. I find this works particularly well with Mavic hubs but makes the maintenance intervals shorter.

6 Reattach Pawls

Slide the pawls back into the hub body and seat the spring in the spring indent. When the pawls are correctly inserted into the hub body, they will hold themselves in place. ▶

7 Install Freehub

Slide the freehub onto the hub body. Use your free hand to hold the pawls down flat on the hub body so the freehub can slide over them. As you install the freehub, rotate it counterclockwise as you slide it down; this helps press the pawls flat against the hub body and prevents binding. ▶

8 Reattach Axle End Cap

When the freehub is slid fully onto the hub body, check that it rotates freely and does not bind anywhere. If it does not freely rotate, a pawl may not be seated correctly, and you'll have to start again. Once the freehub is on, reattach the end cap and adjust the hub if necessary.

Overhauling Hubs or Replacing Cones

If the cup-and-cone hub is making a crunching noise and feels rough while it spins, you may need to replace the axle cones. Over time, the axle cones may become pitted for several reasons—usually either from dirt contamination or from riding on an improperly adjusted hub. It's important to either overhaul the hub or replace the cones once they start to go bad. You can easily ruin your hub as the hub cups become pitted and damaged by the damaged cones and bearings. Overhauling a hub will help considerably; fresh grease and new ball bearings can do wonders. But if you're determined to have the smoothest, perfect hub, you need to completely replace the cones once they're damaged.

Overhauling Hubs

When the hub begins to run a little rough, it may be time to overhaul it. By cleaning and regreasing the hub bearings and races, you'll extend the life of the hubs and maintain optimal performance.

1 Place Wheel in Vise

Place the wheel in a vise, clamping onto the flat surfaces of the locknut. If the locknut does not have a suitable flat surface, use an axle clamp in the vise to hold the axle. ▶

2 Remove Axle End Cap

Hold the cone with a cone wrench, and loosen the locknut with an adjustable wrench. Unthread both and remove from axle. ▶

3 Remove the Wheel From Vise

Hold the axle in place as you remove the wheel from the vise to prevent the axle and ball bearings from falling out and disappearing.

4 Remove the Axle

Slide the axle out of the other side of the wheel. Some ball bearings may fall out as you do this. Be careful to keep track of them. ▶

5 Remove Ball Bearings

Remove the ball bearings from the hub cups. You can use your fingers to grab them, a screwdriver to pop them out, or a magnet to pull them out. The magnet method is the most effective and quickest. Set them aside. ▶

6 Clean All Surfaces

Use a clean, lint-free rag and wipe down the axle, cones, hub cups, and ball bearings. A light degreaser works well for removing any built-up grease or grime. You want all the surfaces polished and shining.

7 Inspect All Parts

Inspect all of the surfaces of the hub parts. If the ball bearings are dull in appearance or notably pitted, replace them. If the hub shell is significantly pitted or damaged beyond use, you'll need a new hub. More frequently, the cones will be pitted and in need of replacement (see next section on replacing cones).

Replacing Cones

A hub cone is the angular surface that serves as the contact point between the axle and the bearings. The cones need to be smooth and well greased for the hub to work properly and run smoothly. On a townie or winter training bike, I'll usually replace only pitted cones when they are extremely rough because an overhaul will usually make them run pretty well. On a race bike, however, any pitting or damage robs you of significant watts.

Cones have three measurements: the axle thread pitch (which axle size they thread onto), their height (specifically the height of the beveled edge that contacts the bearings), and the angle of the beveled edge of the cone. Make sure you have the correct replacement cone for your hub. If in doubt, remove the old cone and compare it to the new one.

1 Replace One Cone

- Place the axle in an axle clamp with the cone and locknut facing up.
- Measure the distance from the surface of the locknut to the end of the axle and write this number down. ▶

- Use a cone wrench to hold the cone, and loosen the locknut with an adjustable wrench. Unthread both. ▶

- Thread the replacement cone on the axle and the locknut over it.
- When the locknut is at the same measurement from the axle end as before, hold the locknut with the adjustable wrench and tighten the cone against it (by turning it counterclockwise) with the cone wrench. Make sure they are quite tight. ▶

2 Install the Ball Bearings

Apply a liberal amount of thick grease onto the surface of the hub cups. Install the clean or new ball bearings one at a time so that they nestle into the shell and are held in place by the thick grease. Typically, there will be the same number of ball bearings on each side of the hub, but this is not always the case. As you install the bearings, it becomes obvious if you have too many or too few—they will fit all the way into the hub cup with no gaps between them and none falling out into the hub body. ▶

3 Install Axle

Slide the axle into the wheel on the side from which it was removed. Go slowly and carefully so that the ball bearings do not unseat during installation. Fully insert the axle with the cone flush against the bearings and hold in place. ▶

4 Replace Second Cone

While holding the axle in place, thread the second replacement cone onto the axle until it is flush with the ball bearings. Thread the locknut over the second cone and finger tighten to keep the axle and ball bearings in place. ▶

5 Place Wheel in Vise

Reinstall the wheel into the vise, clamping the flat surfaces on the locknut of the first side—the side that has been tightened so that the finger-tight cone and locknut are on the top.

6 Adjust the Cone

- Use the cone wrench to adjust the cone in or out, depending on which adjustment needs to be made. Adjusting the hub is a process of trial and error. ▶

- Once the cone is adjusted, hold the cone with the cone wrench and tighten the lock-nut. ▶
- Remove the wheel and check the axle's adjustment. The wheel should turn freely and smoothly with no play in the bearings. If the hub isn't perfectly adjusted the first time, put it back in the vise and start again. It usually takes several adjustments to get it perfect!

7 Check Adjustment in Wheel

When you feel that you have the axle adjustment just right, replace the skewer and put the wheel in the bike. Spin the wheel and check the adjustment. The hub becomes a little tighter when the skewer is tightened, so you may need to have a tiny bit of play in the wheel when it's off the bike to get it perfect when it's in the bike and the skewer is tightened.

Replacing Cartridge Bearings

Cartridge bearings are self-enclosed bearing systems; the ball bearings are packed between two bearing races (the inner and outer shells of the cartridge). When the cartridge bearing is functioning correctly, the inner race will move independently of the outer race, smoothly and quietly. Cartridge bearings are somewhat serviceable, but, in general, if they go bad, they need to be replaced. You can pry the seal off a cartridge bearing to clean the balls inside and inject new grease, but this is usually done more as a preventive measure to elongate the life of the bearings (especially expensive ceramic bearings).

When the cartridge bearing goes bad, it will sound similar to a cup-and-cone bearing with a pitted cone—a crunching noise while the wheel spins and a rough feeling. Unlike cup-and-cone hubs, if you continue to ride a damaged cartridge bearing, it won't harm the wheel at all because the cup part of the bearing is built into the cartridge and not a part of the hub itself.

1 Remove the Axle End Caps

The axle end caps will come off either with an Allen wrench, by loosening a small grub screw, or they will simply pull off. Remove both. ▶

2 Remove the Axle

Usually, but not always, when the end caps are removed, the axle can then be removed. The axle may slide out easily or may need to be tapped out with a soft mallet. On the rear hub, the axle will generally come out of the nondrive side. On a front hub, typically it doesn't matter which side it comes out. *Note:* Some hubs may have a retainer that holds the axle in place. Whether they're thread on, slide on, or other, it's typically easy to figure out how they work and are removed. ▼

3 Remove Cartridge Bearings

Using the flat end of a large Allen wrench (an 8 or a 10 works well), punch out both cartridge bearings from the inside by tapping the Allen wrench with a hammer. Don't do this if you're planning on reusing the bearings because this will ruin them. If you do plan on reusing the bearings, it will require specific bearing punches designed for each bearing size so that the races are not damaged during removal. Place the bearing punch between the bearing and Allen wrench and tap out with a hammer. ▶

4 Install New Bearings

- Wipe down the hub shell and lightly grease.
- Find a socket that is slightly smaller than the outside diameter (OD) of the bearing that you're installing. You want the socket to contact the outermost part of the bearing. If you install a bearing by pressing on the innermost part of the assembly, it will ruin the bearing. ▶

- Place both bearings on both sides of the hub.
- Use a quick-release skewer with the springs removed to hold the sockets over the two bearings. Slowly tighten the quick-release skewer, continually checking that the bearing is going in straight. Continue to tighten until the bearings are flush with the hub body. ▼

Note: You can use the old bearing that was removed in place of the socket to push a new bearing in; this has the advantage of being the exact size of the new bearing. But, if the new bearing is not flush with the lip of the hub shell, the old bearing can become stuck as you're installing the new one. ▶

5 Reinstall Axle

Reinstall the axle in the reverse order of its removal by tapping it in with a soft mallet. Reinstall the end caps, and your wheel will be as good as new. ▶

Rebuilding a Wheel With a New Rim

If you've damaged your rim but the wheel itself is not ruined, it's possible to rebuild the wheel with a new rim. Unlike building a new wheel from scratch, rebuilding the wheel is not a terribly daunting proposition. The hub, spokes, and nipples can all be reused without removing them from the wheel. You will, however, need a tensiometer to properly tension the wheel after relacing the spokes and a decent truing stand to get the trueness, roundness, and dish correct. This section will cover the lacing and initial tensioning of the wheel to learn how to true, round, and dish a wheel.

1 Measure Tension of Wheel

Use the tensiometer to measure the tension of the spokes before unlacing them. Jot this number down. This will give you a good idea of how much the new wheel needs to be tensioned. Follow the directions on your specific tensiometer to get an accurate reading. ▶

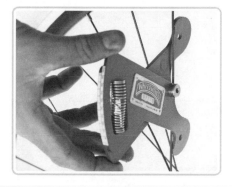

2 Tape New Rim to Old

Line the new rim up to the old so that the valve holes are in the same position. Use electrical tape at the 12, 3, 6, and 9 o'clock positions to tape the new rim to the old. ▶

3 Relace Spokes

- One at a time, unthread the nipple from a spoke.
- Rethread the nipple and spoke onto the new rim. Simply relace each spoke onto the spoke hole directly next to it. ▶
- Apply a drop of linseed oil (or other spoke prep) on the threads, and tighten the nipple until there are three threads showing on the spoke.

4 Tension Wheel

Start at the valve hole and turn each nipple a half turn. Check the tension. Continue tightening the entire wheel, a half turn at a time until the wheel is at the correct tension. ▶

5 Check the Trueness, Roundness, and Dish

To check the trueness, roundness, and dish, see page 68 for detailed instructions.

Choosing the Right Wheels for a Specific Task

Just as no two riders are exactly the same, no two wheels will treat everyone equally. There are several choices when it comes to wheel selection, and finding the perfect pair for your needs can be a difficult proposition. But instead of looking at it as a challenge to be overcome, choosing a pair of wheels should instead be viewed as an opportunity to explore the variety of options.

There are some basic questions that should be taken into account before choosing a wheelset—questions that are less a matter of personal preference but more about pure necessity. Do you have a Campagnolo or Shimano drivetrain? Are you running an archaic six-speed cogset or top-of-the-line offerings? Is your bike built for 650C wheels? These are some of the large-picture questions that have to be addressed first.

If you walk into any bike shop and tell the laconic, underpaid teenager working behind the counter, "I'm looking for new wheels," you'll likely get a blank stare in return. Some of the more cognitively capable individuals might formulate an appropriate response: "For what?"

That, fundamentally, is the only question that matters when you're selecting a wheelset. For what are they going to be used? If you're a middle-of-the-pack age-group triathlete, your needs are going to be much different from the needs of a professional road sprinter, just as his or her needs will be much different from the needs of an octogenarian lawyer who likes to cruise the bike path and look at the creek. I believe there are, in essence, three major criteria that distinguish one pair of wheels from another. They are, in no particular order, build, weight, and aerodynamics.

The build refers to the basic design of the wheel. The design of the wheel includes the broader questions, such as 8- or 10-speed or Shimano or Campagnolo, but also some of the more preferential concerns. Decide whether you want clincher or tubular (more on that in chapter 7). Some wheels have nifty features like ceramic bearings or dimpled rims. Some wheels are sturdier than others in certain situations. If you're a physically heavier rider, this can be a major concern.

The weight question is pretty straightforward. How light do you want your wheels to be? Some super-lightweight wheels may accelerate like rockets and help you shave minutes off your climbing PRs, but they can have poor ride quality and be unable to withstand even the lightest abuse. Take into account your build and riding style when deciding whether you need a super-lightweight pair of wheels.

The aerodynamic aspects of a wheel usually go hand in hand with the weight. Aero wheels are usually heavier but are faster on the flats. Are you a time trialist or a triathlete? Get some deep-dish aero wheels and forget about the weight penalty. If you're a 110-pound (50 kg) climbing specialist, get the lightweight wheels, which will help you excel at your specialty.

One of the largest factors to consider is the price of the wheelset. There's an old adage in the bike industry: "Strong, light, and fast. Pick two." With today's modern technology and ingenuity, it's really a new paradigm: "Strong, light, fast, and cheap. Pick three."

So next time you're in the market for a new pair of wheels, ask yourself one question—for what?

CHAPTER 7

Tires

"**K**eep the rubber side down!" is a maxim that you've probably heard at one time or another if you've spent any time at all on a bike. It's both a funny and prescient sentiment because your tires are, ultimately, the only real point of physical interaction between your bike and the road.

Tires began to take their familiar modern-day rendition when the safety bicycle was introduced in the late-19th century. Originally invented in the middle of the century in England, the pneumatic bicycle tire wasn't commercially produced until 1888 by a Scottish doctor named John Boyd Dunlop. The original pneumatic tire was a clincher type; a vulcanized rubber tube was fitted inside the tire, which was then attached to the rim by a series of clamps. These tire systems were bulky and unreliable, and so a new technology was developed around the turn of the century—the tubular tire.

Still in use today, tubular tires are similar to clinchers in that there's a tube inside of the tire that is inflated to provide ride quality. Unlike clinchers, however, the casing of a tubular tire fully surrounds the tube and the entire tire and tube combo is glued to the rim using a special type of cement. The modern clincher tire came about in 1978 when Specialized introduced the Turbo folding clincher. Popular among casual cyclist for its ease of installation and reliability, clincher tires have now surpassed tubulars as the more popular road tire. With no messy, strong cement to deal with, clinchers made installing tires and, especially, repairing them easy and hassle free. They've also become the more economical choice—when you flat a tube, you don't have to replace an entire, expensive tubular tire.

Tubular tires are far from dead, though. They offer several advantages that some riders, especially racing cyclists, still prefer. Almost all of the professional cycling teams that I know of still use tubular tires, despite the advances in clincher technology and construction. Because there is no hook-and-bead interaction between a tubular tire and the rim (as there is on a clincher), the tire deforms more uniformly as the bike is leaned into a corner. This provides better traction and better predictability while diving down a sketchy descent. Also, because there is no stiff bead on the tubular tire, the entire casing can be made out of more supple materials, giving the tubular an unmatched ride quality—what the French call, *souplesse*. Last, and this definitely applies mainly to racing cyclists, a tubular tire can much more easily be ridden while flat, allowing you to keep going while waiting for your team car or wheel support to get to you.

The latest technology to be introduced to the road market comes directly from mountain biking. Tubeless tires are exactly what their name implies—without tubes. Based on the technology used for car tires, tubeless tires require specialized rims that are airtight and equally specialized tires that create an airtight seal when the two are used in conjunction. The main benefits of tubeless systems are flat prevention (specifically pinch flats—there's no tube to pinch) and better ride quality (you can safely run them at lower pressure than standard clinchers).

Installing Clincher Tires

Clincher tires are standardized by size, so, if you have a 700C rim, a 700C tire will be compatible. Tires are labeled the same way that rims are, but also the width is provided in their designation. A 700C x 23 tire has a 700C diameter and a width of 23 millimeters. The same applies for the tubes used in clincher wheels, although there is some leeway as far as width is concerned. A 700C x 18 to 23 tube (one that is designed for an 18–23 mm wide tire) will probably work fine in a 700C x 25 tire but may explode in a 700C x 34 cyclocross tire.

1 Inspect the Rim

This is especially important if you're installing a tire on a used rim. Closely inspect the rim for damage that may prevent the tire from being installed correctly or that may damage the tube. Any burrs or gouges should be filed down until smooth.

2 Inspect the Rim Tape

- The rim tape (usually made of cotton or plastic) covers the spoke holes on the rim so the tube does not push through them and tear. Make sure each hole is covered and there is no significant sign of wear. *Note:* Some rims, like those on Mavic's Ksyrium and R-Sys wheels, do not need a rim strip because there are no spoke holes in the rim surface.

- If new rim strips need to be installed, start by lining up the valve hole in the rim strip with the valve hole in the rim. Drop a screwdriver in the valve hole to hold the rim strip in place as you install it on your rim. ▶

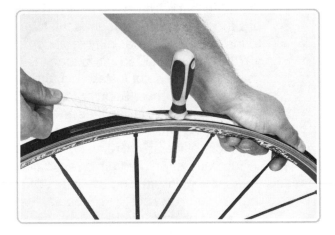

3 Install Tire's First Bead

The tire beads are the stiff rings on the inside edges of the tire that hook onto the rim. To install a tire's first bead, follow these instructions:

- Find the tire's label and always put the tire's label directly over the valve hole so that if you get a flat, you can line up the tube with the tire and wheel to help determine what caused the flat.

- You should be able to put the entire bead of the tire on the rim with your hands, but, if the tire is extremely tight, you may need to use a tire iron to pry the bead onto the rim. A tire iron hooks over the lip of the rim and acts as a lever on the tire to lift it onto the rim. ▶

4 Inflate Tube and Install in Tire

Put a small amount of air in the tube (just enough to give the tube some shape, maybe 5 psi at most), and place the tube's valve in the valve hole. Push the tube into the tire around its entire circumference. ▶

Note: Almost all modern road bikes use tubes that have a Presta valve, but some may have a Schrader valve—the same valve used in car tires. Make sure that the valve you have is compatible with your rim. It will be obvious if you have the wrong type because the rim valve holes for Presta and Schraeder valves are very different in size.

5 Install Tire's Second Bead

The tire beads are the stiff rings on the inside edges of the tire that hook onto the rim. Starting at the valve hole, use your thumbs to install the tire's second bead. Hold the wheel in front of you, and pry the bead up and over the lip of the rim in incremental steps. If you become efficient at doing this, you may be able to install the entire bead with just your hands. If the last bit becomes too difficult to do by hand, use a tire lever to pry the last bit on. Be very careful not to pinch the tube between the tire and the tire lever because this will tear a hole in the tube. ▶

6 Check That the Tire Is Seated Correctly

Put a bit of air in the tire, around 30 to 40 pounds per square inch. Check that the bead is seated correctly in the rim. If the bead is seated correctly, there should be no place where the bead is coming off the rim or where the bead is stuck down inside the lip of the rim. In either case, deflate the tire and adjust by hand.

Note: If you're having difficulty seating the rim correctly, it may help to lubricate the tube with talcum powder. Place the tube in a self-locking bag, and put a couple of shakes of talcum powder in with it. Close the bag and shake so the tube is covered evenly. Reinsert the tube in the tire and try again.

7   Inflate Tire

Inflate the tire to full pressure (the recommended pressure is usually labeled on the tire), and recheck that the tire is properly seated in the rim. Smaller riders can use less pressure, while larger ones may need more to prevent pinch flats, but the max I recommend for clinchers is 120 pounds per square inch. Very light riders can get away with as little as 105 pounds per square inch, but I would not recommend ever going lower. Use about 5 pounds per square inch less in wet conditions to improve traction. *Note:* Tubes come with a valve cap and a little knurled nut that is supposed to hold the valve in place. Do you need these? No.

Repairing a Flat Clincher Tire

The greatest advantage of clincher tires is the ease of repairing a flat. Any at-home mechanic can quickly patch or replace a tube or tire. The tools for patching can easily be carried with you while you ride.

1   Remove Wheel From Bike

It will be impossible to fix a flat or repair a tire if the wheel is still on the bike, so you must remove it.

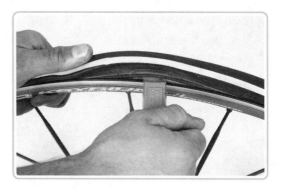

2   Unhook Bead

- Using a tire lever or your bare hands to pry the tire, unhook the bead from one side of the tire. ▶
- Insert the tire lever between the rim and tire and pry the bead up.
- When the bead is unhooked, slide the tire lever forward to continue unhooking the bead. ▶
- Continue until one side of the tire is off the rim.

Note: If you cannot unhook the bead with one tire lever, you can use two. Most tire levers have a hook so that you can pry up a section of bead and then hold the tire lever there by hooking it to the spokes. Then use a second tire lever, about 4 or 5 inches (10 or 13 cm) from the first, to pry up the bead and continue unhooking the tire. ▶

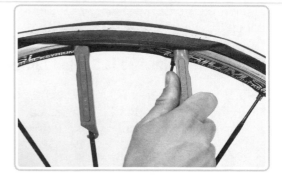

3 Remove the Tube

Start at the valve hole and pull the tube out of the tire. ▶

4 Determine What Caused the Flat

Figuring out what caused the flat is important because something may be stuck in the tire, like a thorn, or some damage have been done to the rim that may cause your new tube to immediately flat after installing it.

- Pump up the tube until it swells. Find the hole by visually inspecting the tube and by listening for escaping air. If you cannot easily find the hole, you may need to rotate the tube directly under your nose—the fine hairs of your upper lip (even if you have a great big Burt Reynolds mustache) are very sensitive and can feel even the smallest stream of air coming from a hole.

- When you locate the hole, figure out what caused it. If it's on the top of the tube, then something punctured the tire. If it's on the bottom, then there may be damage to your rim or rim strip. A pinch flat occurs when the tube is pinched between the tire and rim, often when you strike an object forcefully or the tire is not inflated enough. A pinch flat has two small holes next to each other; this is often why pinch flats are called "snake bites."

- Place the tube next to the wheel and find which part of the wheel corresponds to the damage to the tube. You may easily find what caused the flat, whether it's a tear in the rim strip or a nail sticking through your tire. ▶

- If you can't find what caused the flat, stick your thumb or finger into the tire and run it along the entire inside of the tire's casing. You may feel a piece of glass or other sharp thing sticking into the tire that may not be visible from the outside. Remove anything you find.

5 Patch or Replace Tube

If the hole in the tube is smaller (less than 3 mm), you can patch and reuse the tube. If you're on a ride, it will be faster and easier to replace the tube (you did remember to bring one, right?) and save the patching until after your postride latte.

- Scuff the area immediately around the hole with the sandpaper or scraper supplied with the patch kit. ▶

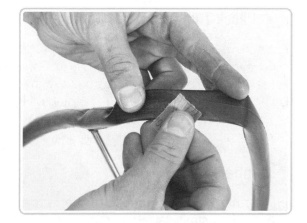

- Apply the supplied glue lightly and evenly to the area around the hole, making the diameter of the cement slightly larger than the patch. ▶

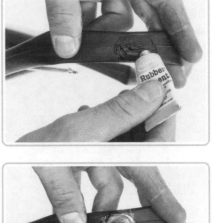

- Wait a minute or two for the cement to dry, and then press the patch firmly over the hole. Hold the patch there for 20 to 30 seconds until you're sure it's adhered well. ▶

- Pump up the tube a bit and check that the patch is holding air.

6 Inflate Tube and Install in Tire

Put a small amount of air in the tube (just enough to give the tube some shape—maybe 5 psi at most), and place the tube's valve in the valve hole. Push the tube into the tire around its entire circumference.

7 Install Tire's Unhooked Bead

Starting at the valve hole, use your thumbs to install the tire's unhooked bead. Hold the wheel in front of you, and pry the bead up and over the lip of the rim in incremental steps. If you become efficient at doing this, you may be able to install the entire bead with just your hands. If the last bit becomes too difficult to do by hand, use a tire lever to pry the last bit on. Be very careful not to pinch the tube between the tire and tire lever because this will tear a hole in the tube. ▶

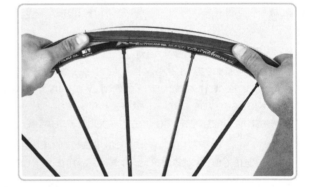

8 Check That the Tire Is Seated Correctly

Put a bit of air in the tire, around 30 to 40 pound per square inch. Check that the bead is seated correctly in the rim. If the bead is seated correctly, there should be no place where the bead is coming off the rim or where the bead is stuck down inside the lip of the rim. In either case, deflate the tire and adjust by hand. ▶

9 Inflate Tire

Inflate the tire to full pressure (the recommended pressure is usually labeled on the tire), and recheck that the tire is properly seated in the rim.

Installing a Tubeless Tire

Tubeless tires may provide greater ride comfort and eliminate pinch flats, but they are more difficult for the at-home mechanic to install. You will need either an air compressor or a CO_2 inflator to get the tubeless tire to seat in the rim correctly and hold air.

Tubeless sealants are not necessary as long as you're using a tubeless specific tire and rim, but they do make installation easier (the tire seats more easily) and are a cheap flat preventative. Stan's NoTubes, Effeto Mariposa's Caffélatex, and Vittoria Pit Stop are all great, low-priced sealants that seal small holes in the tire well.

1 Clean the Rim

Thoroughly clean the rim before attempting to install a tubeless tire. Any dirt, mud, or grime may interfere with the tire's ability to create an airtight seal. Use water and soap or rubbing alcohol if they are particularly dirty.

2 Install Valve

Tubeless rims require the use of special valves that seal the valve hole completely. Make sure the o-rings and other seals for the tubeless valve are not damaged and seal well. If they're dry, a small amount of thick grease, such as Phil Wood Waterproof Grease, helps them seal better. ▸

3 Install Tire's First Bead

The tire beads are the stiff rings on the inside edges of the tire that hook onto the rim. To install the tire's first bead, follow these instructions:

- Find the tire's label and always put the tire's label directly over the valve hole so that if you get a flat, you can line up the tire and rim to help determine what caused the flat.

- You should be able to put the entire bead of the tire on the rim with your hands, but if the tire is extremely tight, you may need to use a tire iron to pry the bead onto the rim. A tire iron hooks over the lip of the rim and acts as a lever on the tire to lift it onto the rim. ▸

4 Pour in Sealant

- If you're using sealant, and I recommend you do, start with the wheel in front of you, resting on your feet. Pour in the recommended amount of sealant (usually between 25 and 50 mL). ▸

- Use your thumbs to hook the bead of the tire onto the rim at the top of the wheel—the opposite of where all the sealant is sitting.

- When you have half of the tire on the rim, hold the tire and wheel and rotate so the sealant pours into the half of the tire that's seated. ▸

5 Finish Seating Tire

Being careful not to spill the sealant, hook the rest of the tire's bead onto the rim. Tubeless tires are extremely tight (to help make them seal better), so you'll probably need to use a tire iron. ▶

6 Evenly Distribute Sealant

Rotate the wheel 360 degrees and shake. You're trying to get the sealant to cover the entire inside surface of the tire, so don't be afraid to get creative—it can be a pretty funny looking endeavor!

7 Pump Up Tire

You will need either an air compressor or a CO_2 inflator to get the tire to seat properly and become airtight. A regular pump will not push the tire's bead into place fast enough to seal all the way around the rim. You'll hear several very loud pops as the tire seats in the rim. I've been doing this for many, many years, and it still discomforts me! Tubeless tires can be run at lower pressure than clinchers because there is not a chance of pinch flatting. Run them 10 to 20 pounds per square inch less than you normally would in a clincher tire. ▶

Repairing a Tubeless Tire

One of the nicest features of the tubeless setup is the ability to use a standard tube if you damage your tire. If the tire has a hole that is too large for the sealant to plug effectively, simply boot the tire and install a tube and you're good to go.

1 Try the Sealant Again

If you've flatted your tubeless wheel and the sealant has not effectively plugged the hole, don't give up right away! Try inflating the tire again with a CO_2 inflator, and rotate the wheel to get the sealant to the hole. It may just need a second try to seal well. If the hole still will not seal, then you will need to install a boot as outlined in the following steps.

2 Locate the Hole

This is usually pretty easy because sealant will be pouring out of the hole and getting all over your bike. This is probably the tubeless system's biggest detriment; it can be quite messy at times.

3 Install a Boot

A lot of companies make tubeless-specific boot kits. These are in essence patches that are held on with super glue. If you have one, clean the area around the hole with rubbing alcohol well before installing the boot. If you don't have a tubeless boot, use something equally strong between the tire and hole as a boot. A energy bar wrapper or a dollar bill work very well. *Note:* Tubeless boots should be able to patch a tire well enough to continue using it tubelessly. I don't recommend trying this during a ride, though. It's better to use a tube to get home before attempting to permanently repair a tubeless tire—they can be finicky! ▶

4 Inflate Tube and Install in Tire

Remove the existing tubeless valve from the rim. Put a small amount of air in the tube (just enough to give the tube some shape, maybe 5 psi at most), and place the tube's valve in the valve hole. Push the tube into the tire around its entire circumference.

5 Install Tire's Unhooked Bead

Starting at the valve hole, use your thumbs to install the tire's unhooked bead. Hold the wheel in front of you and pry the bead up and over the lip of the rim in incremental steps. If you become sufficient at doing this, you may be able to install the entire bead with just your hands. If the last bit becomes too difficult to do by hand, use a tire lever to pry the last bit on. Be very careful not to pinch the tube between the tire and tire lever because this will tear a hole in the tube. ▶

6 Check That the Tire Is Seated Correctly

Put a bit of air in the tire, around 30 to 40 pounds per square inch. Check that the bead is seated correctly in the rim. If the bead is seated correctly, there should be no place where the bead is coming off the rim or where the bead is stuck down inside the lip of the rim. In either case, deflate the tire and adjust by hand. ▶

7 Inflate the Tire

Inflate the tire to full pressure (the recommended pressure is usually labeled on the tire), and recheck that the tire is properly seated in the rim.

Installing a Tubular Tire

Tubular tire gluing is rapidly become a dying art form. Walk into most bike shops and ask about tubular gluing and you're likely to get a blank stare in response. Most racers learn to glue their own tires until they get good enough to have a team with a competent mechanic working for them.

Tubular gluing can be nerve wracking; a tire that rolls off the rim can result in a disastrous crash. But when done correctly, the bond between tire and rim can be much, much greater than the bond on a clincher tire and rim combo.

1 Prep the Wheel

Rims (specifically carbon-fiber rims) can come from the factory with a coating of surfactant (i.e., slick stuff) on them. It's necessary to completely remove this, or your first layer of glue will not stick to your rim, which will lead to a catastrophic failure. Grab a pair of nitrile gloves and a clean lint-free rag. Put a little acetone on your rag, and wipe the gluing surface down until the rag comes away clean, shouldn't take more than a couple of passes. If you have a previously glued rim, you don't need to clean off the rim completely. Just try to even out any spots where the glue is too thick or too thin.

2 Prep the Tire

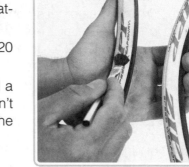

- Some tires, like Vittoria tires, come with a latex coating over the base tape and some don't. If your tires do, try to scrap the coating off with a serrated butter knife or a clean bastard file.
- Once the base tape is clean, pump up the tires to around 20 pounds per square inch or just enough that they take shape.
- Pinch the tire in your hand, and with your other hand spread a layer of glue with an acid brush on your base tape. It doesn't need to be thick, just enough to soak the base tape. Get all the way to the edges of the base tape. ▶
- Let dry overnight in a warm place.

3 First Wheel Pass

- Place the wheel to be glued in a truing stand.
- Using an acid flux brush, spread an even, light layer of glue on the rim. Make sure that you spread the glue all the way to the edge of the rim, but be careful not to get too much glue on the braking surface. It can be cleaned off later, but it's a pain. ▶
- Let dry overnight in a warm place. This first layer needs to be cured at least 12 hours, preferably 24, so that it is fully adhered to the rim.

4 Second Wheel Pass

After the wheel has cured for 12 to 24 hours, apply a second light layer of glue to the rim. Allow to dry for 3 to 6 hours.

5 Third Wheel Pass

So, with two layers of glue and one layer on the tire's base tape, all that's left is one more pass before sticking the tire. Spread this layer on just like all the others—light and even. Let sit for 3 to 4 minutes, or enough time for it to become tacky to the touch.

6 Install Tubular Tire

- Pump up the tire to around 20 pounds per square inch (or just enough to take shape).

- Take the wheel with the somewhat tacky glue on it and place it on the ground, leaning against your knees. Use some kind of protection on the ground; an old wheel bag or pair of nylon shorts works well. Don't use anything that has lint or something that you don't want ruined. ▶

- Insert the valve into the valve hole and grab the tire about 8 inches away from the valve on each side. ▶

- Pull downward forcefully as you stick the tire on to the rim. ▶

- When you reach the other side of the wheel, lift it up and roll the last bit on to the rim. If you've been pulling hard enough on the tire, this last bit of the tire shouldn't be too much of a struggle. ▶

7 Straighten Tire

Spin the wheel and check the straightness of the tire. You can move the tire left and right while the glue is still wet. When it's as straight as you'll get it, pump it up to around 120 pounds per square inch and leave to cure overnight before riding it. ▶

Repairing a Tubular Flat

Whenever you're riding on a pair of tubulars, unless you're in a race situation, it's important that you carry a spare tubular tire. Many companies make tubular-specific saddle bags that can fit and protect a spare tire and have room for a multitool and a couple of dollar bills.

This section will cover replacing a tubular on the road, but to repair a flat tubular (or more specifically, the tube inside the tubular tire), you'll have to find someone who specializes in that type of procedure. There are several companies that can be found online (such as Tire Alert) that can repair a tire for you.

1 Remove Flatted Tire

Pulling a well-glued tire off of a rim can and should be extremely hard to do. If your tire comes off easily with just a little hand force, then it wasn't glued on well enough in the first place! With enough hand pressure and some rocking back and forth, you can usually get a tubular off without tools.

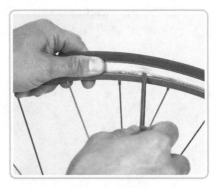

- To get a very well-glued tubular off, you'll need a flat-blade screwdriver. Use the blade to push against the tire just above the junction of the rim and tire. ▸

- As the tire pulls up, slip the screwdriver in a little farther until you can get in all the way under the tire. Do *not* pry the tire up using the rim as a fulcrum for your screwdriver—this will ruin the rim, especially if it's made of carbon.

- Once the screwdriver is under the tire, roll it backward toward you. This will lift the tire up and unstuck it from the rim. Once you have a good 8- to 12-inch (20–31 cm) section unstuck, you should be able to pull the rest off with your hands. ▸

2 Install Replacement Tubular Tire

A used tubular tire is best because it will still have some glue on the base tape that will help it stick to the rim. To install the replacement tubular tire, follow these instructions:

- Pump the tire up to around 20 pounds per square inch (or just enough to take shape).

- Place the wheel on the ground, leaning it against your knees. ▸

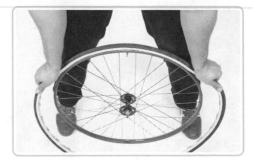

- Insert the valve into the valve hole, and grab the tire about 8 inches (20 cm) away from the valve on each side. ▸

- Pull downward forcefully as you stick the tire on to the rim. ▶

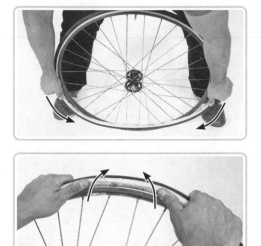

- When you reach the other side of the wheel, lift it up and roll the last bit on to the rim. If you've been pulling hard enough on the tire, this last bit of the tire shouldn't be too much of a struggle. ▶

3 Inflate Tire

Inflate the tire fully. Tubulars with lower pressure are more likely to roll off.

4 Limp Home

Be extremely careful as you ride home. The wheel will have just enough glue left on it, and there will be just enough pressure in the tire to keep the tire on the wheel. Take any corner gingerly, and you should be able to get back in one piece.

PRO'S POINT OF VIEW

Emergency Flat Repairs: How to Get Home When All Else Fails

It's Murphy's law—the day that you have two spare tubes and three patches, you'll get six flats. If you ride long enough, it's only a matter of time before you run into an impossible situation. Either you're out of tubes and tube repair or you have no way of pumping up your tires.

The easiest way of preventing this scenario is to get and maintain a well-provisioned seatbag. I always carry two tubes, a fully stocked patch kit, a tire lever, a multitool, two CO_2 canisters and an inflator, a mobile phone, and a $1 and a $20 bill. On long road rides, I'll also carry a frame pump because they'll work as long as you have arm strength.

If your tire is damaged but the tube is okay, you can boot the tire well enough to finish your ride. An energy bar wrapper or, even better, that $1 bill you keep in your seatbag makes an excellent boot. The sturdy cloth fibers in an American dollar are almost as strong as the tire itself. Plus, if you've forgotten about the boot, it can be a pleasant surprise next time you change your tire!

So what can you do if you're out of tubes or patches? One thing you can do is to tie the tube so that it seals off the hole. Fold the tube where the hole is and tie it with an overhand knot. You'll be able to inflate the tube and get home, albeit with a really, really annoying flat spot in the wheel.

If you have multiple holes in the tube or have no way of pumping up the tire, you'll have to find something to replace the tube. Grass and other vegetable matter stuffed into the tire can get you limping home—it saved my butt on one memorable mountain bike excursion.

Probably the most important tool you can carry is a mobile phone. It can be a lifesaver in emergency situations. You can use it to call the local sheriff's department when an irate driver tries to run you off the road, and, more important, it can be used to call for a desperate ride home.

And that $20 bill? That's for buying your buddy a hot cup of coffee or a cold beverage for saving your neck!

CHAPTER 8

Brakes

Anyone who's driven through downtown traffic or descended the slopes of a mountain will realize the importance of effective and reliable brakes. Braking performance is not only crucial for emergency stopping power but also provides the modulation necessary for competent bike-handling skills.

The first bicycle brakes were the simplest of all—the rider's own two legs. Early bicycles used fixed gears (i.e., whenever the rear wheel spins, the crankset must spin with it). Braking was done by applying rear pressure on the pedals. With the advent of the penny-farthing, or big-wheel bicycle, using only leg power to stop became impractical because the large front wheel created too much leverage to be overcome by backpedaling. The solution was the first mechanical brake, the so-called spoon brake. This brake consisted of a metal or leather pad that pressed onto the tire by means of a rod-actuated lever.

Spoon brakes soon became obsolete as the cycling industry began using pneumatic tires instead of the solid rubber tires found on penny-farthing bikes. Spoon brakes would rub through the thin casing of pneumatic tires too quickly to provide sustainable braking performance. Caliper rim brakes were patented in 1887 and are still the basic design that's used today. Caliper rim brakes consist of two arms that affix to a single point above the front or rear wheel that have brake pads affixed to the ends of them. The brake cable is attached to one arm of the brake, and the brake cable housing is stopped on the opposing arm. When the brake lever is squeezed, the pull of the brake cable against the immovable brake housing causes both arms to pivot the brake pads into the rim. Most modern brakes are actually a dual-pivot design that allows each arm of the brake to pivot independently of the other, producing greater mechanical advantage. This was actually an old design that was rediscovered by Shimano in the early 1990s.

Installing a Brake Lever

Whether you're using an integrated brake and shifter lever combination or you have a brake lever only setup (for a single speed or similar), the installation is the same. There is a metal clamp band that wraps around the handlebar and is tightened with a bolt from the front of the brake lever.

1 Loosen Clamp Bolt

Peel back the gum hood (the rubber cover on the brake lever) and find the clamp bolt on the brake lever. It may be to one side (like older Shimano levers), on the top (SRAM, Campagnolo, or newer Shimano), or directly behind the brake cable anchor point (older-style aero levers). ▼

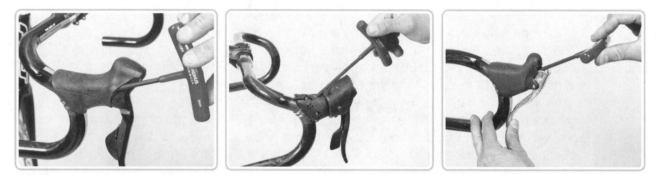

2 Slide Lever Onto Handlebar

Slide the clamp band onto the handlebar and up to your riding position. Tighten the band enough to keep the lever from slipping, but keep it loose enough so that you can find your perfect position.

Note: A good way to measure and record your brake-lever position is to use a tape measure and measure from the very bottom of the lever body to the end of the handlebar. If you're measuring from a similar-shaped handlebar, this will give you a very good idea of where you should put your levers. ▶

3 Install Second Lever

Install the second lever in the same manner as the first. You can use a tape measure (measuring from the base of the lever body to the end of the handlebar) to re-create the position of the first, or you can eyeball it. The human eye is very adept at measuring distance. I usually line them up by sight with great results. ▶

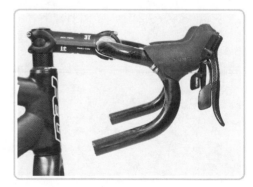

4 Tighten Levers

When you have the position of both levers perfect, tighten the clamp bolts to the point where the levers won't slip. I use a T-handle Allen wrench because it's hard to overtighten a clamp bolt with one.

Installing Brakes

All of the major manufacturers have standardized their brake attachment systems so that they're completely interchangeable. The brake has a single pivot bolt that runs through either the fork or the frame and is affixed with a specific sunken nut on the opposite side. Different width forks and rear brake mountings will require different length sunken nuts; most brakes come with several sizes, and many frames and forks come with specifically made sunken nuts. The front-brake caliper will have a long brake bolt, while the rear will have a very short one—it's obvious which is which if you see them together.

1 Remove Sunken Nut From Brake

Remove the sunken nut from the brake bolt with an Allen wrench or your hand on whichever caliper you are installing.

2 Insert Brake Bolt in Frame or Fork

Insert the brake bolt into the frame or fork. There will be a washer that goes between the brake caliper and the frame or fork. ▶

3 Thread on Sunken Nut

Using an Allen wrench, insert the sunken nut into the frame or fork on the opposite side of the brake caliper. Make sure the nut is fully inserted in the frame or fork so that it will reach the brake bolt. If the sunken nut does not reach the brake bolt or tightens after only a few turns, use a longer sunken nut. If the sunken nut is fully tightened and the brake is not tight against the frame or fork, use a shorter sunken nut. ▶

4 Center Brake Caliper

Get the brake caliper somewhat centered around where you think the wheel will be. No need to be precise here; final centering of the brake will occur after installing and adjusting the brake pads.

5 Tighten Sunken Nut

When the brake caliper is centered, hold it with one hand while you tighten the sunken nut with the other. Tighten until the brake no longer rotates easily with one hand. ▶

Note: The brake calipers come with washers that go between the brake caliper and the frame or fork. Some of the washers are knurled and prevent the brake from pivoting without loosening the sunken nut. Some of the washers are flat and allow you to fine-tune the brake's centering without loosening the sunken nut. Typically, the more expensive brakes will have the knurled washers because they tend to stay in adjustment longer.

Installing and Adjusting Brake Pads

Brake pads come in two major varieties, but each style functions identically. Standard brake pads have the actual braking pad permanently attached to the mounting hardware, while cartridge pads have replaceable pads independent from the mounting hardware. Cartridge brake pads allow you to change the pads without readjusting the mounting hardware.

Brake pads come in many different materials that are ideally suited for different applications. The standard brake pads use rubber and are best for aluminum rims. Carbon rims require either cork or specially designed rubber pads that work better with the hard carbon braking services.

1 Install Brake Pads

Insert the brake pad into the caliper arm and fix in place with the brake pad mounting bolt. Note that there is a left and a right brake pad, relative to the rider's point of view. The brake pads will be clearly labeled left and right. ▶

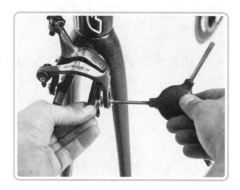

2 Close Brake Caliper

With one hand, close the brake caliper so that the brake pads hit the rim. Use a three-way or a T-handle Allen wrench to center the brake pad on the rim and tighten. The brake pad should be flat against the rim, centered vertically, and both the front and back should be centered horizontally along the braking surface. Toe-in is unnecessary and not recommended for road bike applications. ▶

3 Tighten Brake Pad Mounting Bolt

Still holding the brake caliper in one hand, tighten the brake pad mounting bolt with the other. If the pad turns as you tighten the bolt, you may need to hold the pad with your fingers as you tighten it.

4 Check Pad Adjustment

After tightening both brake pads, squeeze the caliper with your hand and check that the pads are adjusted correctly. A pad that is too high will rub the tire's casing and cause a blowout. A pad that is too low can damage the rim or even slip under the rim after it has worn a bit, causing the brake to lock up. ▶

Installing a Brake Cable and Housing

Brake cables are distinguishable from derailleur cables by their large, distinctive mushroom-shaped heads. Brake housing is also easily differentiated from derailleur housing in that it has a spiral structure that is visible when cut, while derailleur housing has many wire strands.

Brake housing is almost always 5 millimeters in diameter, while derailleur housing can be either 4 or 5 millimeters thick. SRAM and Shimano have completely compatible cables and housing. Campagnolo's housing is identical to SRAM's and Shimano's, but the head of the Campagnolo brake cable is slightly smaller in diameter. SRAM and Shimano brake cables can be used with Campagnolo brake levers if you file the head down enough to fit.

1 Measure Housing

If you're replacing brake housing, you can use the old piece as a measuring stick to determine the length of the new housing piece. If you have no previous template, insert one end of the brake housing into the brake lever and run the housing to the housing stop (on the brake caliper for the front or on the frame for the rear). Mark that spot with your fingernail or with a pen. ▶

Note: The housing should be long enough not to kink or bind when the handlebars are turned but do not need to be much longer. More housing results in more cable drag and a messy appearance.

2 Cut Housing

Use a good pair of cable cutters and cut the housing where you marked it. Double-check that the housing's length is correct. ▶

3 Finish Housing Ends

The cable cutters can leave a jagged edge to the housing; either cut off any jagged bits with a pair of side cutters or file the end smooth with a file. Then use a dental tool or sharpened spoke to open up the end because it may have been crush or distorted slightly when it was cut. ▶

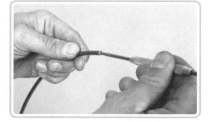

4 Install Brake Cable

Insert the brake cable into the brake anchor pivot on the brake lever. Simply pull the lever toward the handlebar to expose the brake anchor pivot. The cable should easily slide through the lever and out of the back of the lever body. If it doesn't go through easily, adjust the angle of the brake cable and try again. Pull the cable all the way through until the cable head is seated in the brake anchor pivot. ▶

5 Install Brake Housing

Insert the brake cable into the brake housing and slide the brake housing along the cable's length until it seats into the back of the brake lever body. ▶

Note: Shimano and Campagnolo brake housings do not require a ferrule between the lever body and housing. SRAM brake levers do require the use of a ferrule, which is a small metal sleeve that fits over the end of the housing.

6 Insert Brake Cable into Caliper Arm

- The brake caliper arm will have an adjusting barrel for fine-tuning the cable tension. Turn the barrel in until it bottoms on the caliper arm, then back out two full turns. This will give you plenty of fine-tuning adjustment later. ▶

- Loosen the brake cable fixing bolt and slide the brake cable into the caliper arm and through the fixing bolt. The fixing bolt will have a notch for the brake cable. ▶

7 Adjust Cable Tension

Squeeze the brake with your hand until the brake pads are about 5 millimeters (about .25 inches) away from hitting the rim. Pull the brake cable tight with your other hand to remove any slack. ▶

  Tighten the brake cable bolt and check the throw of the brake lever. Add or release tension to dial in the feel of your brakes.

8 Center Brake

When you squeeze the brake lever, check that the brake pads hit the rim at the same moment. If they do not, loosen the brake bolt, center the brake, and then retighten the brake bolt. Fine-tuning the brake's centering can be done with either the centering screw (Shimano and Campagnolo) or with a flat wrench (SRAM). ▶

9 Finish Cable End

Cut the cable about 1.5 inches (4 cm) past the brake cable bolt. Put a cable crimp on the end of the cable and crimp using a pair of side cutters or needle-nose pliers. ▶

Installing and Adjusting Special Brakes

Some bikes may not have the traditional dual-pivot caliper brakes for various reasons. Cyclocross bikes use cantilever brakes for increased power and better clearance with muddy brakes. Similarly, tandems may use cantilever brakes, V-brakes, or even disc brakes for their increased stopping power.

  Adjusting all of these types of brakes is essentially done in the same manner as adjusting a dual-pivot caliper brake—even the disc brakes. Adjust the brake pads, adjust the cable tension, and then center the brake.

Cantilever Brakes

Cantilever brakes began to be commonly used when mountain bikes hit the market, their wide design being able to handle mountain bikes' wide tires. They have since been replaced with V-brakes and disc brakes on mountain bikes, but they continue to be the most popular choice for cyclocross bikes because of their excellent mud clearance.

1 Install Cantilever Brakes

Cantilever and V-brakes use special posts that are welded to the frame and fork. These posts also have one to three small holes in which the brake's tension spring is fitted. Slide the brake arm onto the post and insert the brake's spring tab into the center hole (if there are multiple holes). Using different holes changes the spring's initial tension: moving the spring tab to the upper hole increases tension, while moving it to the lower decreases tension. In my experience, the center hole works the best for most brakes. The brake bolt is then inserted through the brake arm and threaded into the post. ▶

2 Adjust the Brake Pads

Older-style cantilever brakes use a post-style brake pad—meaning a post is attached to the pad and is clamped to the brake arm with a nut. Newer styles of cantilever brakes use the V-brake–style brake pads. The post is threaded, and a nut is used to attach the pads to the brake arms. Also, cantilever brakes pivot below the rim so the brake pad moves in a fixed arc as it travels toward the rim. For this reason, it's important to check the brake pad adjustment often because, as the pads wear, they will start to hit farther down on the rim (they travel farther along the arc). ▶

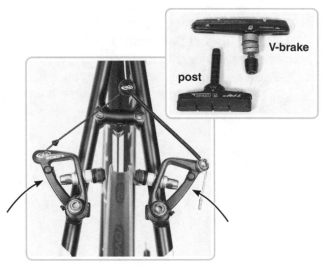

- With post-style brake pads, push the brake arm in until the pad hits the rim by holding the arm and pad in one hand as you tighten the clamp with the other. It's notoriously tricky to get the adjustment just right, so you may need to adjust them several times. ▶

- With the V-brake–style pads, use a T-handle or three-way Allen wrench on the brake pad's nut and push the pad into the rim. You can adjust the pad's position with the Allen wrench and then hold the pad in one hand as you tighten the wrench to clamp the brake pad in place. The brake pad should be flat against the rim, centered vertically, and both the front and back should be centered horizontally along the braking surface. ▶

Note: If you experience loud squealing or shuddering while applying the brakes, toe in the brake pads. Adjust the pads so that the front of the brake pad hits the rim first. ▶

3 Adjust Cable Tension

Cantilever brakes may have either a fixed or an adjustable straddle cable.

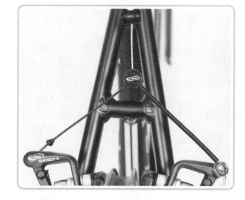

- A fixed straddle cable has one arm that is a fixed distance from the straddle hanger. The brake cable runs through the straddle hanger and is clamped directly on the brake arm. Tightening the brake cable moves the brake pads in and moves the straddle hanger higher. ▶

- An adjustable straddle cable has a straddle hanger that is independent from the straddle cable. Adjust the straddle hanger so that it sits two finger-widths above the top of the tire. Slide the straddle cable through one side of the brake and the straddle cable hanger, and then attach to the other arm with the brake cable bolt. The tightness of the brake is adjusted by adding or releasing tension on the straddle cable. ▶

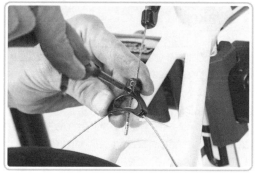

- Adjust the straddle cable tension until the brake is engaged when the lever travels halfway to the handlebar or less, depending on preference.

4 Center Brake

- On brakes that have a fixed straddle cable or that have a straddle cable hanger with no clamp, spring tension is used to adjust the brake's centering. Dialing in the brake's spring tension will bring that side of the brake away from the rim while bringing the other side of the brake closer. ▶

- Some brakes that use an adjustable straddle cable do not have adjustable tension on their brake springs. The straddle cable hanger will have clamps so that it can be affixed to a certain point on the straddle cable. Moving the hanger left moves the brake's center right and vice versa. ▶

5 Finish Cable End

Cut the cable about 1.5 inches (4 cm) past the brake cable bolt. Put a cable crimp on the end of the cable and crimp using a pair of side cutters or needle-nose pliers. ▶

V-Brakes

V-brake is the common vernacular for what's technically called a direct-pull cantilever brake. The arms on a V-brake are longer than on a traditional cantilever brake. The brake cable pulls the two arms together with no intermediary parts, hence the name direct-pull cantilever brake.

V-brakes have a higher mechanical advantage than traditional cantilever brakes (along with more stopping power) and so are often used on tandem bicycles. Because of their higher mechanical advantage, standard road brake levers will not work with V-brakes because they pull too much cable. There are some specially designed road levers for V-brakes, but, if you'll be using any type of standard brake and shifter combo, you'll need to use an adapter.

1 Install V-Brakes

Both cantilever and V-brakes use special posts that are welded to the frame and fork. These posts also have one to three small holes in which the brake's tension spring is fitted. Slide the brake arm onto the post, and insert the brake's spring tab into the center hole (if there are multiple holes). Using the different holes changes the spring's initial tension: moving the spring tab to the upper hole increases tension, while moving it to the lower decreases tension. In my experience, the center hole works the best for most brakes. The brake bolt is then inserted through the brake arm and threaded onto the post. ▶

2 Adjust the Brake Pads

Most V-brakes work similarly to a cantilever brake in that the brake arm pivots below the rim so that the brake pad moves in a fixed arc. It's important to check the pads' adjustment often because, as the pads wear, they will start to hit farther down on the rim (they travel farther along the arc). Some V-brakes use a linkage system so that the brake pads travel along a horizontal plane instead of an arc. These maintain the same pad position as the pads wear.

Use a T-handle or three-way Allen wrench on the brake pad's nut and push the pad into the rim. You can adjust the pad's position with the Allen wrench by holding the pad in one hand as you tighten the wrench to clamp the brake pad in place. The brake pad should be flat against the rim, centered vertically, and both the front and back should be centered horizontally along the braking surface. ▶

Note: If you experience loud squealing or shuddering while applying the brakes, toe in the brake pads. Adjust the pads so that the front of the brake pad hits the rim first. ▶

3 Adjust Cable Tension

The brake cable housing will stop in the V-brake's "noodle," a curved cable guide that bends the brake cable 90 degrees as it enters the brake. The noodle will sit in a metal stirrup on one arm, and the brake cable will be clamped on the other. Opening the brake for wheel removal is accomplished by removing the noodle from the metal stirrup. Often, a rubber seal, shaped like an accordion, fits over the end of the noodle to keep contamination out of the brake housing. Adjust the cable tension until the brake is engaged when the lever travels halfway to the handlebar or less, depending on preference. *Note:* If you are using a standard brake lever, the adapter that allows the use of V-brakes replaces the noodle entirely. ▶

4 Center Brake

Each arm of the V-brake will have a tension adjustment screw or bolt on each side. Dialing in these screws or bolts will increase spring tension (moving that arm away from the rim), while dialing them out decreases tension. Adjust each side until both brake pads hit the rim evenly and the brake releases from the rim crisply. ▶

5 Finish Cable End

Cut the cable about 1.5 inches (4 cm) past the brake cable bolt. Put a cable crimp on the end of the cable and crimp using a pair of side cutters or needle-nose pliers. ▶

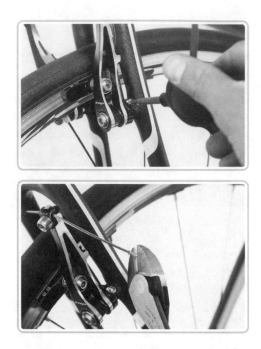

Disc Brakes

While not very common on road bikes, disc brakes have become ubiquitous on mountain bikes because of their excellent stopping power and ability to dissipate heat well (an overheated rim can cause a tire blowout or brake-pad failure). For these same reasons, disc brakes are becoming more popular for tandem bikes, where brake performance is so crucial.

Several manufacturers produce cable-actuated disc brakes that are specifically designed for use with road brake levers. Unlike V-brakes, no adapters are available to retrofit a mountain bike disc brake with road levers.

1 Install Disc Brakes

Disc brakes are usually attached to the frame or fork with fittings that are 51 millimeters apart, called the International Standard (IS) mounting. Less common is the 74 millimeter post mounting. The brakes are bolted directly to the post mounting, or an adapter is used to bolt them to the IS mounting. New mounting bolts will come with Loctite applied. If you're reusing mounting bolts, apply a dab of blue (removable) Loctite before tightening the bolts. ▼

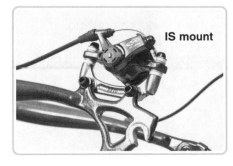

IS mount

post mount

2 Install Rotors

To use disc brakes, you must have disc brake–specific wheels. The rotors are either bolted directly to the hub (six-bolt design) or slid onto a spline on the hub and affixed with a lockring (center-lock design). For six-bolt rotor mounting, apply blue Loctite to bolts and tighten them in a star pattern. For a center-lock rotor, slide the rotor onto the spline and use a Shimano or SRAM cassette lockring tool to tighten the lockring on the hub. ▼

3 Center Brake

Cable-actuated disc brakes will usually have what is called a "fixed pad" design. One of the two brake pads will be fixed in place, while the other pad moves toward the rotor when the brake lever is pulled. The moving brake pad will push the rotor into the fixed side, and the resulting friction will result in braking. Both brake pads will have an adjustment knob separate from the cable pull for moving the pads in and out. ▶

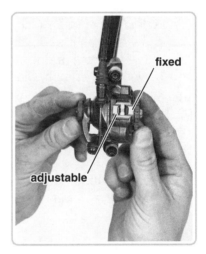

With the wheel installed, loosen the caliper mounting bolts. Dial both of the pad adjustment knobs counterclockwise until they are fully turned out. Turn the outer adjusting knob (the moving side) clockwise half a turn. Then turn the inner adjusting knob (the fixed side) clockwise until the rotor is secured between the two pads. Now that the caliper is perfectly aligned with the rotor, tighten the caliper mounting bolts. ▶

4 Install Cable and Housing

Measure and cut the appropriate length of brake cable housing. Install the brake cable and housing on your bike, ending at the disc brake. With the rotor still locked in place by the pad adjustment knobs, pull the brake cable until there is no slack and the brake arm does not move up at all. Tighten the brake cable bolt. ▶

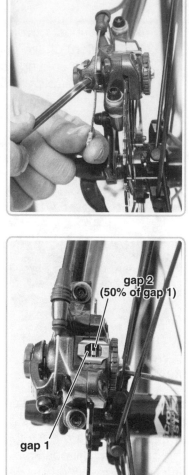

5 Adjust Brake Pads

Turn the outer (moving) pad adjustment knob counterclockwise a quarter turn. Then turn the inner (fixed) pad adjustment knob out a half turn. The gap between the inner pad should be twice as large as the outer pad for optimal performance. Dial in the feel of your brakes by moving the pads in or out. ▶

Note: If the rotor is rubbing in certain spots but not others, it is out of true—just like an out-of-true wheel. You can watch as it goes through the brake pads to determine where it is out of true and bend it with a small adjustable wrench. Clean the wrench thoroughly with rubbing alcohol first to avoid getting contaminants on the rotors.

6 Finish Cable End

Cut the cable about 1.5 inches (4 cm) past the brake cable bolt. Put a cable crimp on the end of the cable, and crimp using a pair of side cutters or needle-nose pliers.

Brake Failure and a Hair-Raising Descent

At some point in their lives, amateur riders need to wrap their heads around one immutable fact—professional riders are better than you are. Sprinters can sprint faster, climbers can climb better, rouleurs can ride longer, and every last one of them can descend like a rock. Undoubtedly, some riders are better than others, but, as a rule, if you can't descend well, you'll never make it into the pro ranks. Dave Zabriskie was one of those guys who seemed like a horrendous descender when viewed from the backseat of a team car. I mean, really bad. But the reality is, having ridden with him, he's much better than I am and probably better than I will ever be.

It really puts into perspective those riders who stand out in the pack as great descenders. Far and away, the best I've ever seen is a burly racer named Brad Huff. I worked with Brad for several years on the TIAA-CREF pro road team, which would later grow into its current iteration as the Garmin-Cérvelo pro tour team. "Huffy," as he is memorably nicknamed, is a phenomenal sprinter and an even more phenomenal bike handler. As if that weren't enough, he's also one of the nicest people I've ever known, always ready with a kind word and a thank-you.

The most impressive descent I've ever seen from Brad (or anyone for that matter) was at the 2007 USPRO national championships in Greenville, South Carolina. Traditionally held in conjunction with the Philadelphia Classic road race in Pennsylvania, the USPRO championship became its own dedicated race in 2006 and featured the grueling 3.5-kilometer climb up Paris Mountain, which the riders would have to tackle four times during the 180-kilometer race. The last ascent of this steep pitch has, every year so far, been the deciding factor in the battle for the coveted stars and stripes jersey of the USPRO national champion.

It was a particularly hot day, even for balmy South Carolina. Brad was having a great year and was to be our wildcard if the race somehow came down to a sprint. It was never fated to be, however. Two laps into the race, the heat and Paris Mountain were taking their toll on the sprinters. Huff was already dangling at the back of the pack on the second climb, meaning that two more laps would surely put paid to his day. Sure enough, on the third lap, Brad was off the back on Paris Mountain—"in the cars," as we'd say. He was riding behind the field but still within the race caravan of team cars, media vehicles, and sag wagons. Jonathan Vaughters, our team director, and I thought that was the last we'd see of Huffy that day.

After cresting the top of the climb and beginning the descent, we got back to focusing on the race in front of us and our team's best bet for the win, an in-form Danny Pate. Uttering a surprised expletive, Jonathan spotted Brad in the rearview mirror of our BMW . . . not only still in the cars but making up ground on us! We were flat out on one of the trickiest descents on the pro circuit, and Huff was diving around and past cars like they were on a bumper car track.

Brad caught us on the left side just as we were making a sharp right. He flew past and immediately dove straight across our hood and to the inside of the Kelly Benefits Strategies car we were following. His bike was leaning so much that I actually saw the leading edge of his front wheel pass *under* the rear bumper of the KBS car. The next 5 kilometers were the most scared I've ever been in a race. I'm lucky Jonathan is an excellent driver. We followed Brad through the caravan as he took unimaginable risks to get back to the lead peloton, which he did just as the descent leveled off.

It was all for naught, however. Brad would get dropped again the next time up Paris Mountain and would lose too much time to make up, despite his descending abilities. Pate would go on to make the front group and finish just off the podium in fifth, with California native Levi Leipheimer taking the championship.

But for me, the ride of the day was that descent off of Paris Mountain. It was truly a superlative experience from a superlative bike rider.

CHAPTER 9

Cranks and Chainrings

The crank and bottom bracket are central to the drivetrain's operation. The drivetrain is the direct link between the rider's pedaling legs and the mechanical power that drives the rear wheel. Any drag or damage to this system will result in an immediate loss of power-transferring efficiency, meaning you'll work harder to go slower.

Like many of the features found on the modern bicycle, the first chain-powered drivetrains were popularized on the "safety bicycle" design of the early 1880s. Previous designs of the bicycle (such as the penny-farthing) incorporated the cranks into the front wheel's axle assembly. By using a chain linkage to attach the power source (the rider) and the means of propulsion (the rear wheel) independent of the wheel's position made it possible to put the rider's weight equidistant from each wheel, creating a much more stable, enjoyable ride.

The crank and bottom bracket system consists of a spindle that rotates on bearings that are housed in the frame, two cranks attached to the spindle, and a chainring that's affixed to the drive-side crank. As the rider turns the cranks, the power is transferred from the front chainring to the rear wheel by means of the chain.

The earliest cranks were attached to the spindle with cotter pins while the bottom bracket bearings were housed in cups built into the bicycle frame. This design remained relatively unchanged until the advent of the square taper, or "cotterless," bottom brackets. The spindle and bearings were incorporated into one unit that was threaded into the bottom bracket shell, and the cranks were pressed onto the spindle with crank bolts. There were several variations on the cotterless design, notably the Shimano Octalink spindle (using a star-shaped interface instead of a square), the ISIS standard (a similar star shape), and one-piece cranks (the spindle and cranks are one S-shaped piece).

Most modern bike drivetrains use external cartridge bottom brackets. The bearings are housed outside of the bottom bracket shell, resulting in greater stiffness by making the bearing placement wider and allowing the use of larger spindle diameters. Shimano and SRAM spindles are attached directly to the drive-side crank, which slides through the bottom bracket. The nondrive-side crank is attached to the spindle with either a pinch bolt or a traditional crank bolt. Campagnolo uses a similar external bottom bracket, but each crank is attached to half of the spindle, which is joined in the middle by means of a Hirth joint and bolt, commonly used in industrial applications. Shimano, SRAM, and Campagnolo external bottom brackets are not compatible with each other. Shimano (as well as Race Face and FSA) uses a 24-millimeter straight gauge spindle. SRAM (Truvativ) uses a "stepped" spindle, which is 24 millimeters on the drive side and 22 millimeters on the nondrive side.

Campagnolo uses a straight 24-millimeter spindle but unique bottom bracket shells that have a wave washer on the nondrive side and a retaining clip on the drive side.

A new standard is rapidly becoming popular that does away with the threaded bottom bracket shell altogether. Cannondale first introduced BB30, which refers to the oversized 30-millimeter spindle used in the system. Cartridge bearings are installed directly into the frame in much the same way as integrated headsets. Trek uses a similar integrated bottom bracket design, called BB90, but it will accept the standard 24-millimeter spindle that Shimano and SRAM use.

Installing Cartridge and External Bottom Brackets

The first piece of information that you need to know before installing the bottom bracket is which type is needed for your frame. Bottom brackets are measured by their width, thread pitch, and the direction of the drive and nondrive threads.

The two major standards are the English bottom bracket (68 mm width, 137 x 24 tpi thread pitch, and left-hand drive-side thread orientation) and the Italian bottom bracket (70 mm width, 36 x 24 tpi thread pitch, and right-hand drive and nondrive-side thread orientation). Of the two, the English standard is by far the more popular, but many Italian- and Belgian-made bicycles, such as Pinarello and Eddy Merckx, still use the Italian standard.

Many more less common bottom bracket types are still out there, but, by and large, they've not been used in the past 20 years. The bottom bracket type will usually be listed in the owner's manual of your bike, or the information can easily be attained by a couple of minutes of surfing on the Internet.

And, like everything else on your bicycle, if it doesn't seem to fit, don't force it! You may be trying to insert a square peg into a round hole.

1 Clean Bottom Bracket and Shell

Use a clean, lint-free rag and wipe clean the threads of the bottom bracket shell and the threads of the bottom bracket. Any dirt or particles trapped between the shell and the bottom bracket can damage the threads, prevent the bottom bracket from being inserted straight, or cause a loud creaking while pedaling. If it is difficult to get the threads clean, a mild degreaser such as Simple Green can be used, but be careful not to get degreaser on the bearings.

2 Apply Grease to Threads

Apply a liberal amount of thick bicycle grease to the threads inside the bottom bracket shell and to the threads on the bottom bracket. It's impossible to overgrease the bottom bracket, so don't be stingy. *Note:* On bikes that are regularly exposed to wet and muddy riding conditions, I use a layer of Teflon plumbing tape on the bottom bracket to better seal the threads from contamination.

3 Install Drive-Side Bottom Bracket Cup

Begin by hand threading the drive-side bottom bracket cup into the frame. It should start threading smoothly and should look straight as it is inserted into the shell. If the bottom bracket is English, the drive side will have left-hand threads (i.e., turn the BB cup left to tighten). If it is Italian, it will have right-hand threads (i.e., turn the BB cup right to tighten).

Use the appropriate tool to fully tighten the drive-side bottom bracket cup. Most bottom brackets require 35 to 50 Newton-meters of torque, which is quite a lot—it's hard to over-tighten a bottom bracket. Refer to the bottom bracket's manual to find the exact torque specifications. As mentioned, the appropriate tool must be used for each style of bottom bracket; however, many of them are compatible with each other. As a general rule, the Shimano square-taper and splined systems are compatible with each other and with most ISIS-splined bottom brackets but not with the eight-notch SRAM Truvativ or Bontrager style. Campagnolo uses its own proprietary installation tool on its square-taper design—the exact same tool used for Campagnolo cassette lockrings. Luckily, the three major manufacturers (Shimano, SRAM, and Campagnolo) have completely interchangeable tools for their external bottom brackets, which are the most common found on bikes today. ▶

Note: Traditional cartridge bottom brackets (square taper, Octalink, and ISIS) generally have shallow tool splines. To hold the tool in place and prevent slipping or accidental damage, use the rear skewer to hold the tool tight against the threads.

4 Install Nondrive-Side Bottom Bracket Cup

Using the same method as used with the drive side, first hand thread the nondrive-side bottom bracket cup into the bottom bracket shell. Then use the appropriate bottom bracket tool to fully tighten the bottom bracket cup. ▶

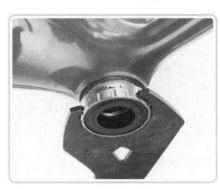

Installing Adjustable Bottom Brackets

Much less common on today's bicycles, the adjustable bottom bracket was a staple on racing bikes before the 1990s. Again, the rise of cartridge and integrated bottom brackets is analogous to the evolution of the modern headset. Just like adjustable headsets, the bottom bracket cups hold loose ball bearings on which the spindle turns. One side of the bottom bracket cup will be fixed, and the other side will have an adjustable cup and a lockring.

1 Clean Bottom Bracket and Shell

Use a clean, lint-free rag, and wipe clean the threads of the bottom bracket shell and the threads of the bottom bracket. Any dirt or particles trapped between the shell and the bottom bracket can damage the threads, prevent the bottom bracket from being inserted straight, or cause a loud creaking while pedaling. If it is difficult to get the threads clean, a mild degreaser such as Simple Green can be used, but be careful not to get degreaser on the bearings.

2 Apply Grease to Threads

Apply a liberal amount of thick bicycle grease to the threads inside the bottom bracket shell and to the threads on the bottom bracket cups. It's impossible to overgrease the bottom bracket, so don't be stingy. *Note:* On bikes that are regularly exposed to wet and muddy riding conditions, I use a layer of Teflon plumbing tape on the bottom bracket to better seal the threads from contamination.

3 Install Fixed Cup

Determine which side is the fixed cup. It will have a lip built into it so that the bottom bracket cannot be inserted into the frame too far. Spread a layer of thick grease into the cup, and insert the ball bearings into the cup (typically the bottom bracket will use nine ball bearings per side). The grease will hold the bearings in place.

Hand thread the fixed cup into the drive side of the bottom bracket shell until you feel resistance.

Use the appropriate bottom bracket tool. A fixed cup tool is a specially designed wrench that fits the cup's flat. Fully tighten the cup into the frame. ▶

4 Insert Spindle

The spindle may or may not be marked left and right, right being the drive side. If it is not labeled, whichever side is longer (in reference to the bearing cones on the spindle) will be the drive side. Slide the drive side of the spindle into the frame and through the cup, being careful not to disturb the bearings before the spindle cone makes contact with them. ▶

5 Insert Protective Sleeve

A plastic sleeve fits between the cup and around the spindle and bearings. This is to prevent contamination of the bearing by anything coming through the frame tubes, whether it's water, dirt, or rust.

6 Install Adjustable Cup

Spread a layer of grease into the cup, and insert the ball bearings onto the cup's surface. The grease will hold the bearings in place. Hand thread the adjustable cup into the frame until you feel resistance. Tighten the adjustable cup until there is no play in the spindle but it still moves smoothly on the bearings. The adjustable cup will have either flats that are adjusted with a large adjustable wrench or holes in the face of it that are used to adjust the cup using a pin spanner. ▶

7 Install Lockring

The lockring will be a large ring with notches on it. Hand thread the lockring onto the adjustable cup until it is flush or close to flush with the frame. Use the large adjustable wrench or pin spanner to hold the adjustable cup in place as you tighten the lockring with a lockring tool. Periodically check the adjustment of the spindle. It may become overtightened as you adjust the lockring. Tighten the lockring as much as you can. ▶

Note: There are many styles of lockrings. Make sure that your lockring tool and lockring mate perfectly because the notches on the lockring can be easily damaged as you're tightening it.

Installing BB30 Bottom Brackets

BB30 bottom brackets will only fit in frames that are designed for the BB30 standard. You can use adaptors with a BB30 bottom bracket to allow the use of standard 24-millimeter spindle cranksets, but, if you do not have the appropriate frame, you cannot use a BB30 crankset. BB30 cranks are popular because the 30-millimeter spindle is considered to be stiffer than the standard 24-millimeter size commonly used and the integrated bearings are simpler and lighter than those used in the threaded cartridge systems.

1 Clean Bottom Bracket Shell

Because the bearings will be resting directly on the bottom bracket shell, it's important to have a very clean surface. Use a lint-free rag and a little degreaser, and wipe out the inside of the bottom bracket shell.

2 Insert Retaining Clips

Inside of the bottom bracket shell will be two grooves in which the bearing retaining clips will sit. Apply a thin layer of grease and insert the retaining clips into these grooves. If the retaining clip has holes on both ends, use a pair of snap ring pliers to tighten the retaining clip as you insert it in the groove. If it does not have any holes, push it into the bottom bracket shell, inserting the square end into the groove first, and use this as a starting point to work the rest of the clip in. ▶

3 Install Drive-Side Bearing

A headset press is used with BB30 inserts to install the bearings. There will be two bearing inserts and a "dummy" bearing with a lip that fits into the frame.

- Grease both sides of the bottom bracket shell and the retaining clips.

- Slide the bearing insert and bearing onto one side of the headset press and slide the press into the drive side of the frame. ▶

- Insert the dummy bearing onto the other side of the headset press. The dummy bearing keeps the headset press straight as you install the bearing. ▶

- Tighten the headset press until the bearing is flush with the retaining clip. Do not overtighten because both the retaining clip and the bearing can be damaged.

4 Install Nondrive-Side Bearing

- Leave the headset press in the frame, but remove the dummy bearing.

- Slide the bearing and bearing insert into the nondrive side of the frame, and tighten with the headset press. While tightening the nondrive-side bearing, the drive-side bearing and bearing insert keep the headset press straight. ▶

5 Install First Bearing Shield

The bearing shields will sit on the outside of the bearings with the writing facing out. These protect the bearings from contamination and dirt. Slide the first bearing shield on the drive side of the crank spindle. ▶

6 Install Spindle in Bottom Bracket

Slide the spindle into the drive-side bottom bracket bearing until it is fully seated in the frame. You may need to gently tap the spindle into the frame with a rubber mallet.

7 Install Second Bearing Shield and Wave Washer

After installing the spindle into the bottom bracket, install the second bearing shield on the nondrive side. There will be several plastic washers and a metal wave washer that goes between the nondrive-side bearing shield and the left crank. When the left crank is attached, the wave washer should be somewhat compressed but not completely flat. If the wave washer is either flat or not compressed at all, remove the crank and either install or remove the plastic washers as needed. ▶

8 Bearing Removal

A bearing removal tool with lips that fit the inside diameter of the bearing is used to tap out the bearing with a mallet. If the retaining clip is not damaged, it does not need to be removed when installing new bearings. ▶

Installing BB90 and Other Press-Fit Bottom Brackets

BB90 (Trek's proprietary system) and other press-fit bottom brackets are similar to the BB30 standard in that they do not have threaded cups. Unlike BB30, however, they do not have retaining clips that hold the bearings in place in the bottom bracket shell. With BB90 bottom brackets, the retaining clip is built in to the bottom bracket shell. Simply slide the bearings into the bottom bracket shell by hand, and the rest of the crank installation is the same as with a standard external bottom bracket.

Other press-fit bearings (such as Press-Fit BB30, BB86, or BB92) have the bearings permanently housed in plastic cups. The bearings and housing are installed in the bottom bracket using a headset press and the appropriate inserts in the same way that BB30 bearings are installed, only press these in until the lips of the plastic housing are flush with the bottom bracket shell. They do not need to be installed forcefully.

Installing Square-Taper, Octalink, and ISIS Cranks

Square-taper, Octalink, and ISIS cranks all use the same means of holding the crank on the spindle. Both cranks sit on the spindle 180 degrees from each other and are held in place by a crank bolt that threads into the end of the spindle.

Removal requires a special tool that threads into the crank and then pushes the crank off the spindle by means of a second bolt. Also, grease should be used on the spindle when installing Octalink and ISIS cranks but not when installing square-taper cranks. The square taper is, well, tapered, so when grease is applied, the crank can move too far up the taper and damage both the crank and the spindle.

1 Prep the Spindle

Use a clean, lint-free rag, and wipe the spindle and the inside of the crank clean. Any contaminant or dirt left on this interface will create a very annoying creak while you ride. If the crank is not a square taper, apply a thin layer of grease to the spindle.

2 Install Drive-Side Crank

Slide the drive-side crank onto the spindle. It doesn't matter in which direction it's put on; it's only important that the other arm is installed 180 degrees away. Apply grease to the crank bolt and insert into the spindle. Tighten forcefully (34–44 Nm).

Note: When installing Octalink cranks, it's possible to begin tightening the crank bolt when the crank is not properly aligned with the splines, ruining the spindle and crank. To double-check, after turning the crank bolt a couple of times, remove the crank bolt and look at the interface. It will be apparent if the splines are not aligned correctly.

3 Install Nondrive-Side Crank

Slide the nondrive-side crank onto the opposite side of the spindle, 180 degrees away from the drive-side crank. Apply grease to the crank bolt and insert into the spindle. Tighten forcefully (34–44 Nm). ▶

4 Install One-Key Removal Cap

Some crank bolts come with a one-key removal cap. These thread onto the crank over the crank bolt and facilitate removal of the crank without the special removal tool. Backing out the crank bolt pushes against the cap (which is still attached to the crank) and pulls the crank off the spindle. Use a couple of drops of blue Loctite on the cap threads, and using a pin spanner install until tight. ▶

5 Removal of Crank

Standard crank bolts that do not have a one-key removal cap are removed using a crank removal tool. These consist of a large nut that is threaded into the crank while a second threaded stud is inserted into the nut and pushes against the spindle, pulling the large nut (and crank) off the spindle.

- Unthread the stud until the tip is flush with the end of the nut. ▶

- Thread the large nut into the crank and snug with a wrench. ▶

- Then tighten the stud until resistance is felt. Continue tightening until the crank comes off. ▶

- Unthread the large nut and repeat on the nondrive side.

Installing Shimano and SRAM External Bottom Brackets and BB30 Cranks

Shimano and SRAM (as well as FSA, Rotor, and most other crank manufacturers) cranks and bottom brackets, while not compatible with each other, are installed in the same manner. The spindle is permanently attached directly to the drive-side crank and the left crank is attached to the spindle, either by a pinch bolt or a traditional crank bolt. Some means of preloading the bearing is used, whether it is a threaded bolt or a wave washer or just by the compression of the crank bolt.

1 Install the Drive-Side Crank

Apply a light layer of grease to the spindle, and slide it into the drive side of the bottom bracket. A bearing shield should be between the crank and the drive-side bearing. You may need to tap the crank into the bottom bracket with a mallet because it's a very tight fit. Fully insert the crank until it is flush with the bearing shield surface. ▶

2 Install Spacers or Wave Washer

If the crank uses plastic spacers or a wave washer (such as BB30 cranks), slide them onto the spindle on the nondrive-side arm. When the left crank is attached, the wave washer should be somewhat compressed but not completely flat. If the wave washer is either flat or not compressed at all, remove the crank and either install or remove the plastic washers as needed. ▶

slightly
compressed
wave washer

3 Install Left Crank (Pinch Bolt)

- Apply a light layer of grease on the crank spindle.

- Make sure the pinch bolt(s) is loose, and slide the left crank onto the spindle, 180 degrees from the drive-side crank.

- A crank bolt is used to preload the bearings. Grease the threads and insert into the spindle. *Note:* Shimano supplies the tool needed to tighten the bolt. Other cranks usually require an Allen wrench. ▶

- Finger tighten the Shimano bolt or tighten the Allen wrench bolt to the torque specifications supplied in the crank's manual. This bolt needs to be tightened only enough so that there is no play in the crankset. ▶

■ Tighten the pinch bolt(s) to torque specifications. They are usually printed on a sticker that is placed on the crank. If there are two pinch bolts, tighten them evenly, a little bit at a time, until you reach the correct torque. *Note:* Shimano cranks will have a small plastic clip that is pinched between the torque bolts. This helps prevent the pinch bolts from unthreading. If the plastic clip is not flush with the crank, loosen the pinch bolts, push the clip in until it is flush with the crank, and retighten the pinch bolts. ▶

4 Install Left Crank (Crank Bolt)

■ Apply a light layer of grease to the spindle.

■ Slide the left crank onto the spindle.

■ Almost all cranksets that do not use a pinch bolt will incorporate a one-key removal cap, either built into the crank or threaded on the crank. You may need to thread the crank bolt in a couple of turns before the spindle splines reach the crank. ▶

■ When the spindle splines reach the crank, align the crank correctly, and tighten the crank bolt to torque specifications, which are usually printed on the crank. *Note:* Unlike traditional bottom bracket and crankset interfaces where it's hard to over-tighten the crank bolt, it's very important to follow torque specifications when installing cranks that use external bottom brackets. The crank bolt is used for preloading the bearing, so overtightening it may damage the bearing or result in considerable drag while pedaling. ▶

5 Removal of Cranks

■ For pinch bolt cranks, loosen the pinch bolts, and completely remove the crank bolt. The left crank will slide off the spindle (you may need to tap out with a mallet). Then the right crank and spindle will slide out of the bottom bracket (again, you may need to tap with a mallet). ▶

■ Cranks that use a traditional crank bolt will have a one-key removal cap, so simply back out the crank bolt until the left crank comes off. The right crank will slide out of the bottom bracket (you may need to tap out with a mallet).

Installing Campagnolo Ultra-Torque Cranks

Campagnolo differs from other manufacturers by not having the entire spindle attached to one crank but rather each crank attached to half the spindle. The two halves are joined in the middle of the bottom bracket by means of a Hirth joint, a system of teeth that lock together, which is often used in jet and car engines, surgical equipment, and other mechanical devices. Also different from other systems, the bearings are not incorporated into the bottom bracket cups but are installed on the spindle halves before they are slid into the bottom bracket.

1 Install Bearings on Spindle Halves

Lightly grease the spindle halves (including the Hirth joint), and slide the bearings onto each half. They should smoothly and easily slide down the spindle until they reach the crank. ▶

2 Remove Retaining Clip

A bearing retaining clip fits into the drive-side bottom bracket cup. If this is installed, remove with a pair of needle-nose pliers and set aside. ▶

3 Install Drive-Side Crank

Generously apply grease to the drive-side bottom bracket cup. Slide the drive-side crank into the bottom bracket until the bearing seats into the bottom bracket cup. ▶

4 Insert Retaining Clip

When the bearing is fully seated, insert the bearing retaining clip into the drive-side bottom bracket cup. There are two small holes on each side of the cup into which the two clip ends will seat. You should not be able to pull the crank out when the clip is seated correctly. ▶

5 Install Wave Washer on Left Crank

A wave washer, similar to that used on BB30 cranks, is installed between the nondrive-side bearing and the bottom bracket cup. Slide onto the spindle until it rests on the bearing face. ▶

6 Install Nondrive-Side Crank

Generously apply grease to the nondrive-side bottom bracket cup. Slide the left crank into the bottom bracket cup until the two halves of the Hirth joint connect. Be sure that the cranks are oriented 180 degrees from each other. You will need a 3-inch adaptor and a 10-millimeter Allen wrench for your torque wrench to install the bolt that holds the Hirth joint together. Apply a dab of grease to the bolt before installation and torque to 42 Newton-meters. ▶

7 Remove Cranks

To remove cranks, completely remove the bolt holding the Hirth joint together. Remove the bearing-retaining clip with a pair of needle-nose pliers, and both cranks will slide out of the bottom bracket. ▶

Installing and Replacing Chainrings

Chainrings are the front sprockets that attach to the drive-side crank, which propels the chain as the bicycle is pedaled. Chainrings are measured in two ways—the teeth size and the bolt circle diameter (BCD). The more teeth the chainring has, the larger the gearing—meaning more force is required to pedal but the bicycle will go farther with each crank revolution. The BCD is a reference to the measurement of the chainrings' attachment points to the cranks. A 53-tooth chainring with a BCD of 130 millimeters will be the same gear sizing as a 53-tooth chainring with a BCD of 135 millimeters, but they will not fit the same cranksets.

A traditional-size crankset accepts chainring sizes of 38 teeth or larger (inner) and 52 teeth or larger (outer). A new standard, called compact cranksets, will allow the use of smaller chainrings (typically a minimum of 34 teeth and 50 teeth combination) that makes climbing easier without resorting to a triple crankset. A triple crankset, just as it sounds, has three chainrings instead of the standard two. This allows the use of very small chainrings popular with touring riders and those who like very small gearing for climbing.

The two most popular sizes of standard cranksets are 130-millimeter BCD (compatible with Shimano, SRAM, and FSA chainrings) and 135-millimeter BCD (compatible with Campagnolo chainrings). Both the Shimano and SRAM compact chainrings and the Campagnolo compact chainrings are 110-millimeter BCD, but they are not compatible with each other due to how they fit on the crankset.

1 Identify Chainring Direction

Each chainring will have an inside and outside and will line up in a certain way in relation to the crank. The large chainring will have a pin that lines up behind the crank to prevent the chain from getting wedged between the two if it falls off. The inner chainring will have some sort of notch or other indication that lines up with the crank. ▶

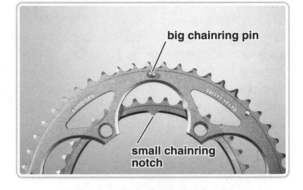

2 Install Small Chainring

Slide the inner chainring onto the crankset, and line up with the notch (or other indication) aligned with the crank. The side of the chainring that has the beveled edged around the chainring holes will be the side that faces toward the bike. Hold in place with your hand. *Note:* For triple cranksets or certain models of standard cranksets, you may need to remove the drive-side crank to remove or install the inner ring. ▶

3 Install Large Chainring

Slide the large chainring onto the drive-side crank, and align the chain pin (prevents the chain from being wedged between the crank and the chainring) with the crank. In the same way as the small chainring, the side of the ring with the beveled edges on the chainring holes will be the side that faces away from the bike. Hold both the inner and outer rings in place with your hand. ▶

4 Install Chainring Bolt

Begin by placing the backing of one chainring bolt through the small chainring. It does not matter which chainring hole you start with. The backing will be the female side of the chainring bolt (will have a smooth surface), while the actual bolt is the male side and will be threaded. Hold the backing in place with one finger as you thread the chainring bolt through the large chainring and into the backing. Stop threading when hand tight. ▶

Note: There are three main styles of chainring bolts. The traditional style will use a 5-millimeter Allen wrench to tighten the bolt while the back is held with a special chainring bolt tool that fits into two slots on the backing. Newer styles incorporate a 6-millimeter Allen wrench to hold the backing while a 5-millimeter or T25 Torx wrench is used to tighten the bolt. Some chainrings, such as the Shimano 7900 and Cannondale MKV rings, have one chainring with threaded holes and do away with the backing pieces altogether.

5 Install the Rest of the Chainring Bolts

One by one, install the rest of the chainring bolts in the same manner as the first. Thread only until hand tight.

6 Tighten Chainring Bolts

Begin with the bolt immediately to the right or left of the crank. Hold the backing with the appropriate tool and tighten the bolt forcefully. Most bolts require a torque of 8 to 12 Newton-meters. Continue tightening in a star pattern, in the same way a child draws a five-sided star. This keeps the chainring flat. Tightening a chainring in a circle pattern can actually bend it, resulting in uneven torque and a loss of shifting performance. ▶

Do You Need a Triple Crankset?

The triple crankset was originally developed for the mountain bike market to aid in the ascent of super-steep trails. Around 15 years ago, the triple was introduced in the road market as a way of attracting new road riders from the growing mountain bike market. The idea was, riders used to the gear range of a mountain bike would be more attracted to a road bike with similar gears. The idea worked and worked well. Soon, triple cranksets were an option on even the most high-end road bikes. Touring and casual riders loved the idea of having standard chainrings (53 teeth/39 teeth) and a "granny" gear of 30 teeth for the steep hills. It seemed everyone was happy; casual riders had a triple for every situation, and hard-core cyclists stuck with their beloved racing double setup.

Then FSA threw a wrench in the works. The first "road compact" crank, popularized by disgraced professional cyclist Tyler Hamilton during the 2003 Tour de France, was introduced in early 2002. The 52-tooth/36-tooth crankset allowed Hamilton, who was suffering a broken collarbone at the time, to remain seated and spin a smaller gear on the climbs, thus alleviating the need to get out of the saddle on steeper climbs. Compact cranksets now are mostly standardized to a 50-tooth/34-tooth chainring setup. Nowadays, if riders decide that the standard 39-tooth inner ring isn't enough climbing gear for them, they still have to make the additional decision between a compact double and the traditional triple. So how do you decide? Well, there are several things to consider.

Let's start with gear range first. Gear range is usually the reason that most riders opt out of the standard double in the first place. Assuming that you're using the same cassette on the rear wheel (let's say a 12/25 tooth) then the overall range of gearing is not that dissimilar. The distance that the bike will travel after one full revolution of the crankset is measured in *gear inches*. A 30-tooth chainring and a 25-tooth cog in the rear will measure 31.5 gear inches, while the 34/25 tooth will result in 35.7 gear inches. This is a slightly smaller gear than the 30-tooth/23-tooth combination, so basically, by using a compact double, you're losing *not quite* one full gear in the rear. The same result is found when comparing the high gear: the 53/12-tooth combo measures 116.1 gear inches, while the 50 tooth/12 tooth has 109.5 gear inches. Again, this is slightly larger than a 53/13-tooth combination, so you're losing just under one gear. Because the smallest cogs can be made only with 11 teeth (size limitations of the freehub body), you will never be able to match the high-end gearing of the standard triple with a compact setup. But that's not really why people buy triples and compacts anyway.

For the same reason, the compact will never have a small gear as a triple, as well. But at a certain point, this argument becomes moot. Cassettes come in very wide ranges now (SRAM even has an 11/32-tooth cassette in its Apex range), so you can get as small a gear as you could need with a double compact. A 34-tooth chainring and a 28-tooth cog is such a small gear that no one would ever miss having a 30-tooth granny gear.

In addition to an adequate range of gears, the double compact has a couple more advantages. The lack of a third chainring means less weight overall, definitely a consideration for any serious road bike. Compact doubles work fine with standard double shifters, as well, so there's no need to buy a specific front shifter. There's also the ego factor. Many strong riders want smaller gears but don't want the stigma of riding with a wimpy granny ring.

Sounds like the double compact is the clear choice, right? Not quite yet. The reason triples have not vanished from the face of the Earth is the same reason that cassettes keep growing more gear options. To get an adequately low gear with a compact double, you have to get rid of some of the intermediary cog sizes. A double compact with an 11/28-tooth cassette has the same overall gear range as a triple with a 12/25-tooth cassette but has a three-tooth gear jump between the last three gears (as opposed to two teeth with the triple) and does away with the 16 altogether.

So, for riders who are only concerned with having the small climbing gear option, the lighter weight and compatibility with other double setups make it a great choice. But for the touring rider looking for the most gear options, the triple is impossible to beat.

CHAPTER 10

Shifters and Derailleurs

These days, it's hard to imagine road bikes before the advent of the rear derailleur. But it's actually a fairly recent invention. The first rudimentary shifter and derailleur were not developed until 1940. Before the first derailleur, rear wheels were equipped with a cog on each side of the hub. To change gearing, you had to dismount your bike, and take out the rear wheel and flip it around, making efficient wheel changes an integral part of racing strategy.

Frustration with these systems led to Tullio Campagnolo, founder of the eponymous component manufacturer, to develop the Cambio Corsa derailleur, a simple rod and paddle that were attached to the right seatstay. To shift the chain from one cog to the other (originally there were only two!), you had to reach behind your legs and flip the rod; the paddle attached to the rod would push the chain onto the next cog. The Cambio Corsa reigned supreme on road bikes for the better part of a decade until both Campagnolo and Hercules developed parallelogram derailleurs, which were cable actuated and shifted with a down tube mounted lever. In 1964, Suntour introduced the first slant parallelogram rear derailleur, which is the design still used today.

The front derailleur's development followed a similar trajectory. Several manufacturers, including Campagnolo, Simplex, and Huret, produced a rod-actuated paddle front derailleur that worked in a manner similar to Campy's Cambio Corsa rear derailleur, but when Campagnolo introduced the parallelogram front derailleur, they all became obsolete. The design has barely changed since.

Friction down tube shifters were the standard until the mid-1980s. The derailleur cable was pulled along the entire throw of the lever. Stopping the shift in a specific gear was dependent on the rider's skill. Index shifting, which has predetermined ratcheting stops built into the shifter, quickly became the standard when Shimano introduced it in 1985.

The last great innovation in shifting was also introduced by Shimano in 1990—the integrated brake lever and shifter system. Dubbed STI (Shimano Total Integration), the integrated brake lever and shifter quickly became the standard as Campagnolo came out with its Ergopower levers. When SRAM introduced its first complete road group in 2006, it included its version, called DoubleTap shifters. Today's modern shifter and derailleur combos provide incredibly quick, precise, and effortless shifting in a reliable, lightweight system.

Installing Shifters

There are no hard and fast rules concerning the shifter's position on the handlebars. It all comes down to your personal preference. Traditionalists prefer a slightly lower shifter hood placement, reminiscent of the older style of brake lever. The recent trend is to have the shifters pointed up slightly, maybe in response to the super-low front ends on modern racing bikes. The only thing that matters is that your hands are in a comfortable position and that you can easily brake and shift while holding both the hoods and the drops of the bars.

1 Locate the Clamp Band Bolt

The shifters are held onto the handlebars by a metal band that is attached to the shifter by a band bolt. When the band bolt is tightened, the clamp constricts and holds the shifter in place. On Campagnolo, SRAM, and Shimano newer-style levers (Dura-Ace 7900, Ultegra 6700), the hood lever has to be pulled back to get to the bolt, which is on top of the lever body. ▶

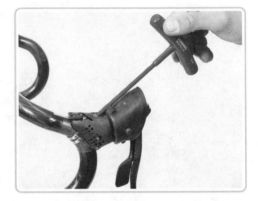

Shimano's older shifters (Dura-Ace 7800 and earlier models) and its new Di2 electric shifters have a channel on the outside of the lever body that allows an Allen wrench to be slid under the hood to get to the bolt. ▶

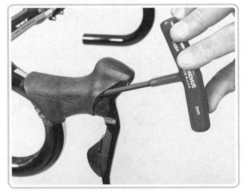

2 Slide the Shifter Onto the Bar

Loosen the band clamp bolt enough so the shifter will easily slide onto the handlebars. When you have the shifter in the appropriate position, tighten the band clamp bolt with a 5-millimeter Allen wrench. Tighten enough so that the shifters will not move, but be careful not to crush the carbon bars. ▼

3 Install Second Shifter

Once you have one shifter in position, install the second shifter in the same manner. I've found the best way to get both levers even with each other is to squat down next to the bike and eyeball them—the human eye is incredibly adept at measuring spatial differences!

4 Fine-Tune the Position

It's a good idea to get the levers as close to perfect now before installing the cable and housing. Put your bike on a trainer to simulate what it will feel like, or just get on your bike and lean against a wall as you fine-tune the position of the levers. Most people prefer their lever hoods either flat or slightly raised, but it's completely a matter of personal preference. ▶

Installing Cable and Housing

Derailleur housing is stiffer than brake housing and usually a smaller diameter. The stiffer housing provides quicker, more precise derailleur actuation but means more drag in the system when the housing is bent at an extreme angle. For this reason, derailleur housing is often a smaller diameter than brake housing. Shimano and SRAM derailleur housings typically have a 4-millimeter diameter, and Campagnolo's has a 4.5-millimeter profile.

Derailleur cables are also a smaller diameter than brake cables, but all of the major manufacturers use the same size cable. However, the head of Campagnolo's cable is slightly smaller than the cable employed by Shimano and SRAM but is completely compatible with each.

1 Measure Housing Length

Shifters will usually come with precut housing, but these housings are quite long so that they can be used on multiple bike sizes. Place one end of the shifter housing into the shifter, hold it in place, and see how the cable will fit into the cable stops on the frame. When you've determined the proper length, mark how much to cut off, either with a marker or by making a divot with your fingernail. For Campagnolo's, SRAM's, and Shimano's newer handlebar-routed shifters, it's best that the cable housing crosses a bit in front of the head tube. For Shimano's nonhandlebar-routed shifters, the cable housing should not cross at all. ▼

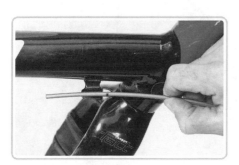

SRAM, Shimano, Campagnolo

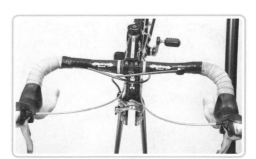

older Shimano

The rear derailleur housing should be fairly straight as it enters the barrel adjuster on the rear derailleur. However, you want the housing to be as short as possible without having a bend at the barrel adjuster—too short and the cable is bent, too long and there's more drag in the housing. ▶

2 Finish the Housing Ends

Use a sharp pair of cable cutters, and cut the housing at the marks that you've made. Finish the ends by opening them with a dental tool. Both ends of each piece of shifter housing will use cable ferrules. ▶

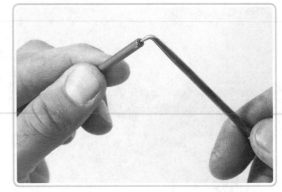

3 Install Rear Derailleur Cable

Make sure the right shifter is shifted all the way down (as it would shift to the smallest gear), and insert the shifter cable into the shifter. With Campagnolo and new Shimano shifters, the cable is inserted through the bottom of the shifter body. For SRAM shifters, the cable is inserted through the inside of the lever body. For older-style Shimano shifters, pull the brake lever back slightly and insert the cable from the outside of the lever itself. ▼

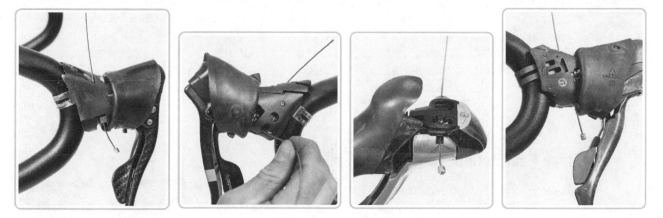

4 Install the Cable Housing

- Slide the derailleur cable into the first piece of derailleur housing.

- Insert the cable through the cable stop on the down tube and through the cable guide on the bottom bracket, and then slide the cable into the rear derailleur housing. ▶

- Insert the rear derailleur housing into the cable stop on the chainstay, and slide the cable through the barrel adjuster of the rear derailleur, seating the housing into the derailleur.

- You should adjust the tension and limit screws on the rear derailleur (see pages 146-147) before installing the front housing. The front derailleur cable and housing are installed in the same manner as the rear, except that, at the bottom bracket guide, the cable is redirected toward the front derailleur, where it is clamped. ▶

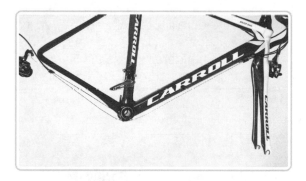

Installing and Adjusting the Rear Derailleur

The rear derailleur is basically two pulleys that tension the chain and a cage attached to a spring that pulls the derailleur outward and up. When the shifter pulls the cable (shifting up), it acts against the spring, moving the chain inward (toward a smaller gear) and downward (so that the upper pulley will clear the larger cog). When the shifter releases the cable (shifting down), the derailleur's spring pulls the chain outward (toward a larger gear) and upward (to keep the upper pulley close to the smaller cog).

The rear derailleur has built-in stops, called limit screws, which prevent the derailleur from moving too far in either direction. This keeps the chain from shifting off the smallest and largest cogs. Rear derailleurs can come in various sizes, basically a measurement of their cage length. Derailleurs with a longer cage length can accommodate a larger discrepancy in cog sizes (or can be used with a triple crankset) but shift slower because the cage must move farther to actuate a shift. Most standard road derailleurs will work with up to a 27-tooth cog with a double crankset. If you're using a larger cassette or a triple, you'll need a long-cage derailleur.

1 Install the Rear Derailleur

The rear derailleur bolts onto the derailleur hanger on the back of the chainstay with a 5-millimeter Allen wrench. The derailleur has a small screw (called the B-tension screw) immediately behind the attachment bolt. This screw rests against a lip at the bottom of the derailleur hanger.

- Pull the derailleur backward as you install it so that the B-tension screw clears the lip of the hanger. When the screw is over the lip, release the derailleur so the B-tension screw rests against the lip as you finish tightening the derailleur bolt. ▶

2 Adjust the H-Limit Screw

The H-limit screw (or high-limit screw) keeps the chain from falling off the smallest cog. The limit screws are usually labeled clearly but, if in doubt, turn one. If, with no cable tension (shifted all the way down), the screw moves the cage inward or outward, that's the H-limit screw. Inversely, if the screw doesn't move the cage at all, the other screw is the H-limit.

Adjust the H-limit screw until the upper pulley is directly underneath the smallest cog. Turning the screw clockwise will adjust the pulley inward (to the left). Adjusting it counterclockwise will move it outward (to the right). ▶

3 Adjust the L-Limit Screw

The L-limit screw adjusts how far the derailleur can move inward. With no tension on the derailleur cable, push the derailleur inward. Adjust the L-limit screw until the upper pulley stops directly under the largest cog. *Note:* If the chain is installed, you'll have to turn the crank as you push the derailleur inward. Adjust the L-limit screw until the chain easily moves onto the largest cog but goes no farther. Turning the L-limit screw clockwise moves the upper pulley outward (to the right), while turning the screw counterclockwise moves the upper pulley inward (to the left). ▶

4 Install the Chain

If the chain is not already installed, you will need to install the chain (see page 164).

5 Attach the Derailleur Cable

Double-check that the shifter is shifted all the way down. Pull the derailleur cable finger tight. Clamp the derailleur cable with the derailleur cable bolt on the side with a slight indentation. If you clamp the cable on the wrong side of the bolt, it will not shift correctly.

On SRAM rear derailleurs, the cable will curve around a bend as it travels to the bolt. On Shimano and Campagnolo derailleurs, the cable travels straight to the bolt. ▶

SRAM   **Shimano/Campagnolo**

6 Set the Ferrules

Hold the rear derailleur in place, and gently pull the rear derailleur cable with your hand below the down tube. This tensions the cable and helps the cable ferrules and housing seat well. Usually, this creates slack in the cable. Loosen the derailleur clamp bolt, and pull the cable finger tight before retightening. ▶

7 Adjust the Cable Tension

The cable tension is fine-tuned with the derailleur's barrel adjuster. Start at the smallest cog and test the shifting. If the chain is slow to shift up (toward the larger cogs), add tension by turning the barrel adjuster counterclockwise. If the chain is slow to move down (toward the smaller cogs), release tension by turning the barrel adjuster clockwise. ▶

8 Adjust the B-Tension Screw

The B-tension screw determines the body angle of the rear derailleur in relation to the chainstay. Adjustments are made with the B-tension screw so that the upper pulley clears the largest cog. Shift to the largest cog and see if the pulley clears. If the pulley overlaps or is very close, tighten the B-tension screw to pull the upper pulley away from the cog. If there is a large gap between the upper pulley and large cog (which results in slower shifting), loosen the B-tension screw to bring the pulley in. There should be about a 2- to 3-millimeter gap between the pulley and the cog. ▶

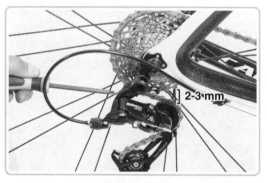

9 Finish the Cable End

Cut the derailleur cable about 1.5 inches (4 cm) after the cable clamp bolt. Put a cable crimp on the end of the cable, and crimp using a pair of side cutters or needle-nose pliers. ▶

Installing and Adjusting the Front Derailleur

The front derailleur works in the same manner as the rear derailleur. A strong spring pulls the derailleur cage inward, while the tension on the derailleur cable pulls it outward. Also like the rear, the front derailleur body is a slant parallelogram, meaning that it stays close to the chainrings as it moves through its shift.

Unlike some mountain bike versions, all road derailleurs are what's called a bottom-pull derailleur—the cable is routed from beneath. If you have a bike with top-cable routing (such as many cyclocross bikes have), it's necessary to have some sort of pulley mounted below the front derailleur to reroute the cable in the proper direction.

The derailleur is attached to the seat tube with a clamp that either wraps around the tube or attaches directly to the frame itself. Clamps come in various sizes, so make sure that you have the proper clamp for your specific frame. The direct-mount style is called a braze-on derailleur because it bolts directly to a tab that is attached to the seat tube (traditionally braze welded, hence the name).

1 Position the Height of the Front Derailleur

Attach the front derailleur to the seat tube using a clamp or by attaching it to the braze-on. Position the derailleur so that the bottom of the outer cage sits 1 to 2 millimeters above the tallest point of the chainring teeth. ▶

Note: Most chainrings have shorter, ramped teeth to make shifting easier. Do not measure the distance to the cage from these teeth because it would result in the front derailleur cage hitting the taller chainring teeth.

2 Align the Derailleur Cage

With the height properly set, align the front derailleur so that the outer cage is parallel with the large chainring. Fully tighten the clamp or braze-on bolt and double-check the alignment. ▶

3 Adjust the L-Limit Screw

Just like the rear derailleur, the front derailleur has limit screws that keep the cage from traveling too far in either direction. The L-limit screw prevents the chain from falling to the inside of the small chainring when shifting down.

Shift the rear derailleur to the largest cog. Look at the front derailleur from above. The inner plate of the cage should just barely clear the chain. If there is a large gap or the cage is rubbing, adjust the L-limit screw (usually the inner screw if not labeled). Turning the L-limit screw clockwise moves the cage outward (toward the large chainring), while turning the screw counterclockwise moves the cage inward (toward the seat tube). *Note:* It helps to turn the crank while adjusting the L-limit screw. Turn the screw in until you hear the inner plate rubbing the chain, then back the screw out a quarter turn. ▶

4 Attach the Derailleur Cable

Check that the front shifter is shifted down. Pull the cable finger tight and clamp with the cable clamp bolt. An indentation on the derailleur body shows which side of the bolt the cable should be routed. ▶

5 Set the Ferrules

Gently pull the front derailleur cable with your hand below the down tube. This tensions the cable and helps the cable ferrules and housing seat well. Usually, this creates slack in the cable. Loosen the derailleur clamp bolt, and pull the cable finger tight before retightening. ▶

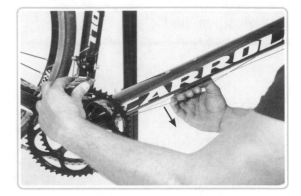

6 Adjust the H-Limit Screw

The H-limit screw prevents the chain from moving off the large chainring when shifting from the small to large ring. Shift the rear derailleur to the smallest cog. Shift the front derailleur to the large chainring, and check the gap between the outer plate of the derailleur cage and the chain. It should just barely clear. Turning the H-limit screw clockwise moves the cage inward (toward the small chainring), while turning the H-limit screw counterclockwise moves the cage outward (away from the small chainring). ▶

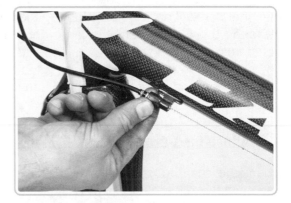

7 Adjust Cable Tension

Shift the rear derailleur to the middle of the cassette and test the front shifting. If the chain is slow to shift to the large chainring, add tension to the cable. If the chain is slow to shift to the small chainring or the shift is difficult to make, release tension on the cable. Most cable stops on the frame will have a barrel adjuster that can be turned to adjust tension (counterclockwise to add tension, clockwise to release tension). If your frame has no barrel adjuster, you'll have to adjust the tension at the cable clamp bolt. ▶

8 Finish the Cable

Cut the derailleur cable about 2 centimeters (about 1 in) after the cable clamp bolt. Put a cable crimp on the end of the cable, and crimp using a pair of side cutters or needle-nose pliers. You may need to bend the end of the cable inward so that it clears the crank as you're pedaling. ▶

Troubleshooting Shifting

Shifting ailments are probably the most common source of frustration for cyclists. Today's 10- and 11-speed drivetrains are, at best, finicky and easily fouled up. Here are some of the most common causes for poor shifting performance.

Bent Derailleur Hanger

The rear derailleur hanger is easily bent whenever your bike is crashed, dropped, or even looked at wrong. It was common practice on the pro teams that I've worked for to replace derailleur hangers *any time* the bike was crashed—even if the shifting was still perfect.

The only way to accurately check the derailleur hanger alignment is with a hanger tool, which threads into the derailleur hanger and uses various points of the wheel as a reference. Luckily, just eyeballing the hanger usually works well enough—use the cogs on the cassette as a reference. If it looks a little bent, replace the derailleur hanger, and your shifting troubles might be over. If your frame doesn't have a replaceable derailleur hanger (more common on steel and ti frames), take it to a professional so it can be bent straight for you. ▶

Dirty Cables

If your derailleur hanger isn't bent but your shifting is still off, you may have dirty cables. Over time, water and other contaminates may seep into the cable housing and cause the cables to gunk up with dirt and grime. Remove the cables from the housing and wipe them down. Apply a couple of drops of dry lube to the cables before reinstalling them and they should work like new. If, when you remove the cables, they're significantly corroded, frayed, or damaged in any way, you should replace them. The same applies to the cable housing. See "Install Cable and Housing" on page 154 for instructions.

Worn Chain or Cassette

As the linkage in the chain wears during use, the chain will stretch. Because the distance between each link is longer on a stretched chain, it will no longer fit perfectly with the teeth on the cassette, which will result in poor shifting. Replacing the chain before it can stretch too much (using a chain wear tool) will ensure crisp shifting. See "Installing Chains" on page 164 of chapter 11 for instructions. ▶

Continuing to use a stretched chain will damage the cassette, too. As the chain stretches, it wears the teeth on the cassette. Often, you won't notice this wear until you attempt to install a new chain. The worn teeth won't hold the new, tighter chain well enough so that, as you pedal, it will slip, causing a loud pop, especially in the smaller cogs where there are fewer teeth to hold the chain. At this point, you must replace the cassette. See "Installing a Cassette" on page 170 of chapter 11 for instructions.

Worn Pulleys

Very often overlooked, the pulleys on the rear derailleur play a large role in shifting performance. Replace them when the teeth are noticeably worn, and lubricate the bushings with a drop of light oil any time you lube the chain.

Worn or Dirty Shifter

Just as dirt and grime can foul the cables and housing, shifter internals can become contaminated by the elements. If there is no longer a positive click while shifting or if there is play in the lever, you may need to clean out the internals. Use a light spray lube and generously spray it into the shifting mechanism. Have a rag handy because this can get quite messy. The idea is to displace the dirty, old lube with the fresh lube you're spraying in. The old lube will be pushed out of the bottom of the shifter body.

If lubing the internals of the shifter doesn't seem to help, the internals may be worn. Shimano and SRAM shifters can't be rebuilt; they must be replaced. Campagnolo shifters can be rebuilt with new internals, but the process is very complicated and should be left to a trained professional.

Installing and Adjusting Special Shifters and Derailleurs

Just as there are many handlebar types, there are specialized shifters to go along with them. Bikes with aero bars and extensions will use aero levers instead of the traditional road levers. Similarly, road bikes set up with flat mountain bike–style handlebars will need mountain bike–style shifters. A brand new technology, Shimano's Di2 electronic shifting system, requires specialized setup, as well.

Installing Time-Trial Shifters

Time-trial bikes are specially designed to be as aerodynamically efficient as possible. Part of this design incorporates shift levers installed on the ends of the aero bar extensions rather than built into the brake levers as they are with road bikes.

These time-trial (TT) shifters (or bar-end shifters as they're sometimes called) are held in the aero bar with an expansion plug and mechanically work in a fashion similar to standard road shifters. Pull the lever one way, and the cable pulls the derailleur into a shift. Push the lever in the opposite direction, and the cable is released, allowing the derailleur to pull the chain onto a new cog.

1 **Isolate the Expansion Plug**

The TT shifter may come disassembled or fully built. You'll need to separate the shift mechanism from the body of the shifter to install the expansion plug. A screw or Allen bolt will hold the shift mechanism on the body. Remove this and the pieces will separate. Try to remember how the pieces fit together as they came apart. This will make it easier to reinstall them later. *Note:* Keep the parts from the right and left shifters separate. Most of them will not be interchangeable. ▶

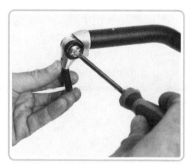

2 Install the Shifter Body

Loosen the expansion plug by means of the Allen bolt on the face of the body. Typically, this bolt will be reverse threaded. Check by turning the bolt to the right; the plug should contract. Slide the plug into the lever, and straighten and tighten the expansion plug with the Allen bolt. *Note:* The head of the Allen bolt is easily stripped. Tighten it only enough so that the shifter doesn't rotate in the aero bar. ▼

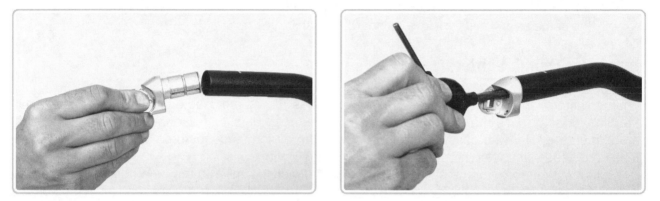

3 Install Shifter Mechanism

Install or reinstall the shifter mechanism on the shifter body. Shimano shifters have a lever body cover that sits between the lever body and the shifter mechanism. An indentation on the round part of the cover points down. Campagnolo and SRAM shifters mount directly to the lever body, but SRAM return-to-center shifters will have a second bolt (opposite the fixing bolt) that can be used to adjust the angle of the shifter. ▼

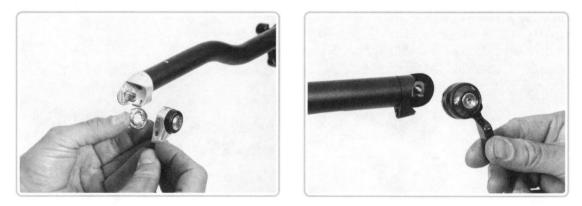

4 Install Cable and Housing

Shift the lever all the way down, placing the chain in the smallest cog. The derailleur cable will seat in the face of the lever and slide through the back of the mechanism. The cable housing, with a ferrule, sits into the back of the shifter body before being routed to the derailleurs. From here, derailleur setup is exactly the same as it would be with a standard road shifter. ▶

Installing Thumb Shifters

Thumb shifters, or trigger shifters, as they're sometimes known, are used on road bikes that have flat handlebars as opposed to the more traditional curved road bars. Flat-bar road bikes are becoming much more popular with casual cyclists who want the performance features of the skinny tire road bike combined with the comfort of the mountain bike's upright position.

While mountain bike thumb shifters may look and function similar to their road bike counterparts, they are more likely than not to be incompatible with road derailleurs. Make sure you have the correct shifters for your derailleur type.

1 Slide the Shifter Onto the Bar

Quite possibly the easiest shifter of all to install, simply slide the shifter into position on the bar and tighten the clamp bolt. ▶

2 Insert Derailleur Cable

Shift the lever all the way down, placing the chain in the smallest cog. The cable attachment point can be located in the shifter body, either behind a plastic screw (Shimano) or under the body of the shifter (SRAM). ▼

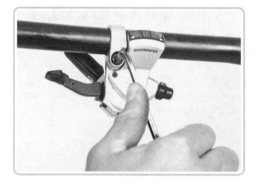

Shimano

SRAM

3 Adjust Derailleur

From here, the derailleur adjustment is exactly the same as it would be for a standard road shifter. There will be a second barrel adjuster on the shifter itself to fine-tune the cable tension, but this should be used for on-the-bike adjustments. Do the setup adjustments with the derailleur's barrel adjuster. ▶

Installing and Adjusting Shimano Di2 Shifting Systems

In 2009, Shimano introduced the first all electronic shifting system dubbed Di2 (Digital Integrated Intelligence). Since its introduction, Di2 has become the benchmark for shifting performance, offering riders unmatched precision, speed, and ease of shifting. A small, 100-gram battery powers the two servomotors housed in the front and rear derailleurs. The shifter buttons are placed on the brake levers in the same position as the standard mechanical shifters so that learning the new shifting is pretty painless.

Several different wiring kits are available for either external or internal routing of the cables. If you're running external, there are three sizes of wiring kits for different size bikes. Setup and adjustments are all handled in a small control box mounted to the brake cable housing at the front of the bike so it can easily be adjusted while riding.

Installing Shimano Di2 Shifting Systems

Shimano Di2 shifters and derailleurs look very similar to their mechanical counterparts but function quite differently. Some of the installation and adjustments are similar to the mechanical system's, but most of it is specialized, so read the following instructions carefully before installing a Di2.

1 Install Shifters

The shifters are mounted in the same manner as older Shimano Dura-Ace shifters. A 5-millimeter Allen wrench is slid under the outside of the lever body, under the hood to access the clamp bolt. Loosen the clamp bolt until the clamp easily slides onto the handlebars. When you have the lever in your preferred position, tighten the clamp bolt clockwise until the lever no longer moves easily by hand. ▶

2 Install Rear Derailleur

Exactly the same as a mechanical rear derailleur, the Di2 rear derailleur mounts directly to the derailleur hanger using a 5-millimeter Allen wrench. The derailleur has a small screw (called the B-tension screw) immediately behind the attachment bolt, which rests against a lip at the bottom of the derailleur hanger. Pull the derailleur backward as you install it so that the B-tension screw clears the lip of the hanger. When the screw is over the lip, release the derailleur so the B-tension screw rests against the lip as you finish tightening the derailleur bolt.

3 Install Front Derailleur

The front derailleur mounts to the frame in the same manner as a mechanical front derailleur but also uses a small post bolt that butts against the seat tube to provide extra stability because the servomotor is quite strong. ▶

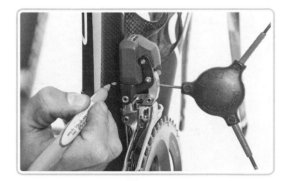

- Mount the front derailleur normally, and make a mark on the seat tube where the post bolt will hit. Remove the front derailleur, and attach the included backing plate at that mark (the backing plate has adhesive tape on it). The backing plate prevents the post bolt from damaging the frame. ▶

- Mount the front derailleur again so that the bottom of the outer cage is 1/32 to 1/16 inch (1–2 mm) above the tallest point of the teeth on the outer chainring and the cage is cocked inward slightly, not parallel with the chainrings as it normally would be. Fully tighten the mounting bolt. ▶

- Screw in the post bolt until it hits the backing plate. Continue to screw in the post bolt until the front derailleur cage is perfectly parallel with the chainrings. The tension between the mounting bolt and the post bolt provides a stable platform for the powerful front shifts. ▶

4 Install Rear Wiring Kit

Each frame that incorporates internal routing will have very specific ways of mounting the wiring kits, so for this book we'll cover only the external mounting kits. Choose the correct size for your bike. Shimano recommends small kits for bikes 52 centimeters or less, medium kits for bikes between 52 and 56 centimeters, and long kits for bikes larger than 56 centimeters.

- First, attach the cable junction to the bottom bracket shell without fully tightening the bolt. The cables that run to the front derailleur, rear derailleur, and the battery mount may be quite long. Slack is taken up by wrapping the extra cable around the different slots in the junction box. There is no set way to do this, just trial and error. When you're happy with the junction box setup, run the longest cable (runs to the front of the bike) through the tab at the front of the junction box, and bolt it to the bottom bracket. Double-check that the correct amount of slack is in the cables to reach the derailleurs and battery well.

- Bolt the battery mount underneath the front water bottle cage. Check that there is enough room to remove the battery when the cage is mounted. If there isn't, you'll need a bottle cage adapter, which is sold by Shimano. Use a zip tie to attach the mount to the down tube, running the zip tie over the battery wire and the front wire. ▶

- Using a zip tie, attach the wires to the frame at the chainstay, the down tube, and the seat tube.

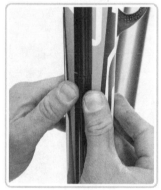

- Wipe down the down tube and chainstay with rubbing alcohol around where the wires are routed. Use the included adhesive covers over the wiring to prevent any snags or damage. ▶

- Insert the wiring ends into the front and rear derailleurs. It should be readily apparent how they are inserted. *Note:* While it's okay to insert the wire ends into the derailleurs by hand, *never* pull them out by the wire. This will ruin the connection. Always use the included Shimano tool to remove the wire ends. ▼

5 Install Front Wiring Kit

The front wiring kit includes the control box, the attachment point for the rear wiring kit, and two wires for each shifter. The shifter wires are labeled red and white—red for the right shifter, white for the left.

- Open the flap on the inside of the shifter body, and, using the cylindrical end of the Shimano Di2 tool, push the wire ends into the shifter body. There are two open slots in the lever body. It does not matter which one you use. The second slot is for accessory shifters (bar-end or remote shift levers). ▶

- Mount the control box to the front brake cable with small zip ties, which are included with the front wiring kit. Take up the slack in the shifter wire by folding the wire over itself under the bar and taping it down. Keep it close to the brake housing so that when the bar is wrapped, you won't be able to feel it. ▶

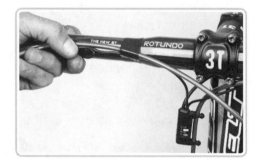

- The junction for the rear wiring has a clip that attaches to the brake housing, either on the front housing (if running the wire on the drive side) or on the rear housing (if running the wire on the nondrive side). Connect the front wiring kit to the rear. ▼

Adjusting Shifting

Because the shifting action is controlled electronically, each shift moves a precise distance each time the shifter button is pressed. All rear derailleur adjustments are done using the control box on the front wiring kit, while the front shift is adjusted using the H- and L-limit screws on the front derailleur. Because the range of shifts on the rear is also electronically controlled, the derailleur limit screws are used only as a fail-safe in the event the derailleur is physically moved past the upper or lower cog (such as might happen in a crash).

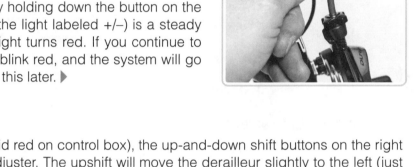

1 Turn on Adjustment Mode

Shift to the middle of the cogset (the 15 or 16 will work fine), and turn on the rear derailleur adjustment by holding down the button on the control box until the second light (the light labeled +/–) is a steady red. Release the button once the light turns red. If you continue to hold the button down, the light will blink red, and the system will go into crash recovery mode. More on this later. ▶

2 Adjust the Shift

While in shift adjustment mode (solid red on control box), the up-and-down shift buttons on the right shifter act as a very precise trim adjuster. The upshift will move the derailleur slightly to the left (just the same way that shift would move the derailleur), while the downshift does the opposite. This is similar to adjusting the tension on a mechanical rear derailleur. If it's slow moving up the cassette, use the shift button that would shift in that direction (just like you would turn the barrel adjuster in that direction on a mechanical derailleur).

   Tap the upshift button until the chain starts to make noise (similar to the noise of the chain trying to shift). Then tap the downshift button exactly four times, and turn off the adjustment mode (hold down the control box button until the solid red light turns off). The shifting should be perfect now, but, if you need to make small adjustments, use the adjustment mode to make the shift quicker in either direction.

3 Adjust Limit Screws

The limit screws on the rear derailleur are used to prevent the chain from coming off in the event of a crash or if the bike falls, not to physically stop the derailleur from moving. Shift into the smallest cog, turn in the H-limit screw until it touches the stop, and then back it out a quarter turn. Do the same on the largest cog and the L-limit screw. ▶

   Note: If the limit screw stops the derailleur from moving while it's trying to shift, the derailleur will think that it has been crashed and will disengage the servomotor. If this happens, you'll have to use the crash recovery mode to reattach the servomotor (see page 160).

4 Adjust the Front Limit Screws

- Shift the rear derailleur onto the largest cog. Shift the front derailleur onto the small ring.
- Adjust the L-limit screw (the uppermost screw) until the inner part of the cage almost touches the chain. ▶
- Shift into the smallest cog on the rear and the large chainring on the front.
- Adjust the H-limit screw (the lowest screw) until the outer part of the cage almost touches the chain. The H-limit screw adjusts in the opposite manner compared to a mechanical front derailleur; turning it clockwise will move it outward. ▶

Using Special Di2 Features

Shimano's Di2 has several special features that many overlook or simply don't know about. Here are the major ones:

Battery Indication   By holding down any of the shift buttons for a full second, the battery indication light on the control box will turn on. If the light is green, 50 to 100 percent of the battery life is left; if the light is yellow, 25 to 49 percent is left; and if the light is red, less than 25 percent is left.

Low Battery Shift Conservation   As the battery charge approaches empty, the front derailleur will stop working before the rear derailleur does because shifting the front derailleur requires much more power. If the front derailleur stops working, you'll have approximately 100 shifts left in the rear derailleur before the battery is completely drained, usually leaving enough battery power to get you home.

Crash Recovery Mode   The rear derailleur will automatically disengage the linkage from the servo-motor if the derailleur is physically moved, like when it takes a whack during a crash. This is to protect the expensive motor from damage during an accident. If you crash, your bike tips over on the drive side, or any number of other things happen and the rear won't shift, use the crash recovery mode to reengage the motor to the linkage.

While pedaling the bike, hold the control box button until the indication light flashes red (this happens after the solid red of the adjustment mode). Release the button, and the rear derailleur will go through the entire cassette and relearn the shifts. If your derailleur hanger alignment wasn't altered in the crash, the shifting should be as well adjusted as it was before.

How to Make the Most of a Fixed Gear

Fixed-gear bikes are the oldest and simplest of all bicycles. Before the advent of the derailleur, all bicycles were fixed. Now they're only commonly found on track bikes and under skinny, jeaned hipsters. But there are many great reasons for average cyclists to incorporate fixed-gear cycling into their routines. Fixed gears are so called because of their inability to coast: every time the rear wheel turns, the crank must necessarily turn as well. Adjusting the gears can change the ratio of how many revolutions the crank makes in relation to the wheel, just like on a standard bike, but you can choose only one gear at a time. You're "fixed" in that gear.

If you've never ridden a fixed gear before, you should try it at least once. It's a completely different riding experience; the purity and simplicity of the design is quite unique. Most road cyclists, when first learning to ride a fixed-gear bike, eventually forget that they can't coast, causing a crash or the rider to be violently bucked. After a couple of weeks and a couple of incidents, you pretty much unlearn the coasting instinct while riding a fixie.

Fitness benefits are to be had by riding a fixed gear, as well. Because you can't simply shift to a smaller gear while out riding, any hill you encounter becomes a massive Pyrenean col to be conquered, standing and stomping on the pedals just to get up it. On the other side of that hill, you'll reap the benefits of improved efficiency, too. Without coasting, to get to any great speed, such as on a descent, you'll become very proficient at pedaling quickly and smoothly. This smoothness, which the French call *souplesse*, will make you a more efficient and better cyclist.

The current fixed-gear craze among urban hipsters began in the bike messenger cultures of San Francisco and New York. They would prove their toughness by riding fixed-geared bikes that had narrow little handlebars and no brakes through the craziest of traffic. As with any fashionable fad, it's become endemic in our society, so much so that outside any college bar or indie rock club there will inevitably be a dozen fixed-geared bikes locked up. To make a fixed-gear bike, all you need is an appropriate frame and a wheel with a track hub built into it. Track frames and older steel frames with horizontal dropouts are ideal because you can slide the rear wheel forward and back to get the appropriate chain tension (there's no derailleur to pull the chain taut).

Regular frames with vertical dropouts can be used for this purpose but only with very specific gear ratios because there's no adjustment possible with them. The late Sheldon Brown's website has an excellent resource for determining which gears would be appropriate for each frame's dimension. If you are using a track frame, get a track hub because the rear dropout spacing for each is 120 millimeters. Standard road spacing is 130 millimeters, so you'd need to use a specially designed fixed-gear hub in that spacing or find a spacing kit compatible with your track hub. You'll also want to use a standard road fork so you can mount a front brake. Some purists, especially the aforementioned bike messengers, forgo a front brake and employ only backpedaling, which is applying backward pressure on the pedals, to slow down. Not only do I think this is reckless, but it is downright asinine. In a hairy situation, a front brake and backpedaling will work as effectively as two road brakes, but simply backpedaling could lock up the rear wheel, sending you into an uncontrollable skid.

So, if you're an average cyclist looking for a new challenge or a racing cyclist looking to take advantage of fixed-geared riding's benefits, do as the hipsters say—fix the gear, fix the problem!

CHAPTER 11

Chains and Cogsets

Bicycle chains have not gone through much technological advancement compared to other parts of a bike, such as frames and pedals. Sure, new styles of chains are narrower and have fancy shapes that facilitate lightning-fast shifts, but, in essence, all the chains made after 1980 are basically of the same design. And all of the chains used before 1980, all the way back to the first safety bicycle, are of the same basic design.

Before the safety bicycle, the drivetrain of a bike was attached directly to one of the wheels—think of the crankshaft running through the front wheel of a penny-farthing. This meant that the mechanical advantage of pedaling was always 1:1—for each revolution of the wheel, the crank had to turn one revolution. The safety bicycle (and subsequent bikes) used an industrial roller chain design, which had been used in agricultural and other heavy machinery. These chains had inner and outer plates that were linked with a bushing and a rivet. The chain links would rotate on the bushing as the chain links drove the cogs.

In 1980, Sedis developed the first "bushingless" chain, which is the design used today. Instead of a full bushing inserted between the plates, the bushingless design incorporated the outer plates to act as a bushing. Essentially, each outer plate had half of the bushing attached to it, making the chains lighter, easier to lube (the bushing was split in the middle), and much more flexible laterally (again, because of the split bushing).

Cogsets, on the other hand, have had many advances in the past century. The first wheels used fixed sprockets to power the rear wheel, while the mechanical advantage could be changed by using different-sized sprockets. There was no coasting; each time the wheel turned, the sprocket and cranks had to turn as well.

Sachs patented the first successful freewheel in the late 19th century, and it quickly became the norm. The sprocket incorporated an internal ratcheting mechanism that engaged while pedaling but allowed for coasting while not pedaling. As derailleurs became available, freewheels simply became wider to accommodate more sprockets. When multiple sprockets are clustered together, they are no longer termed sprockets but instead become cogs, hence the name cogset. This design worked well until the freewheel became so wide that it made the wheel inherently weak; the width of the freewheel meant that the bearing supporting the drive side of the wheel was continually being pushed farther inboard.

Shimano introduced the freehub design in the 1980s to deal with the issue of ever-increasing cogset sizes. The internal ratcheting system was removed from the cogset and built into the body of the hub itself. This allowed the drive-side bearings to be as wide as the axle. The individual cogs are slid onto the freehub body. When all of the cogs are together, it's called a cassette. Each cog has specially designed teeth to improve shifting performance. Often, especially with 9-, 10-, and 11-speed component groups, the cassettes and chains are specifically designed to function with each other and can create compatibility issues if you try to mix and match from different manufacturers. See figure 11.1 for an example of a chain and its parts.

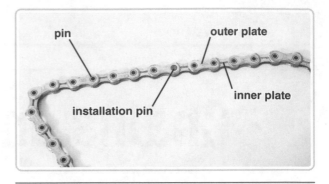

Figure 11.1 Parts of a chain.

Installing Chains

Bicycle chains will come in a length that is long enough to fit almost all bike sizes and must be shortened to fit your drivetrain. After shortening the chain, it must be connected, either with a special installation pin or with a quick link, a link that can be joined and removed without a tool.

Compatibility among various drivetrains from different component makers can get a little confusing. Different manufacturers' 9-speed drivetrains are so similar that there tends to be no compatibility issues (e.g., Shimano chains work with SRAM cassettes, SRAM chains work with Campagnolo cassettes, etc.). With 10-speed drivetrains, SRAM and Shimano drivetrains work fine with each other, but neither drivetrain is compatible with Campy's drivetrain. And 11 speed . . . well, currently, Campagnolo is the only company making 11 speed, so it's a bit of a moot point.

1 Determine Chain Length

Unlike mountain bike and cyclocross chains, road chains should be left as long as possible so that you can use more of the cassette while in the large chainring. A chain that is too short will cause a significant amount of drag while using the larger cogs or may even bind completely. ▶

- Shift the derailleurs into the smallest cog on the rear and the small chainring on the front.
- Route the new chain through the front and rear derailleurs so that both ends are hanging from the bottom of the bike. ▶

- Pull the two ends toward each other until the bottom of the chain just clears the upper pulley. ▶
- Mark how many links should be removed to attain this length.

2 Shorten the Chain

Use the correct chain tool (9- and 10-speed chains use the same tool; 11-speed chains require a special tool), and break the chain at the appropriate link. Fully insert the link's rivet into the chain tool at the point that needs to be broken, and turn the chain tool's handle in until it makes connection with the rivet. Check that the chain is fully inserted into the tool before pushing the rivet all the way through the back plate of the chain. ▶

If you are using a chain with a quick link (SRAM, Wipperman, KMC), you should account for the extra length of the quick link when determining the chain length. When you break the chain, you should have two male ends. For Shimano and Campagnolo 11-speed chains, you will have one female and one male end. ▶

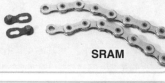

Shimano/
Campagnolo

SRAM

Campagnolo 10-speed chains are connected using a so-called HD-Link, which is two links connected to two female ends specifically designed to be joined after breaking. Deduct the length of this piece from the chain length before breaking. One end of a Campagnolo 11-speed chain will have a small zip tie through it. You must shorten the chain from the *other* end. The end with the zip tie is specifically designed to be joined after breaking. ▶

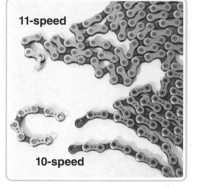

11-speed

10-speed

3 Connect the Chain

Each type of chain has a very specific way in which it needs to be installed. Use the specific guidelines for each type of chain as follows:

Shimano

Shimano chains must be connected with a special rivet pin, which comes included with the chain. One end will be tapered and the other blunt.

- Pull the chain off the front chainring so that there will be no tension as you insert the rivet pin. Push the tapered end through the open link from the outside (so that the tapered end moves toward the bike). ▶

- Pull the chain back onto the small chainring to tension the chain. Fully insert the link with the rivet pin into the chain tool with the blunt end facing the handle of the tool. Slowly turn the handle clockwise, and push the rivet pin through the chain. You will feel the pressure on the handle release as the rivet is fully seated. The blunt end will be flush with the outer plate of the link. ▼

- Use the open end of the chain tool or a pair of pliers to break off the exposed piece of the rivet pin. Use a quick side-to-side motion to cleanly break the pin. Inspect the rivet; it should be flush with both sides of the link with no deformities or twisting. ▶

SRAM

SRAM, Wipperman, and KMC chains use a quick link instead of a rivet pin to connect their chains. SRAM links do not have an inside or outside position of the two halves, but some connectors do. Check the instructions that come with the chain to ensure proper installation. *Note:* Some quick links are reusable (SRAM 9-speed chains), while some are not (SRAM 10-speed chains). Check with the manufacturer to determine whether they can be reused.

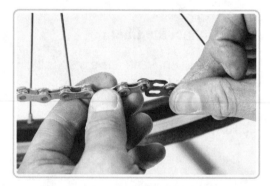

- Insert both halves on the two male ends of the broken chain, and connect with each other. ▶
- Pull the two ends away from each other, and the quick link will partially seat itself. ▶

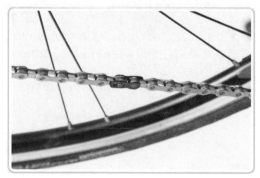

- Pedal the drivetrain forward until the quick link is on the top of the drivetrain. ▶
- Hold the rear brake, and apply forward pressure on the pedals. You will hear the link pop as it fully seats itself.

Campagnolo 10-Speed Chains

Campagnolo 10-speed chains are joined using the HD-Link and two special rivets that are hollow and have guide pins.

- Place the guide pin into the rivet and insert into the link to be joined. ▶
- Push the rivet from the inside of the chain toward the outside (away from the bike) with a chain tool for 9- and 10-speed drivetrains. It's important to keep the chain fully seated in the tool while pushing the rivet; use your thumb over the top of the chain to hold it down. ▶
- When the rivet is fully seated, simply pull the pin out of the rivet.

Campagnolo 11-Speed Chains

Campagnolo 11-speed chains are narrower than 10-speed chains, so the tolerances for installation are much tighter. A special 11-speed chain tool must be used, which also has a solid plate (on a lever) that is used to peen (flatten) the deformed end of the installed rivet.

- After breaking the chain to the appropriate length (remember to shorten only from the end of the chain that does not have a zip tie through it), insert the pin rivet through the link so that it can be joined from the inside (so the rivet moves away from the bike). ▶
- Put the chain on the front chainring so that it is tensioned, and fully insert the chain into the chain tool. The Campagnolo 11-speed chain tool has two sliding prongs, which hold the chain in place.
- Push the rivet pin through the link until you feel no pressure on the handle of the chain tool. The rivet should be flush with the outer plate of the link. ▶

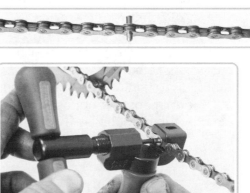

- Use the open end of the chain tool to break the exposed piece of the rivet pin. ▶

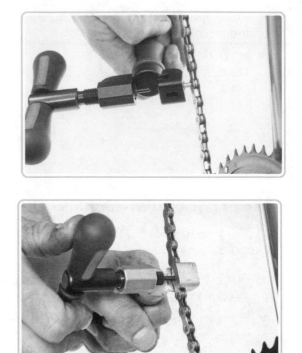

- After the rivet is installed, you must perform the additional step of peening the broken end of the rivet. This flattens the surface so that the chain operates smoothly. Flip the lever on the chain tool down, and insert the chain link into the tool in front of the plate, with the handle facing toward the bike. Turn the handle so that the chain tool pin pushes against the broken end of the rivet while the back end of the rivet is held in place against the backing plate. Turn the handle forcefully until the end of the rivet is flush and resembles the surrounding rivets. ▶

4 Remove the Chain

The chain can be removed for replacement or cleaning by using a chain tool to fully push out one rivet and disconnect the link. Quick links are even easier; simply push the link together and remove (Park makes an excellent tool that does this). ▼

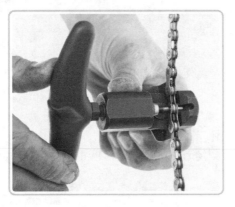

Note: Never break the chain where it had been previously connected (the connection rivet will look markedly different from the surrounding rivets). Pick a link on the opposite side of the chain to prevent any structural weakness in the chain. ▶

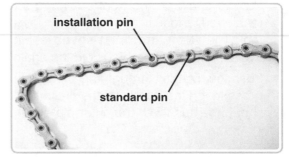

installation pin

standard pin

EMERGENCY CHAIN REPAIRS

If your chain breaks while riding, it's a good idea to replace it with a new one as soon as possible—but that won't get you home very quickly! It's a good idea to always keep a chain tool in your seatbag while riding for just such an emergency.

Use the chain tool to remove the broken link. When breaking the chain at the female end, do not fully push the rivet out as you would when installing a new chain. Push the rivet just to the point that the chain will come apart with the rivet still inserted in the chain plate. Turn the handle a bit at a time. When the rivet is close to coming out, remove the chain and check to see that it will come apart. Repeat until the chain link is disconnected. ◄

Place both halves of the chain into the chain tool, and push the disconnected rivet back through the link. Replace the chain as soon as possible because this is only an emergency fix and the chain will fail at that link eventually. ▶

Installing a Freewheel

Freewheels, although a tad antiquated, are still often found on single-speed and BMX bikes. Installing them is extremely simple, but removal can be strenuous exercise!

Any freewheel made in the past two decades will have a standard thread pattern (1.375 in. x 24 tpi). Older British and Italian standards did exist, but they are so close to the new standard that they are interchangeable. The one exception is the French thread pattern (1.366 in. x 25.4 tpi). If you have this type of hub, make sure you use the correct freehub.

1 Grease Threads

Grease the threads on the hub shell well. This may save you some sweat when you need to remove the freewheel.

2 Hand Tighten the Freewheel

Thread the freewheel onto the hub and hand tighten. ▶

3 Install the Wheel and Ride

Put the rear wheel on the bike, and go for a short ride around the block. The pedaling action tightens the freewheel on the hub, so no tools are necessary. You may feel the freewheel slip a couple of times as it tightens, but it will become rock solid.

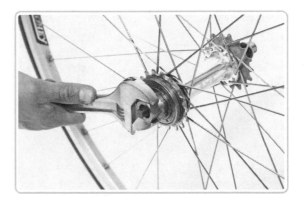

4 Removing the Freewheel

Because the freewheel is tightened any time that you apply pressure to the pedals, removal can be difficult. Find the appropriate removal tool for your freewheel brand, and insert it into the freewheel over the wheel axle. Use a large adjustable wrench to unthread the freewheel by turning the tool counterclockwise. If the freewheel simply won't budge, place the freewheel tool in a vice and put the wheel on top. Then turn the wheel counterclockwise like a large steering wheel to apply leverage and loosen the freewheel.

Note: If you ever need to rebuild a wheel that has a freewheel hub, remove the freewheel before cutting the spokes! It will be impossible to remove the freewheel (and build the new wheel) if it is still attached to the hub.

Installing a Cassette

More than likely, your bike will have a freehub and cassette rather than just a freewheel. Cassettes are easy to install and replace and are basically maintenance free.

Shimano and SRAM cassettes are interchangeable, but Campagnolo uses a different spline pattern on its freehubs. All 8-, 9-, 10-, and 11-speed cassettes will fit on the same freehub, the exception being Shimano Dura-Ace hubs from 2004 to 2007. These hubs were only compatible with 10-speed cassettes because they used taller splines. Shimano 10-speed cassettes will fit on other freehubs using an adapter spacer that comes included with the cassette.

1 Install Spacer

If you are using a Shimano 10-speed cassette, there will be a 1-millimeter spacer that slides onto the freehub body before the cassette. This spacer will not be needed if you are using a Shimano Dura-Ace hub from 2004 to 2007. ▶

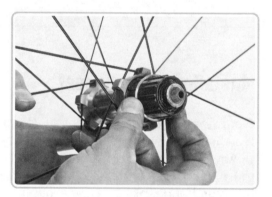

2 Install Cassette Cogs

Starting with the largest cog, install each cog and any spacers one by one. The splines are arranged in a such a way that the cog will fit on the freehub in only one direction as it is slid onto the freehub body. ▶

3 Install Lockring

The lockring threads into the freehub body and holds the rest of the cogs in place. Grease the thread of the lockring, and, using a lockring tool, tighten the lockring by turning it clockwise with a large adjustable wrench. Tighten forcefully. It's easy to cross-thread the lockring, so make sure that it is threaded in straight before you tighten it! ▼

Note: Some older cassettes and freehubs won't have a lockring. Instead, the last cog on the cassette is threaded onto the freehub body. Use a chain whip to tighten this cog.

4 Removing the Cassette

If you turn the lockring tool counterclockwise, the freehub will just spin, so you have to use a chain whip to hold the cassette in place while you loosen the lockring. Drape the chain links on the end of the chain whip across one of the larger cogs, with the handle facing to the right (toward the front of the bike as it would be when installed). Hold the chain whip tight as you loosen the lockring with the lockring tool and a large adjustable wrench. ▼

Maintaining and Repairing Chains and Cassettes

There is probably no single aspect of bicycle repair that inspires more debate and cogitation than lubing the chain. Many companies make a dizzying assortment of lubes for any type of riding condition imaginable. Even the airplane manufacturer Boeing has a bicycle chain lube. Which one is right for your chain?

In my experience, all of the bike lubes work reasonably well in most conditions. Maintaining the chain is more about keeping it clean and properly lubed, not about which lube you're using. Maintaining the chain (and replacing it regularly) will also greatly extend the life of the cassette, not to mention the life of the derailleur pulleys and chainrings.

Keep the Drivetrain Clean

This is probably the most important step you can take to keep the chain working well. A chain that is covered in dirt and grit will work like a file on the cogs, pulleys, and chainrings, wearing them quickly. Regularly washing your bike and the drivetrain (see chapter 2) will keep the chain running smoothly and quietly.

Use the Right Amount of Lube

More is better, right? Wrong. Too much chain lube is actually more harmful to the drivetrain than not having enough. The reason relates to having a dirty chain. Extra lube on your chain attracts dirt and dust, which clumps up and creates an abrasive mixture. Apply the lube sparingly to the chain and wipe off the excess. Applying the lube to the inside of the chain (the side facing the chainrings and cassette) through a couple of revolutions of the pedals is enough lube to apply to a clean chain.

Replace the Chain Regularly

As the chain wears, it stretches. The plates themselves do not literally stretch, but the rivets wear and the links no longer fit tightly together. As the chain stretches, it wears the cassette teeth so that when a new chain is installed, it will not fit tightly and can cause slipping, especially in the small cogs where there are fewer teeth holding the chain.

A modern road chain should last around 2,000 miles (3,219 km), but that distance may vary depending on your riding conditions. Buy a chain stretch indicator tool, and check the chain frequently. This simple tool will let you know when the chain has stretched between .75 and 1 percent of its original length and needs to be replaced. Replacing the chain is much less expensive than replacing a cassette.

PRO'S POINT OF VIEW

David Millar's Bike Toss

In 2008, when I was a mechanic with the Slipstream-Chipotle professional cycling team (which would take the name Garmin-Chipotle during the Tour de France that year), we were invited to our first Grand Tour ever—the 91st Giro d'Italia. Three-week Grand Tours are the pinnacle of cycle sport, and the Giro is second only to the Tour de France in terms of prestige, history, and difficulty.

Needless to say, the team was nervous. Being our first outing on the world stage, the opening team time trial would be crucial for our fledgling squad. In a team time trial, the entire nine-person team will ride together on a specific course, and the time of the fifth rider across the line is given to the entire team for the day. On paper, we had one of the strongest teams in the race in this discipline. Some of the best time trialists in the world were in our lineup, cornered by British champion David Millar; American Christian Vande Velde; and former Paris–Roubaix winner, Magnus Bäckstedt.

Both of our directors wanted to be in the first car that day, so I was assigned the task of driving the second car. The first car stays with the leaders of the team to give advice over the radio and be there if there's a mechanical problem or crash. The second car follows the first rider dropped so that, no matter where a rider is on the course, there will be a follow car behind him if there were a problem.

The fans were rabid, and the race was fast and treacherous; it was exhilarating. We won the day by a slim six seconds, placing Christian in the pink leader's jersey of the race. Christian would continue his excellent form that year, placing fourth overall at that year's Tour de France.

For a new team, it was quite a coup. But our luck was not to last, however. During the second stage, American time-trial champion Dave Zabriskie was involved in a crash going over some railroad tracks, and he cracked a bone in his back. Christian would narrowly lose the leader's jersey in a hectic finale to Italian Franco Pellizotti, a rider who would later be banned for a doping violation.

The culmination of our newfound ill fortune would come on the fifth stage. David Millar slipped into the day's five-man breakaway, the first that would survive to the end of the stage to fight for the win. I was in the first car that day, so it was the second car that was following the breakaway while we were behind the main field. Nearing the end of the stage, the gap between the break and the peloton fell to less than a minute, meaning the second car would have to pull over so that there would be no interference between the team cars and the hard-charging field.

David is an incredibly strong and cunning rider. We knew he had a great chance to take the win from a small group, even more so given the slight uphill finish. We listened to the race radio intently as they approached the final kilometer. Eight hundred meters, 700 meters, 600 meters, and, finally, the voice over the radio spat out, "Meccanico Millar. Meccanico Millar. Vince Brutt." David had a mechanical, and Pavel Brutt had won the day. The car went dead silent.

Nothing is more stressful to a mechanic than hearing that one of your riders had a mechanical. The first thing that goes through your head is, "Was this my fault?" The second thing that goes through your head is, "God, I hope that wasn't my fault."

The second car had David's spare bike on top of it because it had been following him all day, but, with the second car pulled over, the entire field went past Millar before we could get to him with the first car. I jumped out with a pair of wheels and ran to David, who was nonchalantly standing by his bike. "My chain broke," was all he said, deadpan. Without his spare to give him, I was forced to pull Pat McCarty's spare bike from the car, which David slowly pedaled to the finish line, adding insult to injury.

It wasn't until later that night that I learned the rest of the story. David's chain had snapped during the final sprint for the win. If it had held on only 200 meters longer, he could have had an elusive Grand Tour stage in the bag.

Enraged, he immediately dismounted and tossed his bike over the railing. The TV footage was incredible. An elderly Italian fan rushed to retrieve the wayward bike and hand it back to David, who then immediately threw it on the ground again. This same fan patiently climbed over the railing, picked up the bike, and leaned it against the railing, which is where I would find it after sending David off with Pat's spare.

Late that night, David bought us all a round of beers in the hotel pub, and we tried to laugh off the incident. Bad luck, we said.

The next day, a swarm of Shimano engineers came to our hotel to study the broken chain, eventually deciding to issue a recall of the run of chains that had been on David's bike. They desperately wanted to take the chain back to Japan to study, but David made me promise the night before to save that chain for him. I did, and I hope he still has it today.

CHAPTER 12

Pedals and Cleats

Pedals are the last of the three interaction points between the rider and the bicycle (the other two being the saddle and handlebars). While it may seem that adjusting the saddle height or changing stems would make much more of a difference to a rider's position and overall comfort, I would argue that the pedal is probably more important to overall cycling happiness. Because of the incredible amount of repetition involved in pedaling a bicycle, a small problem with the pedal spindle, cleat position, or anything else pedal related can have an amplified impact on your body.

Having the incorrect bar height might give you a stiff neck or numb hands, but this is nothing compared to the damage that can be caused to the joints in your legs and hips if your pedal system is not set up correctly. This may sound like a dire warning, but it's to prove a point—most people overlook their pedals until there's a problem.

There have been two major designs for bicycle pedals with one being all but completely defunct now. But their histories might surprise you! Traditional cage-type pedals have a spindle that attaches to the end of the crank and a cage that rotates around that spindle on bearings. The rider's foot is held in place with a toe clip—a metal or plastic holder for the shoe and a leather toe strap that pulls the foot tight against the cage. Toe clips were invented around 1900, and the modern iteration, including a self-clinching, quick-release toe strap, was introduced by Alfredo Binda in 1947.

The newer style of pedal is called a "clipless" pedal because of its lack of toe clips—a somewhat confusing name because you actually clip into the pedal. A clipless pedal uses a spring-loaded catch to hold a cleat that is affixed to the bottom of a specially designed cycling shoe. To release the cleat, simply twist your foot in either direction, and the cleat will pop out of the retention catch.

Toe clips do amazingly well at keeping your foot attached to the pedal. So well, in fact, that it became the main reason for their downfall. It was impossible to extricate yourself from the pedals without reaching down and undoing the toe strap, meaning that, if you fell, your bike was falling with you. A famous illustration of this danger came from 1987's edition of the Tour of Flanders, when Danish pro Jesper Skibby fell while climbing the Koppenberg hill. A follow car tried to pass on the narrow climb but instead ran over Skibby's rear wheel, barely avoiding his foot—which was still strapped into his toe clip.

Considered to be a modern invention, the clipless pedal actually predates most toe-clip designs. The first patent for a clipless pedal was filed in 1895 by a Rhode Island inventor by the name of Charles Hanson. His pedal featured many of the same designs incorporated into today's pedals, including rotational float and twisting your foot to unlock the shoe. Many other wacky designs followed, including pedals that used magnets to hold the shoe in place and one design that featured powerful suction cups that stuck to the bottom of your shoes. However, early clipless pedals were unreliable, so toe clips reigned supreme for the greater part of the century. It wasn't until Look introduced its groundbreaking clipless pedal in 1985 that the design made inroads on the pedal market, largely spurred on by the success of the Look-sponsored rider Bernard Hinault, who would win the Tour de France in 1985 on Look's prototype clipless pedals.

The Look-style cleat had a three-hole mounting system that quickly became the standard for shoe manufacturers. Many other styles came and went, but almost all road cleats today mount with this three-hole pattern. The one exception is the Shimano SPD cleat, a small, recessed cleat, originally designed for mountain bike use, which has found limited success in the casual road market.

Toe-clip pedals are heavier and less safe than their clipless counterparts, but they haven't become completely extinct yet. Many inexpensive road bikes come equipped with toe clips as a way to make road riding less intimidating because they can be used with normal shoes. Track riders, especially sprinters, still prefer toe clips as well because of their excellent shoe retention.

Installing Pedals

Unlike other bicycle parts, pedals have only one standard—almost. Some inexpensive bikes, cruisers, and BMX bikes may have a .5-inch (1.3 cm) pedal spindle diameter, but all road and mountain bikes have a .6-inch (1.4 cm) standard, so those are the only ones that concern us.

The pedal thread orientations are standardized as well, with the right pedal always right-hand threaded (turn right to tighten), while the left pedal always has a left-hand thread. Early fixed-geared bicycles were the origin for this arrangement. If the pedal axle ever seized and wouldn't turn anymore, the pedal would unscrew itself instead of flinging you over the handlebars.

1 Grease the Pedal Threads

Apply a thin layer of grease to the entire surface of the pedal threads.

2 Hand Thread the Pedal

Begin by threading the pedal axle into the crank by hand. Remember, the right pedal is right-hand threaded, and the left is left-hand threaded.

Note: If the pedal axle will not thread into the crank easily, don't force it! Check that the pedal axle threads in straight and is not cross-threaded (when the threads of the pedal axle and crank are misaligned). Visually inspect the pedal axle and the crank threads for damage. The crank threads can be tapped (essentially recut), but this is best left for an experienced professional.

3 Finish Tightening the Pedal Axle

The pedal axle will have a flat spot for a pedal wrench on it near the threads (for a 15 mm pedal wrench), or the end of the axle will accept an Allen wrench. Sometimes it will have both. In that case, it's preferable to use the Allen wrench. If you're not using a fixed-gear bicycle, it's not necessary to tighten the pedal a great deal; it tightens itself as you pedal and won't come unscrewed while coasting. ▼

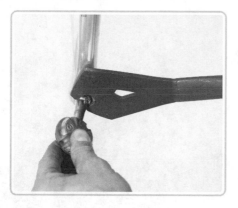 

Note: If you're in a hurry, after you start the pedal thread by hand, you can hold the pedal axle with the pedal wrench and turn the crank backward. This is best done in a stand.

4 Adjust Release Tension

Most clipless pedals (with a few exceptions) have adjustable release tension screws. These are typically small Allen or flat screws that can be found on the pedal body. Turning the screw clockwise will add tension and make it harder to clip out, while turning it counterclockwise will make it easier to clip out. Adjust this screw a bit at a time, then ride the bike to test the cleat retention setting. ▶

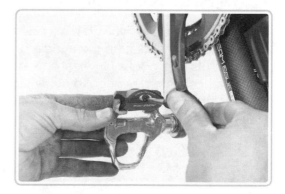

Installing Cleats on Shoes

When clipless pedals were a new innovation, it seemed that every pedal manufacturer had a unique mounting pattern for the cleat hardware. Some shoe and pedal combinations were so unique that they would work exclusively with each other, but luckily those have died out. Today, the original three-bolt pattern incorporated into the original Look clipless pedal has become the standard. All major brands of road cleats will mount to this standard, although some may require an adapter.

Cleats for mountain bike pedals have been standardized as well. The Shimano groundbreaking SPD cleat was so innovative and practical that there has never been any credible challenge to its mounting pattern. The mountain bike cleat is much, much smaller than a road cleat to allow room on the sole of the shoe for tread, necessary for tricky hike-a-bike sections of trail. Because they are easier to get into (mountain bike pedals are double sided) and are easier to walk in, many road riders prefer to use mountain bike pedals and shoes. The downside is that mountain bike pedals aren't as secure as road pedals, which can be hairy during a town-limit sprint or other violent effort.

Shimano, Look, Time, and Campagnolo Cleats

These cleats are usually called "Look-style cleats" because the French bicycle company, Look, was the first to introduce a three-bolt cleat pattern. Now almost ubiquitous, nearly all road shoes are compatible with the three-bolt design. Float, or how much the cleat rotates while engaged, can be changed with different styles of cleats.

1 Grease the Bolts

Lightly grease the cleat bolts, or dab a little bit of grease on the female threads that are recessed in the shoe body.

2 Insert the Bolt Into the Shoe

Most of these style cleats will have washers between the bolts and cleats that will allow lateral adjustment of the cleat, while the fore and aft adjustment is in the shoe. The cleat bolts are inserted directly into the shoe body or adapter plate if you are using one. ▶

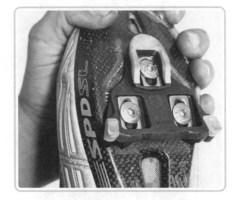

3 Adjust the Fore and Aft Position

A good place to start, if you don't already have your cleat position fixed, is to set the cleat in the middle of the adjustment, using the bolt slots as a guide. On most shoes, the middle of the cleat adjustment slots is designed to be directly under the ball of the foot. For more on fine-tuning, see chapter 13. ▶

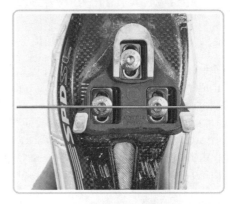

4 Adjust the Lateral Position

Again, unless you have the cleat position fixed already, start with the cleat in the middle of the shoe, using the bolt slots as a guide. ▶

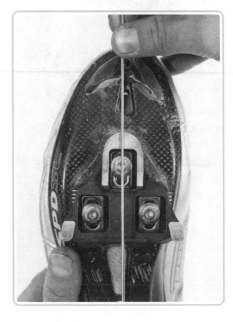

5 Adjust the Angle

Take both of your shoes, and find a flat surface with an edge, such as a countertop or a desk. Place the shoes on the flat surface, and line the rear edge of the cleat on the facing edge. As you hold the cleat against the edge, you can rotate each shoe until it is straight. If you know you are pigeon toed, you can rotate the heel out a little bit and vice versa if you're duck footed. ▶

6 Tighten Bolts

Tighten the cleat bolts snugly to the manufacturer's torque specs. Bring an Allen wrench (or screwdriver if necessary) with you on your first couple of rides because you'll probably want to make small adjustments. Check the bolts' tightness after the first three or four rides, then periodically thereafter.

Shimano SPD Cleats

Shimano SPD cleats are installed in the same manner as in the three-bolt system, but they have a few small quirks for road bike application. Some cleats can change the amount of float, depending on which direction the cleat is mounted.

1 Grease the Bolts

Lightly grease the cleat bolts, or dab a little bit of grease on the female threads that are recessed in the shoe body.

2 Insert the Bolt Into the Shoe

Most of these style of cleats will have a single washer between the bolts and cleats that will allow lateral adjustment of the cleat, while the fore and aft adjustment is in the shoe. The bolts are inserted directly into the shoe or adapter plate if you are using one. If you are using these cleats with road shoes instead of with mountain bike shoes, it's a good idea to use Shimano "pontoons," which make finding the pedal with the cleat easier. These aren't necessary with mountain bike shoes because the tread will act as a guide. ▶

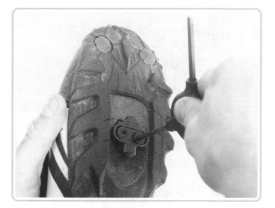

3 Adjust the Fore and Aft Position

A good place to start, if you don't already have your cleat position fixed, is to set the cleat in the middle of the adjustment, using the bolt slots as a guide. On most shoes, the middle of the cleat adjustment slots are designed to be directly under the ball of the foot. For more on fine-tuning, see chapter 13. ▶

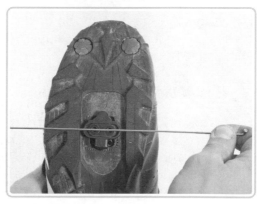

4 Adjust the Lateral Position

Again, unless you have your cleat position fixed already, start with the cleat in the middle of the shoe, using the bolt slots as a guide. ▶

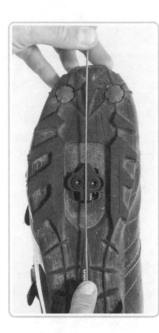

5 Adjust the Angle

Because Shimano SPD cleats are so much smaller than Look-style cleats, small changes in the cleat angle can feel like large adjustments once you're on the bike. Use a long screwdriver or something similar, and line it up with the center line of the shoe, running from the heel to the ball of the foot. Looking from above, use this line as a reference when initially setting up the cleat angle. ▶

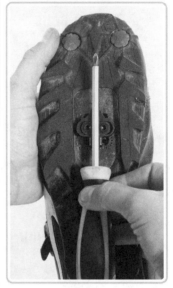

6 Tighten Bolts

Tighten the cleat bolts snugly to the manufacturer's torque specs. Bring an Allen wrench with you on your first couple of rides because you'll probably want to make small adjustments. Check the bolts' tightness after the first three or four rides, then periodically after that.

Shimano SPD-R Cleats

Now obsolete, for a couple of years in the early 2000s, all of Shimano's high-end road shoes and pedals were of the SPD-R design. A special bolting pattern was designed with two cleat holes directly in line with the center of the shoe. The cleats were all metal and quite durable, but they damaged any floors that were softer than concrete when walked on.

Three different cleats were available that had varying degrees of float. Furthermore, the amount of friction of the float could be adjusted by raising or lowering a rubber pad built into the pedal body.

1 Grease the Bolts

Lightly grease the cleat bolts, or dab a bit of grease on the female threads that are recessed in the shoe body.

2 Insert the Bolt Into the Shoe

SPD-R cleats have a pontoon, similar to the SPD pontoon, that is fitted under the rear cleat holder, the cleat, and the rear cleat bolt. The front and rear cleat bolts are not interchangeable; the rear is flat, while the front is a button head. The bolts will be inserted directly into the shoe.

3 Adjust the Fore and Aft Position

A good place to start, if you don't already have your cleat position fixed, is to set the cleat in the middle of the adjustment, using the bolt slots as a guide. On most shoes, the middle of the cleat adjustment slots are designed to be directly under the ball of the foot. For more on fine-tuning, see chapter 13.

4 Adjust the Lateral Position

Again, unless you have your cleat position fixed already, start with the cleat in the middle of the shoe, using the bolt slots as a guide.

5 Adjust the Angle

Use a long screwdriver or something similar, and line it up with the center line of the shoe, running from the heel to the ball of the foot. Looking from above, use this line as a reference when initially setting up the cleat angle.

6 Tighten Bolts

Tighten the cleat bolts snugly to the manufacturer's torque specs. Bring an Allen wrench with you on your first couple of rides because you'll probably want to make small adjustments. Check the bolts' tightness after the first three or four rides, then periodically thereafter.

Speedplay Cleats

Speedplay cleats have a unique four-bolt mounting pattern, which mates with a base plate that is attached to the shoe using the traditional three-bolt pattern. The placement of the base plate determines the fore and aft adjustment of the cleat, while the lateral adjustment is done with the cleat itself.

1 Attach the Base Plate

Speedplay cleats come with several shims that match the curvature of different types of shoes. Select the correct shims for your shoes so that the base plate lays flush with your shoe's sole. Lightly grease the included bolts and attach the base plate to the shoe. Try to adjust the fore and aft position as best as you can because it will necessitate removing the cleat to change later. ▶

2 Attach the Cleat

Place the plastic cleat body and metal cover over the base plate, and attach using the 11-millimeter fastening screws. Before tightening fully, adjust the lateral position of the cleat, and then tighten the screws. Be careful not to strip them; maximum torque on these screws is only 2.5 Newton-meters. *Note:* The side of the cleat that is cut away faces the *inside* of the shoe. This cutaway is for the pedal axle. ▶

3 Adjust Float

If you're using Speedplay Zero pedals, you can adjust the amount of float, or the amount the cleat rotates before disengaging, by adjusting the two small screws on the outside of the cleat. With the screws fully backed out, the cleats have 15 degrees of float; with them fully screwed in, they will have 0 degrees of float (fixed). ▶

Maintaining Pedals and Cleats

It should seem obvious why properly maintained pedals and cleats are essential to your cycling well-being. All riders, if they have been riding long enough, have dicey stories about "that one time my foot came out of my pedal" or of embarrassing themselves by falling over at a stoplight when they couldn't get out at all.

Apart from the danger of suddenly ejecting from the cleat interface, an issue with your pedal or cleat, whether from negligence, improper installation, or simple wear and tear, can wreak havoc on your legs. Small, nagging problems can quickly become large, damaging issues through the repetitive nature of pedaling a bike. Here, I'll cover the mechanical maintenance of the pedals and cleats. For more on positioning, see chapter 13.

Lube the Pivot Points

Clipless pedals employ a spring-loaded retention clasp to hold the cleat (and your foot) in place. It's a good idea to apply a light lube to the springs and the clasp's pivot points periodically or after each wash. The retention system is an often-used, but easily overlooked, moving part on your bike. *Note:* On Speedplay pedals, the clasp retention system is built into the cleat instead of being on the pedal body. Use a Speedplay-approved lube on the cleats' moving parts.

Inspect the Cleats

Cleats, especially the plastic ones common today, are light and strong but are susceptible to wear. A markedly worn cleat will not be held tightly by the pedal and will feel sloppy or will clip out accidentally. Periodically check the cleats for wear or damage. Some cleats have built-in wear indicators; when the wear reaches a certain line, the cleats should be replaced. Cleats are relatively inexpensive and easy to install, so, if you think you might need new ones, go ahead and replace them.

Inspect the Pedal Body

If you're experiencing slip in the pedals but the cleats are in good shape, the pedal body itself might be worn. Inspect the body of the pedal for any parts that are worn in such a way that would affect the interaction between the cleat and the pedal. Most pedal bodies are irreplaceable, and, when significant wear has occurred, the entire pedal must be replaced. Shimano's first generation of SPD-SL pedals had replaceable plastic bumpers that would take most of the wear. These can be easily pried out and new ones snapped in place. Because the cleats are metal and the pedal bodies plastic, Speedplay pedal bodies are designed to be easily replaced. Rebuild kits are readily available.

Grease the Bearings

The bearings inside the pedal body need to be periodically greased to maintain proper lubrication. There are many, many different bearing designs used by pedal companies; some use loose ball bearings, while some use sealed cartridge bearings. Yet others use needle bearings, and many others use a combination of these types.

1 Insert Grease Through Dust Cap

If your pedals have a dust cap or bolt on the end of the pedal spindle, this can be removed to add grease with a grease gun. Others must have the spindle removed to access the bearings. ▶

2 Remove Pedal Spindle to Expose Bearings

To remove the spindle, clamp the pedal body in a vise, wrapping the pedal in a rag to keep from marring it. The spindle will have a retaining collar, which threads into the pedal body. With this collar removed, the spindle can be slid out to expose the bearings. ▶

The collar may have wrench flats for removal or may need a special tool to remove, such as most Shimano and Look pedals require. Typically, the threads for the collar will be in the reverse direction from the pedal spindle. Therefore, the right pedal will have a left-hand thread on the collar and a right-hand thread on the left pedal's collar.

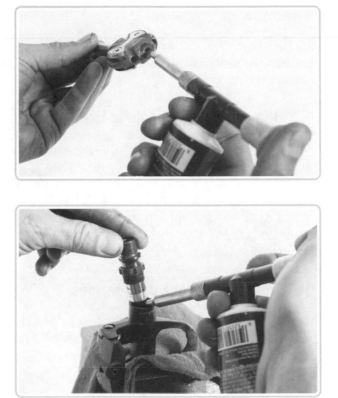

3 Clean and Grease Bearings

After removing the spindle from the pedal body, the bearings (whichever type they are) will be exposed. If they are loose ball bearings or needle bearings, wipe them clean with a lint-free rag and apply a durable grease to them. If they are cartridge bearings and feel rough, they must be replaced. See "Adjust the Bearings" in the next section.

Note: Shimano SPD-SL–style pedal spindles are held in place with a lockring, similar to other pedal spindles, but, unlike other spindles, there is also an adjustable cup that is held in place by the lockring. Each time the pedal spindle is removed, the bearings must be adjusted. If you have SPD-SL–style pedals, continue to the next section.

Adjust the Bearings

If there is play in the pedal body when it is fully inserted into the crank, the bearings need to either be adjusted or replaced. Typically, each pedal will have two bearings on the inboard and outboard sides on which the pedal spindle spins. Because they are fit inside the pedal body, they necessarily must be small and therefore easily prone to wear.

To adjust the bearings, first you must determine which style of bearings your pedals employ. The vast majority of pedals use sealed cartridge bearings, which are not adjustable. Once they have play in them, they must be replaced. Some pedals (Look Keo pedals, for example) do not have replaceable bearings, and the entire spindle must be replaced. The major exceptions to this rule are Shimano pedals. Both the SPD-SL style and the SPD style employ traditional ball and race bearings. Both styles are fully adjustable but in different ways.

Shimano SPD

Shimano's mountain bike–style clipless pedals are sometimes used for road applications by those looking for double-sided entry or those using mountain bike shoes.

1 Remove Pedal Spindle to Expose Bearings

To remove the spindle, clamp the pedal body in a vise, wrapping the pedal in a rag to keep from marring it. The spindle will have a retaining collar that threads into the pedal body. The threads for the collar will be in the reverse direction from the pedal spindle's. Therefore, the right pedal will have a left-hand thread on the collar and a right-hand thread on the left pedal's collar. With this collar removed, the spindle can be slid out to expose the bearings. ▶

2 Clean and Grease the Bearings

To grease the bearings, use a grease gun to push fresh grease into the packed bearings. The old, dirty grease will be pushed out and can be wiped away. If the bearings are particularly dirty, the spindle can be soaked in a solvent and blown dry before inserting grease.

3 Adjust the Bearings

The spindle in the Shimano SPD pedal has an adjusting cone and a small locknut on the outboard side (both are right-hand thread). To adjust pedal play, hold the adjusting cone with a 10-millimeter wrench, and loosen the locknut with a 7-millimeter wrench. If there is play in the bearings, tighten the adjusting cone by turning it clockwise a bit; turn it counterclockwise if the bearings are too tight (the pedal binds as it spins). Adjust in small increments, and test by reinstalling in the pedal body until the pedal turns smoothly and there is no play. ▶

Shimano SPD-SL

The Shimano SPD-SL–style pedal spindles are held in place with a lockring, similar to that in other pedal spindles, but, unlike other spindles, there is also an adjustable cup that is held in place by the lockring. Each time the pedal spindle is removed, the bearings must be adjusted.

1 Remove the Spindle to Expose Bearings

To remove the spindle, clamp the pedal body in a vise, wrapping the pedal in a rag to keep from marring it. The threads for the lockring will be in the reverse direction from the pedal spindle. Therefore, the right pedal will have a left-hand thread on the collar and a right-hand thread on the left pedal's collar. Loosen the lockring with a 20-millimeter cone wrench, and then unthread the adjustable cup from the pedal body (you should be able to do this with your fingers, but the cup has 17-millimeter flats for a cone wrench if needed). With the adjustable cup unthreaded, the spindle can be slid out of the pedal body.

2 Inspect the Bearing Race and Cup

The inside lip of the pedal body acts as the bearing cup, and the bearing race is built into the spindle. If the cup is notably pitted, it cannot be replaced—you'll need a new pedal if it's quite damaged.

The bearings are held on the spindle with a circlip. Unless the ball bearings are noticeably rough as they spin on the spindle, do not remove the circlip. The bearings can be cleaned and greased while still installed. If the bearings are rough on the spindle, remove the circlip with a pair of circlip pliers, and inspect the race surface. If the race is damaged, you'll need a new spindle. The bearings on the outboard side (one set of ball bearings and a set of needle bearings) cannot be removed from the pedal body, so, if after servicing the inboard bearings the pedal is still rough, you'll need to replace the pedals. ▶

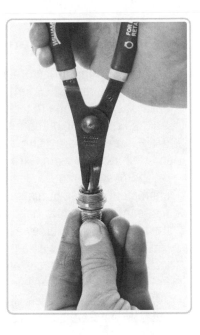

3 Grease the Pedal Body

Fill the pedal body with a durable grease until it is about a quarter full. When the spindle is installed, any excess grease will be pushed out of the pedal.

4 Install Spindle and Adjust Bearings

Slide the spindle back into the pedal body, and tighten the adjustable cup until finger tight. Hold the adjustable cup with the 17-millimeter cone wrench, and tighten the lockring with a 20-millimeter cone wrench. Check the bearing adjustment. The pedal should turn smoothly with no play. Make small adjustments by loosening the lockring and adjusting the adjustable cup. Tighten the adjustable cup to remove play, and loosen the cup if the pedal binds or does not turn smoothly. ▶

A Broken Cleat and One Scary Ride

The annual Tour of California is the largest and most prestigious race on U.S. soil. Covering 600 to 700 miles (965.6 to 1,126.5 km) during eight days of racing, it's proved itself to be an excellent forum for the domestic U.S. teams to test their mettle against the larger European professional outfits.

The first edition of the Tour of California was held in February 2006, when I was working for the TIAA-CREF professional cycling team, an upstart division of three development teams that would, in time, grow into the pro tour team Garmin-Cérvelo.

Thomas Peterson, a young rider who had been nicknamed "Mister Burns," based on the Simpsons' character because of his spindly physique, took the Best Young Rider jersey on stage 2, and it became the team's mission to hold it to the end. Six grueling stages later and Tom was still firmly in control of the silver and blue jersey awarded to the highest-placed racer under the age of 23.

The finale stage was a circuit race around Redondo Beach—10 laps of a flat, twisty 7.65-mile (12 km) course. Circuit races are known to be fast and aggressive, usually coming down to a bunch sprint finish, but the overall leaderboard was tight, so the teams were prepared for a fight for the overall title.

On the first lap, Glen Chadwick escaped with several other dangerous riders. It was early in the race, so the Phonak team's race leader Floyd Landis wasn't too concerned with chasing hard but just keeping the gap to the breakaway at a minimum. Their plans quickly went south as a couple of riders overlapped wheels and a massive pileup occurred. The field was neutralized as riders untangled their bikes and bodies, and the breakaway quickly gained eight minutes, making Chadwick the virtual race leader on the road.

Our guys seemed to have gotten through the crash without any damage. At least they were all up and riding immediately. Our good luck didn't hold out, however. Our team leader, Tom Peterson, had broken the cleat on his shoe, and, worse, he had no spare shoes in the car. After some frantic brainstorming on how to resolve our dilemma (at one point we considered taping his foot to the pedal), Michael Creed, an experienced pro who was in his first season with our team, calmly pulled over and gave Tom his shoe, allowing him to finish the stage.

At this point, the race was on. Phonak was in the front, driving the group hard to catch Chadwick's break and keep the race lead. Needless to say, it was not the ideal time to pull over and change shoes. By the time Tom was riding again, we were a good minute behind the back of the caravan, the procession of team cars that are there to service their riders. That meant we were probably a good two minutes behind the hard-chasing field of riders.

"Brake check!" Jonathan Vaughters, our director, yelled at me as Tom rode up to my side of the car, a common practice used to assist a rider in regaining the main field after a mechanical incident or a crash. The mechanic will lean out of the window and place a hand on the rider while pretending to adjust the rear brake, ostensibly damaged or knocked out of alignment after the incident. With one hand pushing the rider, the driver will accelerate, giving the rider a nice, quick push.

Jonathan was a former professional rider who was well acquainted with all of the tricks of the trade. But his eagerness (read panic) to retain a major jersey in one of the first large races for his fledgling team may have clouded his judgment a slight bit (read a lot). As soon as I was out of the window and had a hand on Tom, he punched the gas and we were rocketing down the course.

I was scared. Based on the look I could see in his face, Tom was scared too. Really scared. It's hard to steer a 16-pound (7 kg) bike as someone is pushing you from behind at an ungodly speed. At one point, Tom, in an effort to gather some semblance of balance, leaned his shoulder against the car.

"Don't let him lean on the car!" Jonathan roared, oblivious to the other cars and riders we were flying past on our way back to the field. I had no idea how he could be driving the way he was and still be able to turn around and see what we were doing.

Several minutes later, Tom was back in the field, crisis averted. "How fast were we going?" I asked JV.

"Seventy-five," he replied. I wasn't sure if he was joking or not. The next lap, we saw Creed calmly sitting on the side of the road watching the race—with only one shoe and an ice cream cone. Tom would finish safely in the main field and win the Best Young Rider jersey, which was a major coup for our young team.

From that day on, it was strict policy that every rider would keep an extra pair of shoes in the team car—just in case.

CHAPTER 13

Achieving the Perfect Fit

Most people I speak to think that there is exactly one way that a bicycle should fit them. They have it in their minds that once they are "fit" on their bikes, they will never have to adjust or play with anything ever again and cycling will be instantaneously blissful. While a good and proper fit will make cycling more enjoyable and can alleviate some niggling (and serious!) problems, it's not a panacea. You still need to listen to your body and trust your instincts.

When I'm fitting someone on a bicycle, the first thing I ask is, "So, what do you want to accomplish?" Each person's fit is unique and should take into account a variety of factors. A 50-year-old casual cyclist looking to complete her or his first century is not going to have the same needs for fit as a Category 1 racer setting up her or his time-trial bike. So, with that in mind, the following guide on bike fit is just that—a guide. It will provide an outline of what a good fit for general road riding should consist of, but always listen to what your body is telling you. If something is uncomfortable or feels wrong, it probably is!

The body makes three contact points with the bicycle, and your fit is a measurement of where these contact points are in relation to each other and to the bike itself. These points, in order of setup, are the cleat and pedal interface, the saddle, and the handlebars. But, before going into the fine points of fitting your road bike, we'll discuss the first thing that everyone encounters when deciding on a bike—which bike size is the right one for me?

Frame Fit

When people speak of a bike's size, they're not actually talking about the entire bike but rather the bike's frame measurement. Specifically, the frame size is a reference to the seat tube length, although, as we'll see, this is a somewhat dubious designation.

Traditionally, steel frames were made with a horizontal top tube that came in only one length. Frame builders would offer different sizes by providing longer seat and head tubes, and a rider would have to customize the length of the bike by choosing longer or shorter stems. In those days, the seat tube measurement truly was the measurement of the frame. A 22-inch (55 cm) frame from one manufacturer would fit similarly to a 22-inch frame from another.

We still use this archaic measurement to label a frame's size, although it's pretty arbitrary what each manufacturer actually measures. With the advent of sloping top tubes, differing top tube lengths, and specialty frame designs, the actual seat tube measurement isn't the best reflection of how a frame is actually going to fit you. The seat tube can be measured from the center of the bottom bracket to the center of the top tube, from the center of the bottom bracket to the top of the top tube, and even from the center of the bottom bracket to an imaginary line where a horizontal top tube would intersect the seat tube (see figure 13.1). ▼

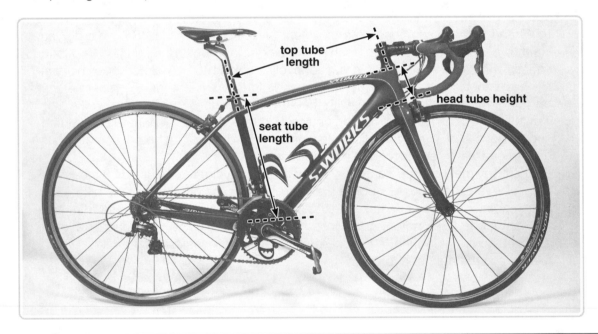

Figure 13.1 Different points of measurement on a modern road frame.

Most bike companies label their frame sizes in increments of 2 centimeters, in either even (52, 54, 56 cm, etc.) or odd (53, 55, 57 cm, etc.) numbers. But, because these are often specious labels, these sizes are really only effective for comparing other bikes by the same manufacturer. Some companies have recently dropped this way of measuring their bikes and instead employ a small, medium, and large system, which makes about as much sense to me as any other system being employed.

Assuming that you can safely stand over the bike's top tube, the seat tube measurement is actually irrelevant. A much more important measurement when determining which frame to buy is the top tube length. With different seatposts, you can pretty much get the proper saddle height and saddle setback no matter what the seat tube length is, but, with the wrong top tube length, you can't compensate with a super-long or super-short stem to get the right reach—it will ruin the bike's handling characteristics.

When looking at frames, do your research and figure out the top tube lengths from the manufacturers that you're interested in. Most will have their frame's geometries easily available in the owner's manual or on their websites, or, failing that, bring a tape measure with you when you're looking at new bikes. So, what exactly is the right top tube length? When seated on the bike with your hands resting on the handlebar's hoods, you want your back at roughly a 45-degree angle (in relation to the saddle) and your arms at a similar angle (in relation to the bars) (see figure 13.2). ▼

Figure 13.2 Rider's back at a 45-degree angle when seated on the bike.

Stand next to the bike in your cycling shoes, and raise the saddle until the top is even with your hip bone—by no means an accurate way to determine saddle height but close enough to decide on a frame size. Sit on the bike, either in front of a mirror or with someone you trust watching you, and check out how your back and arms look on various frame sizes.

Choose a frame that allows you to get a proper position with a stem length of between 10 centimeters and 13 centimeters and a stack height (amount of spacers under the stem) of less than 4 centimeters. When you compensate for an improperly sized frame with either an extremely short or long stem or a large amount of stack height, the bike's handling is negatively affected because the stem was not designed to be used in that manner.

Very small bikes are the exception that proves the rule. Many times, frame builders will design a small bike with a very short stem in mind (particularly on women's bikes) in a range of 8 to 11 centimeters. A small bike built with a (relatively) longer top tube and a shorter stem keeps the frame large enough to allow the use of normal (29 in. [700C]) road wheels, giving more tire and wheel upgrade options.

Saddle Height

Now assuming that you have the proper frame size for you, the next and most important measurement to determine is the saddle height. The rest of the bike's measurements and adjustments are all done in relationship to the saddle height. Any change in the height of the saddle will invariably affect every other measurement.

There are several ways of determining saddle height, and each has its own merits and drawbacks. As always, it's a good idea to use some common sense and feel to double-check your measurements. Although a change in the saddle height will take a little time to get used to, if it doesn't feel right, it may not be right!

Heel Method

Probably the most commonly used and simplistic of methods to determine saddle height is also the easiest to do. With your cycling shoes on, adjust the saddle until your heel rests on the pedal with your leg fully extended and your hips even on the saddle (see figure 13.3). This is a good way to get a general idea of your saddle height, but it doesn't compensate for differences in shoe and cleat combos or an individual's variation of femur, tibia, and foot length.

Figure 13.3 Proper saddle height can be determined when your heel is resting on the pedal, your leg is extended, and your hips are even.

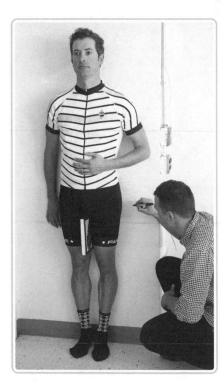

Figure 13.4 Measuring your inseam.

The Inseam Method

The inseam method is also referred to as the 109 percent method due to the calculation that's employed. Based on research done at Loughborough University in Great Britain, it was determined that the optimal saddle height, measured from the center of the pedal axle to the top of the saddle, was 109 percent of your inseam length.

To measure your inseam, stand barefoot with your back against a wall and a thick book placed between your upper thighs (to simulate the width of the saddle) (see figure 13.4). Have a friend mark where the top of the book meets the wall. The measurement from that mark to the floor is your inseam. *Note:* It's a good idea to take a couple of measurements and use the average to get the most accurate measurement.

The Lemond Method

Pioneered by three-time Tour de France champion Greg LeMond, this method was actually developed by his legendary coach, Cyrille Guimard. Your saddle height, measured from the center of the bottom bracket to the top of the saddle, should be 88.3 percent of your inseam length.

Calculate your inseam length using the technique described in the inseam method, then multiply that number by 0.883 to get your saddle height. *Note:* This is another good way to get a first estimate of your saddle height, but it usually produces a different measurement from the inseam method and does not take into account differences in crank length.

The Holmes Method

This is the most scientific of all four of the methods described here but probably the hardest for the home cyclist to do correctly. This method doesn't take into account your inseam length but instead relies on the bend of your knee at the bottom of your pedal stroke. The knee should be bent at an angle of 25 to 35 degrees, usually closer to 25.

To measure the angle of your knee, you'll need a specialized medical tool, called a goniometer, which can be found at medical supply stores. To use the goniometer, place the center of the tool on the side of the knee, just behind the kneecap (see figure 13.5). One arm of the goniometer should run along the length of the tibia and the other along the length of the femur. Read the measurement. If the angle is less than 25 degrees, lower the saddle. If it is greater than 35 degrees, raise the saddle. *Note:* This method is the most preferred by professional bike fitters because it takes into consideration crank length, foot size, and both the femur and tibia lengths.

Figure 13.5 Measuring the angle of the knee using a goniometer.

Crank Length

Determining the proper crank length is even less of an exact science than the various methods of determining saddle height. Changing the length of the crank effectively changes the gear ratio of the drivetrain that you're spinning—the length of the lever (crank) determines the amount of force necessary to pedal.

So, why doesn't everyone ride incredibly long cranks to take advantage of the extra leverage? Longer cranks force your knees to flex more than shorter ones, which exacerbates the "dead spots" in your pedal stroke, when the angle of your knee prevents the quadriceps or hamstrings from working effectively.

Standard cranks usually come in 170-, 172.5-, and 175-millimeter lengths. Shorter and longer cranks can be found, but they are more like boutique items. The best way to determine which works best for you is to simply try various sizes.

Shorter riders (5 ft 4 in. [162.6 cm] and under) should start with 170-millimeter cranks and vary from there, while taller riders (5 ft 11 in. [180.3 cm] and above) should start with 175-millimeter cranks. Cyclists in the middle of that range should begin with 172.5-millimeter cranks. Riders with relatively longer or shorter legs for their height should take that into account when choosing crank length. The longer the leg, the longer the crank, and vice versa. Cranks that are much shorter or longer than the standard sizes do have their place on modern bikes. Extremely short riders should take advantage of shorter-than-average cranks to help reduce the toe overlap that often occurs on a small frame with full-sized wheels. Very large bikes, which very tall riders use, most often have disproportionately high bottom bracket heights so that longer cranks could be employed without the risk of hitting the pedal on the ground while cornering, a concern on standard-sized frames.

Saddle and Cleat Position

After determining your optimal saddle height (including which cranks to use), it's time to determine your saddle setback. The saddle setback determines the ratio of how much work your quadriceps do in relation to your hamstrings and gluteus muscles.

The quadriceps provide explosive, quick power, such as that used in a sprint, while the longer, more efficient hamstrings and gluteus muscles are better equipped to provide endurance work. Sliding the saddle forward engages more of the quadriceps, while sliding it back puts the emphasis of the pedal stroke on the hamstrings and gluteus muscles. It's best to start with a neutral position, and, if you feel like fine-tuning your engagement, adjust from there.

1 Set Cleat Position

The reason that this process doesn't get its own section is simple: there's really only one way to do it. There are some dissenting opinions, but at least 99 percent of the successful cyclists I know set their cleats in one way. Normally, I would eschew the notion that "because everyone else is doing it" is a valid argument, but, in this case, I find it hard to believe that after so many years of trial and error, there has never been a viable alternative to the traditional method.

Attach the cleat so that its center is directly under the ball of your foot. ▶

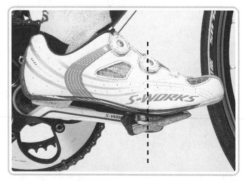

From there, you can adjust the angle of how your foot sits in relation to the pedal, based on personal preference—duck-footed individuals might angle their heels in, while pigeon-toed riders might angle their toes in to get comfortable. *Note:* Road cleats do not have much in the way of lateral adjustment. It's usually more comfortable to set the cleats up so that your shoes are as close to the cranks and chainstays of your bike without actually rubbing or striking them. ▼

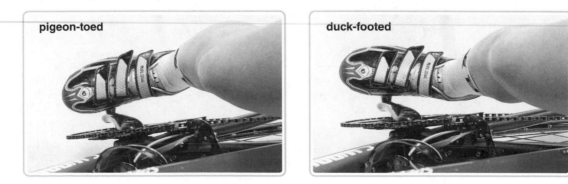

pigeon-toed   **duck-footed**

2 Adjust Fore and Aft

Place your leg at the three o'clock position (with the crank parallel to the ground), and drop a plumb-bob from the tibial tuberosity, the bony bump directly below the kneecap. The line of the plumb-bob should pass straight through the center of the pedal spindle. If it does not, adjust the saddle forward or backward until it does. *Note:* If you don't have a dedicated plumb-bob, you can tie a large nut to a piece of string; it works equally well. ▶

Make sure that you have the correct saddle height before adjusting the saddle setback. If the saddle height is incorrect, it will affect where your knee should be in relation to the pedal spindle. Consequently, if you change the saddle height, you'll often need to change the setback as well.

3 Check Saddle Tilt

The saddle should be perfectly flat. If you find that you need to tilt the nose of the saddle up or down to achieve a degree of comfort, you should be using a different saddle. Tilting the saddle causes you to slide around while pedaling, thus losing biomechanical efficiency. A myriad of excellent saddles are on the market, but finding the right one is personal choice. Riders with wide hips (read sit bones) may need a wider saddle, while some may prefer those with a cutout for comfort. No two riders are exactly alike. Find a saddle that works well for you.

Note: There is much debate on which pedaling style is better. Many advocate dropping your heels as much as possible while pedaling (think about scraping gum off your shoe while you pedal) to engage the calf muscles. Others (most notably cycling legend Lance Armstrong) pedal with their toes pointed down and no movement in their heels, thinking that this is more efficient.

I believe that you will naturally tend toward one style or the other, and both work equally well. Use whichever one is more comfortable for you.

Handlebar Width and Height

For maximum comfort, your handlebars should be about the same width as your shoulders. Hold a prospective bar size up to your shoulders while standing in front of a mirror to determine proper fit. Most manufacturers measure their bars from the center of one drop to the center of the other drop, although many Italian makers measure the outside of the drops. Always double-check a new bar's width with a tape measure. ▶

The bar height is another measurement that is determined solely by your comfort. Most racing cyclists have a very low bar height in relation to their saddles (called bar drop) that achieves an aggressive, aerodynamic position. This requires great flexibility in the hips, a low body-fat percentage (so your stomach isn't in the way!), and a strong lower back. Most nonprofessional cyclists, especially those with less flexibility in their hips, backs, and necks, will have a much more relaxed position with their backs at about a 45-degee angle.

If you're setting up a new bicycle, start with your bars higher than you think you'll need them. It's very easy to drop the bars and shorten the steerer tube as you ride the bike more, but it's impossible to add steerer tube once it's been cut!

Stem Length

Last, deciding which stem length to use will fine-tune your fit on the bike. In addition to affecting how far your arms reach, a shorter or longer stem will also make the steering a little quicker or slower, respectively.

The most reliable starting point for stem length is also the most traditional. With your hands in the drops and your elbows slightly bent, look directly at the front hub. It should be perfectly obscured by your handlebars. If not, try longer or shorter stems until it is.

This is by no means a definitive method for getting the right stem length, but it's a good starting point. Play with various sizes until you feel most comfortable, but remember, if you find you need something drastic (less than 10 cm or more than 13 cm), you may need a smaller or larger bike to begin with.

Special Fit Cases

As I've stated before, no two riders fit exactly alike. Here are some of the common modifications that certain groups of cyclists may need to achieve their optimal fit.

Very Short Riders

Short riders will invariably need correspondingly shorter parts on their bikes. Shorter cranks (less than 170 mm) are needed to keep the knee at a proper angle while pedaling and to prevent toe overlap. Unlike their taller cycling counterparts, short riders usually have very little to no drop from their saddles to their handlebars. Often the bars are higher than the saddle. This is usually due to the inability to get a frame with a short enough head tube to achieve much drop.

Many smaller frames are made to use very short stems (between 7 cm and 10 cm), using different head tube angles and fork rakes to compensate for the tighter steering axis that accompanies shorter stems.

Very Tall Riders

These riders often need custom-built bike frames to achieve a proper fit. Just as short riders need shorter cranks, tall riders need longer cranks (as much as 190 mm) to take advantage of the extra range of knee motion afforded by their long femurs and tibias. Very large frames are often built with taller bottom bracket heights to avoid clipping the pedals while cornering, which can be a problem when using long cranks.

If a custom-made frame is out of your budget or if you're simply on the cusp of being very, very tall, there are many off-the-shelf products that can help you fit your bike. Most companies make stems up to 15 centimeters and seatposts with extra setback to get your saddle in the correct position. *Note:* If you are trying to get an extra-high handlebar height, be aware that most forks with carbon steerer tubes are not recommended to be used with more than 4 centimeters of spacers under the stem for safety. If more spacers are needed, you'd be better off with a fork that has an alloy steerer tube.

Young Riders

Just as with clothes and other sporting equipment, always get a frame one size larger than you think a young rider needs now. You can easily compensate for a larger frame size with a shorter stem—much easier to swap out a year from now than an entire frame!

Young riders' skeletal structures and joints are still developing and care should be given not to put undue stress on them. Almost all racing federations have a ban on juniors using large gearing. This helps young riders develop a smooth, efficient pedaling style. Ninety-two gear inches (a 52-tooth chainring and a 15-tooth cog) is the largest allowed for junior racers.

Female Riders

While female riders do have some obvious physiological differences from males, most of the cycling products labeled as being specific for women are nothing more than marketing gimmickry. Most of the fit needs for women are often the same needs for some men, such as shorter stems, reach adjustments for brake levers (for use with smaller hands), and shorter cranks.

The exception to this rule, I believe, is the saddle. Women's saddles tend to be wider in the rear to support wider sit bones and incorporate different padding designs to accommodate women's anatomy.

Fine-Tuning Fit in a Wind Tunnel

Time trialing is often called "the race of truth," and for good reason. It's the purest essence of cycling: one rider, against the clock, with only him- or herself and a stopwatch to beat. Cyclists who specialize in this demanding discipline are of a different cut of cloth from their road-racing kin—they suffer more, push themselves harder, and intimately know their bodies' limits. But it takes more than simply being strong and fit to be a good time trialist. Because there are no other riders to draft from, aerodynamics plays a disproportionately large role in time-trialing prowess. Solid disk wheels, specialized frames with fairings and hidden cables, innovative clothing and helmets, and other slick bike parts are all employed in an effort to cheat the wind as much as possible.

As much as aerodynamic bicycles are important, a rider's body position on that bicycle counts for much more than any single part possibly could. If a bicycle were a sailing ship, the rider would be the sail—large, bulky, and able to catch the wind at almost any angle. A good rider with a bad time-trial position would be at a considerable disadvantage to a smarter rider who has put thought and time into creating the optimal position for time trialing. That is why, in the cutthroat world of professional cycling, most teams go to unrivaled lengths to obtain the slightest advantage. Using a low-speed wind tunnel is the most effective means of creating empirical data that can be used to test new ideas and determine exactly what the fastest time-trial position is.

In 2007, the team that I was working for, Slipstream Sports, which would go on to become the Garmin-Cérvelo ProTour team, was leading the field in the development of new cycling science, largely due in part to two men—Jonathan Vaughters, team founder and a creative thinker, and Dr. Allen Lim, widely regarded as the smartest man in cycling. Allen holds a doctorate in sports physiology from the University of Colorado and has been the driving force behind many of cycling's recent innovations, including the use of ice vests while warming up on hot days and the now ubiquitous rice cakes, which many pros consume while on their bikes.

That spring, Allen; former U23 world time-trial champion Danny Pate; and I booked time in the San Diego Air & Space Technology Center wind tunnel to fine-tune his position on our new Felt time-trial bikes. A wind tunnel is basically a large, cavernous circle with a fan that pushes air through it at variable speeds. On the opposite side of the fan is a pedestal on which the bike and rider are placed, and, as the wind passes them, data are collected. Aerodynamic drag can be measured in gram equivalents, a value that describes how hard the wind pushes against a rider at a given speed—the lower the number, the more aerodynamic you are. Efficient aerodynamics is akin to free energy. If a rider puts out X amount of force to travel at a certain speed at Y grams of drag, another rider who has a lower Y value can put out the same X amount of force and travel faster, thereby beating the first rider.

We spent countless hours in the wind tunnel (no inexpensive rental, either) to test new ideas and equipment in an effort to get Danny as fast as possible. Allen and the engineers from Felt had many products and theories to test, and each variation was precisely measured and compared to the other measurements to prove which was fastest. At the end of the day, after trying various handlebars, clothing, helmets, wheels, and even gloves, it was the simplest motion that made an exponentially large difference.

Simply by shrugging his shoulders while in the time-trial position, moving them closer to his ears, Danny was able to lower his aerodynamic value from 2,816 grams of drag to 2,749 grams at 30 miles per hour (48 kmh), a difference of 2.3 percent. No other single thing we did that day even came close to making Danny that much quicker.

So, what does a difference of 2.3 percent mean? In the 2011 Tour de Suisse, American Levi Leipheimer used the final day's time trial to wipe out a 1 foot 59 inch (180 cm) deficit to leader Damiano Cunego to win the overall title by only 4 seconds. If Cunego had been 2.3 percent more aerodynamic, he would have ridden nearly 57 seconds faster, easily retaining his lead and winning the prestigious race.

CHOOSING AND WORKING WITH A BIKE SHOP

Bike shops, just like car repair shops, can be quite intimidating to the average customer. There's a specific and sometimes foreign lingo to learn, certain knowledge that's often taken for granted by experienced shop employees, and a bewildering assortment of options—even for the simplest product categories. It's important to find a good bike shop that you feel comfortable working with. Not only will you (most likely) be purchasing expensive equipment from them, you'll also need their expertise when it comes to maintaining your bike. Even the most competent home mechanic will need to rely on the years of experience to be found in a bike repair shop from time to time.

So, what makes a good bike shop? Although it's a somewhat nebulous concept because there are many kinds of shops that cater to many types of clientele, there are certain characteristics to be found in any decent establishment.

First, and most important, you should be able to trust the employees of the shop. You need to have faith that the salespeople have your best interests in mind when selling you equipment. Make sure that they listen to your needs and respect your input and desires. The customer isn't always right, but he or she is always the customer—what you need is what's most important, not what they want to sell you.

The same is true for the repair technicians in the back of the shop. If you have questions or concerns about your repair, they should be able to answer you forthrightly and intelligibly. They should be able to clearly explain why you would need any repair, let alone expensive ones, and give you as many options as possible. I'm wary of any mechanic or salesperson who never says, "I don't know." No one can know everything (in writing this book, I've had to turn to many resources to ensure accuracy), and feigned sagacity is much more dangerous than simple ignorance.

Another asset is cleanliness. If a shop's staff can't keep their environs clean and organized, that's often indicative of how well they can take care of your bike. An organized shop is an efficient shop, especially important when you're paying for repairs by the hour.

You should feel welcome and comfortable any time that you walk into your preferred bike shop. I have had several rude encounters with shop employees who were dismissive. Would they have treated me differently if they'd known I worked in pro cycling? I don't know and I don't care. Competence and courtesy are not mutually exclusive. If you feel as though a shop employee is being rude to you, simply take your business elsewhere! Your money is as green as anyone else's, and if they don't value your patronage, there are other shops that will.

It's important to recognize that you have some responsibility in the shop-and-customer relationship, too. You need to be clear about your needs and wants and be willing to ask questions whenever you're confused. Although it's a horrendous cliché, there are no dumb questions, and any good shop employee will gladly take the time to explain things to you.

Building a relationship with your preferred shop can be mutually beneficial. They'll learn your riding preferences and your bike's quirks and peculiarities and will make each visit more enjoyable. They'll gain a valuable, loyal customer, and you'll both make new and lasting friendships.

à bloc – French for *all out*.

adjustable cup – The side of a bearing system that is adjustable. Usually paired with a fixed cup.

aero – Short for aerodynamic.

aero bars – Handlebars used to obtain an aerodynamic position.

aero levers – Brake levers specifically made for aero bars.

Aheadset – *See* threadless headset.

Allen wrench – A hexagonal tool used to tighten Allen bolts, which are common on bicycles.

anatomic – Describing anything on a bicycle designed to fit the human body (e.g., anatomic handlebars).

anchor bolt – A bolt that fastens a cable to a bicycle part.

axle – The shaft on which bearings turn. Commonly found in hubs and pedals.

ball bearing – A steel or ceramic ball that allows a part to rotate on an axle or spindle. Found in hubs, pedals, bottom brackets, and headsets.

bar – European measurement for air pressure inside a tire.

bar end shifter – Specially designed shifters that mount to the end of an aero bar extension.

barrel adjuster – An adjustable cable stop that enables adding or reducing tension on a cable by turning it in or out.

BCD – Bolt chainring diameter. The measurement used for chainring and crank compatibility.

boot – Anything used to temporarily fix a cut in a bicycle tire.

bottom bracket – The spindle and bearings housed in the frame's bottom bracket shell on which the cranks turn.

bottom pull derailleur – A front derailleur whose derailleur cable attaches from the bottom.

braze-on – Anything welded onto a frame (e.g., front derailleur hanger and cable stops).

bearing cup – A smooth face in which the ball bearings sit.

bearing race – A smooth cone, attached to an axle or spindle, that spins on the ball bearings.

binder bolt – A bolt built into a frame used to hold the seatpost in the frame.

bottom bracket shell – The part of a bicycle frame that houses the bottom bracket.

brake caliper – The brake assembly that is attached to the frame or fork and articulates to engage the brakes.

brake pad – The rubber or other compound that is pushed onto the rim by the brake caliper to engage the brakes.

brake shoe – Attached to the brake caliper and holds the brake pad.

B-tension screw – The screw that adjusts the angle of the rear derailleur in relation to the derailleur hanger.

bushing – A metal or plastic sleeve that acts as a primitive bearing.

cable – Braided wire that is used to actuate the derailleurs or brakes.

cable guide – A piece that is fitted under the bottom bracket shell that guides the derailleur cables to the derailleurs.

cantilever brakes – Brakes typically found on mountain and cyclocross bikes.

carbon fiber – Material used in bicycle components constructed with interwoven carbon threads set in resin.

cartridge bearings – A single unit that houses a bearing cup, ball bearings, and a bearing race.

cassette – A group of cogs.

center pull – An older style of road brake caliper with a single pivot.

center to center – A way of measuring handlebars, from the center of one drop to the center of the opposing drop.

chain – A series of metal links and bushings that are used to propel the bicycle's drivetrain.

chain link – An individual segment of a bicycle chain.

chainring – A round, toothed plate attached to the crankset, which propels the chain.

chainstays – The rear tubes of a bicycle frame that run from the bottom bracket shell to the rear dropouts.

chain suck – When the chain comes off the bottom of the chainring and is sucked between the crank and frame.

circlip – A metal clip that fits in a groove and holds two pieces together.

clincher tire – A tire that incorporates a tube and is attached to a clincher rim with a hooked bead system.

clipless pedal – A pedal that uses a cleat and retention system to hold the shoe on the pedal rather than a toe clip.

cog – An individual sprocket used to propel the rear wheel.

compact crank – Any road bike crankset that uses a chainring combo smaller than 53/11.

cone wrench – A very thin wrench used to adjust hub cones.

cottered cranks – An obsolete crank style that used cotter pins to attach the cranks to the bottom bracket.

cotterless cranks – Any crankset that does not use cotter pins.

crank bolt – The bolt that attaches a crank to the bottom bracket.

crank length – The measurement of one crank.

derailleur (front) – The mechanism that moves the chain between chainrings.

derailleur (rear) – The mechanism that moves the chain between cogs.

derailleur cage – The part of the rear derailleur that holds the derailleur pulleys.

derailleur hanger – The part of the drive-side rear dropout on which the rear derailleur pivots.

derailleur pulleys – Small sprockets attached to the rear derailleur on which the chain runs.

disc brake – A braking system on which the brake pads engage on a disc attached to the hub instead of engaging on the rim as with a traditional brake.

disc wheel – An aerodynamic rear wheel used in time trialing that is solid from rim to hub.

dish – The center measurement of a wheel.

dishing tool – The tool used to measure a wheel's dish.

double butted – Used to describe spokes or frame tubes where the center part has a smaller or thinner diameter than the outer parts.

down tube – The tube on a bicycle frame that runs from the head tube to the bottom bracket shell.

drivetrain – All the parts used to propel the bicycle: the crankset, chainrings, chain, derailleurs, and cassette.

dropout – The point on a frame or fork in which the wheel is affixed.

drops – The lower, curved portion of road handlebars.

dual-control levers – Integrated brake and shifter levers.

dust cap – Any seal used to keep contaminates out of bearing assemblies.

elliptical chainrings – Nonround chainrings (e.g., Shimano Biopace, Rotor Q-Rings, O.symetric chainrings).

English thread – The most common bottom bracket standard, featuring 1.37 inches x 24 threads per inch thread pitch and a drive-side left-hand thread and a nondrive-side right-hand thread.

expander bolt – A bolt and wedge system used to affix a part inside a tube, such as how bar end shifters are affixed.

expander plug – Set inside a steerer tube into which the headset top cap is threaded. *See* top cap.

eyelet – A point on a frame where accessories can be attached, typically employed for fenders or racks.

facing – The act of smoothing out the face of a bicycle part.

ferrule – A small metal cap for the end of a cable housing.

fixed cup – A bearing cup that is not adjustable. *See* adjustable cup.

fixed gear – A bicycle that does not have the ability to coast.

fixing bolt – Any bolt used to anchor one bicycle component to another.

flange – The measurement of the outer diameter of the hub shell in which the spoke heads sit.

fork – The part that turns in the head tube and attaches to the front wheel.

fork crown – The point at which the two legs of the fork meet.

fork rake – The angle of the fork legs in relation to the steerer tube.

frame – The main part of the bicycle, composed of the head tube, down tube, top tube, seat tube, bottom bracket shell, seatstays, chainstays, and rear dropouts.

frame set – A frame and fork combo.

freehub – The part of the rear hub on which the cassette sits that allows the cassette to coast independently of the rear hub.

friction shifter – Used for nonindexed shifting.

front triangle – The front segment of a bicycle frame, composed of the head tube, down tube, seat tube, and top tube.

gauge – A way of measuring spoke size (e.g., 14- or 15-gauge spokes).

gear – The ratio of the chainring and cog being employed (e.g., a 53/11 gear).

gear inches – The distance, in inches, a bicycle will travel forward with one complete revolution of the crankset.

gear ratio – *See* gear.

group, groupset, gruppo – The component group made by a manufacturer, composed of the shifters, derailleurs, brakes, bottom bracket, crankset, chain, cassette, hubs, and headset.

handlebars – The part held by the rider, attached to the fork by way of the stem and used to steer the bike.

handlebar tape – A wrapping to cushion the handlebars and make them less slippery.

hanger – *See* derailleur hanger.

headset – The bearing assembly, housed in the head tube, on which the fork's steerer tube rotates.

head tube – The tube on the frame that houses the headset and fork and is attached to the down tube and top tube.

head tube angle – The angle of the head tube in relation to the wheelbase of the bicycle.

hex key – *See* Allen wrench.

housing – The outer sheath in which the cables run that actuate the derailleurs and brakes.

housing stop – The attachments on a frame that stop the housing and ferrules but allow the cable to continue.

hub – The center part of a wheel that rotates on an axle.

index shifting – Shifting in which the cable is stopped in specific increments.

integrated headset – A headset that has the bearing cups built into the frame.

Italian thread – The second most common bottom bracket standard, featuring 36 inches x 24 threads per inch thread pitch and both a drive-side and nondrive-side right-hand thread.

left-hand thread – Thread direction in which turning the piece left will tighten it.

limit stop screw – The upper and lower limit screws on derailleurs that arrest the derailleurs' movement in either direction.

linear pull brake – *see* V-brake.

locknut – A nut used to hold a bearing adjustment, usually paired with an adjustable nut or race.

lockring – A large, flat locknut, usually found on older-style bottom brackets and cassettes.

lock washer – A washer with serrated edges that prevents a bolt tightened against it from loosening.

MAFAC-style brakes – *See* cantilever brakes.

master link – A breakable chain link used to join two pieces of chain.

metric – Standard of measurement used by the entire world, except U.S. cycling parts, which are measured in imperial units.

monkey wrench – A large adjustable crescent wrench.

mounting bolt – Any bolt used to affix a bicycle component to the frame or another component.

needle bearing – Rod-shaped bearings seated in a cylindrical sleeve.

nipple – A small nut seated in the bed of a rim into which a spoke is threaded.

noodle – The curved tube that guides the brake cable into a V-brake.

one-piece crank – A crank in which the crank and spindle are one piece.

outside to outside – A way of measuring handlebars, from the outside of one drop to the outside of the opposing drop.

overlap – *See* toe overlap.

oversized – Typically refers to the 31.8-millimeter standard for road bars as opposed to the traditional 26.0-millimeter standard.

parallelogram – Design of rear and front derailleurs that allows them to maintain the same vertical distance from each cog or chainring while moving on the horizontal plane.

peanut-butter wrench – A 15-millimeter box wrench made by Campagnolo that is excellent for spreading peanut butter.

pedal – The rotating platform attached to the crank on which a rider's foot rests.

penny-farthing – An antique bicycle style with an extremely large front wheel and cranks directly affixed to the front hub.

pinch bolt – A bolt used to squeeze two parts together and create a clamp (e.g., stem bolts, seatpost bolts).

pinch flat – A flat tire caused by the tube being pinched between the tire and rim.

pins and ramps – Special features on the sides of chainrings that improve upshifting

pin spanner – A U-shaped tool with pins on the ends used to tighten lockrings.

pitting – When a surface becomes rough and damaged.

pivot bolt – Any bolt around which a bicycle component can pivot (e.g., a rear derailleur pivot bolt).

pneumatic tire – Any tire that uses an air chamber to provide comfort and performance.

preload – The amount of adjustment on a bearing before a load is placed on it.

Presta valve – Cycling-specific valve found on bicycle tubes; has threaded nut to prevent air loss.

psi – Pounds per square inch; U.S. measurement for air pressure in tires.

pulley – A small chainwheel in the rear derailleur cages that guides the chain during shifts.

Q-factor – The distance between the outer edges of a crankset.

quick-release skewer – A hub skewer with a lever that can be opened by hand to tighten or loosen a wheel in the frame's dropouts.

quill – An older style of stem that affixes to the steerer tube by means of a wedge bolt.

radial spokes – A spoke-lacing pattern in which none of the spokes cross each other.

rear triangle – The rear part of a bicycle frame, consisting of the chainstays, seatstays, and rear dropouts.

right-hand thread – Thread direction in which turning the piece right will tighten it.

rim – The part of the wheel on which the tire is attached.

rolling resistance – The amount of friction between two rolling articles (e.g., the friction between tire and road).

saddle – The point on which a rider sits.

saddle rails – The two rails underneath a saddle that are clamped in the seatpost and that allow forward and aft adjustment.

safety bicycle – The first bicycle that featured same-sized wheels, a double-triangle frame, and pneumatic tires.

Schrader valve – The inner-tube valve that uses a spring to retain the air seal. Similar to those found on car tires.

sealed bearings – *See* cartridge bearings.

seat angle – The angle of the seat tube in relation to the bicycle's wheelbase.

seat mast – A seatpost that is built into the frame.

seatpost – The part that is attached to both the seat tube and saddle and is adjusted to raise or lower the saddle height.

seatstays – The tubes of the bicycle frame that run from the seat tube to the rear dropouts.

seat tube – The tube of the bicycle frame that runs from the bottom bracket shell to the junction of the top tube and seatstays.

setback – The distance between the tip of the saddle and the center of the bottom bracket, measured on the horizontal plane.

sewn-up tire – *See* tubular tire.

shifter – The mechanism that actuates a derailleur.

shim – Any thin washer or piece of material used to take up space between two parts.

skewer – *See* quick-release skewer.

spacer – Any thick washer used to space two parts.

spacing (cassette) – The number of cogs a cassette has (e.g., 9- or 10-speed cassettes).

spacing (frame/hub) – The distance between the rear dropouts.

spindle – An axle that rotates inside a bearing assembly.

spline – The set of ridges along a tube designed to hold two pieces together.

spoke – The metal or composite rod that attaches a rim to the hub.

spoke count – The number of spokes used in a wheel.

spoke pattern – The pattern of how the spokes are laced in a wheel.

sprocket – A toothed wheel used in conjunction with a chain.

stack height – The amount of spacers between the headset and the stem.

standover height – The distance between a rider's crotch and the top tube when straddling a bike with his or her feet on the floor.

star-fangled nut – A nut that is pounded into an alloy or steel steerer tube that serves as an anchor for the top cap bolt.

steerer tube – The tube attached to the fork blades or crown that runs through the head tube and onto which the stem is attached.

stem – The bicycle component that connects the steerer tube to the handlebars.

straight gauge – Any tube or spoke that is not butted.

tensiometer – A wheel-building tool used to measure the tension on a spoke.

threaded headset – Traditional headset in which the locknut threads onto the steerer tube. Used with quill stems.

threadless headset – Newer-style headset in which the steerer tube passes through the headset and a threadless stem is clamped onto it.

tire bead – The stiff edge of a tire that hooks into a clincher rim and is anchored when the tire is inflated.

tire iron – A plastic or metal tool used to pry the tire bead off of a rim.

toe clips – Traditional straps made of leather or nylon and a cage that holds the foot onto a pedal.

toe in – The process of angling brake pads so that the front hits before the rear.

toe overlap – When the foot, on the pedal, overlaps the front wheel while turning.

top cap – The uppermost part of the headset that, by means of the top cap bolt, adjusts the headset bearings.

top pull derailleur – A front derailleur whose derailleur cable attaches from the top.

torque – A measurement of rotational force.

torque wrench – A tool used to prevent overtightening a bolt by presetting the torque value.

Torx wrench – A diamond-shaped tool used to tighten and loosen Torx bolts.

TPI – Threads Per Inch, a standardized system for measuring thread dimensions on bolts and nuts.

track hub – A hub without any coasting elements, used in fixed-gear applications.

triple – A triple crankset or a crankset with three chainrings.

triple butted – Any tubing or spoke that has three distinct thicknesses.

true – The measurement of the straightness of a rim.

tube (frame) – The discreet parts of a bicycle frame (e.g., the down tube, the top tube).

tube (tire) – The inner tube used to provide an air chamber for a clincher tire.

tubular tire – A tire in which the inner tube is sewn into the casing and the entire tire is glued onto a rim.

V-brake – A side-pull cantilever brake with longer caliper arms and no straddle cable.

velo – French for *bicycle*.

washer – A thin, round spacer used under a nut or bolt to prevent damage.

wheelbase – The distance, measured along the horizontal plane, between the front and rear hubs of a bicycle.

wheel dish – The measurement of a wheel's rim in relation to the center point of the hub.

wheel dishing tool – A tool used to measure a bicycle's dish.

Daimeon Shanks has more than 17 years experience in cycling, a career which has included every facet of the sport from an elite level racer to his current role as a professional mechanic. Shanks graduated from the University of Oregon with degrees in Italian and History where he raced for the University's cycling team, eventually becoming the director and president of that program.

As a mechanic, he has worked professionally in every discipline of the sport including mountain biking, track, road, and cyclocross. His work experience includes stints with the Mavic Neutral Support Program, as the head track mechanic for the U.S. National Team, and as the resident mechanic at the U.S. Olympic Center in Colorado Spring, CO.

Shanks has spent five years as a mechanic with Garmin-Transitions ProTour cycling team, working events such as the Grand Tours of Europe, the pinnacle of road cycling's hierarchy. Shanks is currently the co-owner of The Service Course bike repair shop in Boulder, CO.